MANN KI BAAT

A Social Revolution on Radio

MANN KI BAAT

A SOCIAL REVOLUTION ON RADIO

BlueKraft Digital Foundation

BlueKraft Digital Foundation

LexisNexis®

LexisNexis®

This book is a publication of **LexisNexis**
(A Division of RELX India Pvt Ltd)
14th floor, Building No 10, Tower-B, DLF Cyber City, Phase-II,
Gurgaon-122002, Haryana, India.
Tel : + 91 124 4774444 Fax: + 91 124 4774100
Website : www.lexisnexis.co.in / E-mail : help.in@lexisnexis.com

---

The illustrations used in the book are courtesy Akbar Saheb.

ISBN: 9789350359907

Printed by: Sai Printo Packs Pvt. Ltd., A-102/4, Okhla Industrial Area, Phase-II, New Delhi-110 020

Printed and bound in India.

Message

This book is filled with Prime Minister Modi's enthusiasm for interacting with the people of India, particularly with the youth.

Talking on a one hour radio show once a month, while addressing challenging tasks as Prime Minister, requires tremendous efforts, and I cannot but feel his strong passion for dialogue with his people.

Having met a number of leaders in the international society, I found Prime Minister Modi comes next to nobody in caring for the development of his own country from a strategic and long-term perspective.

Japan and India are the two major democracies in Asia, having a special mission to join hands in leading the peace and prosperity of the Indo-Pacific region.

I hope this book will inspire many Indian youths, who will make their own contribution for further development of India.

Shinzo Abe
Prime Minister of Japan

Authors' Note

A Curiosity-driven and Multimedia-powered Book

'Mann Ki Baat', Prime Minister Narendra Modi's popular and ubiquitous monthly radio address, has developed into a tour-de-force in itself. Ever since the programme began on Vijaya Dashami in 2014 (3rd October 2014) there has been considerable curiosity about the origins of the programme, the idea behind it and the mind of the man behind the inspiring voice that reaches millions every month.

In times of visual bombardment, 'Mann Ki Baat' has become one of the most popular programmes in the history of the radio, not just in India but indeed worldwide.

Here is a man who is perhaps among our most popular leaders ever and has great command over the visual medium, but decides to do a radio programme.

In times of pervasive skepticism, 'Mann Ki Baat' functions as a magnet for positivity by attracting it from all over the nation. It then acts as a megaphone, amplifying positivity with the great reach it has.

Despite having a medium that provides incredible potential for political consolidation, the man speaking on the programme has made it a platform above politics, partisanship and power. The brand that has evolved is completely apolitical with a focus on 'Jan Shakti'–the inherent strength of 125 crore Indians and a message of optimism.

These seemingly counter-intuitive facts have naturally sown a widespread keenness to know more about the origin and evolution of this programme. How and why did Prime Minister Narendra Modi decide to do a radio address? How did the format develop? How does he select the topics and most importantly, how does he keep it detached from politics?

It was while seeking answers to these questions that the idea of a book on 'Mann Ki Baat' originated. This book contains insights from none other than the Prime Minister himself. His inputs provide us a peek into how one of the most popular leaders of our time approaches an idea like 'Mann Ki Baat' and what its historical value may be.

Interactions with the Prime Minister gave substantial detail on how he decides what the core content should be. It also throws light on how he approaches feedback from the people and how he lays emphasis on proper correspondence and follow-up by the respective government departments.

There is also immense curiosity in the public and media perception of 'Mann Ki Baat'. To address this, a comprehensive analysis of the television debates, print media articles and social media reactions was also done.

This book entailed a detailed study of the correspondence that comes to the Prime Minister before every 'Mann Ki Baat' episode–lakhs of letters, emails, posts on MyGov, inputs on the 'Narendra Modi Mobile App' and inputs from various Ministries and MPs. These indicated what the people wanted to hear from the Prime Minister and reiterated his strong personal popularity among the youth.

While preparing this book, a detailed study of every 'Mann Ki Baat' transcript was also undertaken. Beyond the themes and the overall narratives of every episode, each transcript is also a treasure trove of knowledge that deserves to be stored for posterity.

Hence, the book offers a definitive transcript of the first 23 episodes. These are useful in analysing the Prime Minister's monthly addresses in greater detail. The transcripts would be particularly useful for researchers and readers who want to examine the growth of a radio programme that became a movement in itself.

The journey of a radio programme that transformed into an important means of manifesting 'Jan Shakti' has been analysed. It highlights the transformative potential of each Indian and their Prime Minister who used the radio to ignite numerous mass movements for the nation's progress. These movements include instilling a sense of cleanliness, fighting drug menace, road safety, getting more tourists to India, saving the girl child and Divyang welfare to name a few.

There are interesting anecdotes shared by the members of the Prime Minister's team and people from AIR to quench people's curiosity about the minute but interesting details of how the idea of a radio programme came up, how the name and frequency were decided, and how the format was chalked out, among other things.

The core idea of 'Mann Ki Baat' is the Prime Minister's taking to his heart the views of the people. This book takes the reader behind the scenes on how public feedback is received through various channels, processed and followed-up after every episode, including letters which the Prime Minister does not talk about on the programme.

For this book, we are glad to have had the cooperation of the 'Narendra Modi Mobile App' team, which has been working tirelessly to strengthen the Prime Minister's bond with the people of India. At the end of every transcript is a QR code that enables the reader to hear the corresponding episode in 22 languages. The thorough work by the 'Narendra Modi Mobile App' team converts this book about a radio address into a 'multimedia book'–a beautiful confluence of the conventional and the modern, much like the programme itself.

The insights and analysis received from the All India Radio and MyGov teams were equally valuable. The scale at which feedback is received and processed at these places is revealing in its magnitude and efficiency.

The artwork in this book has been prepared by Akbar Saheb, a well-wisher of the Prime Minister and a very well-respected artist based in UAE.

Feedback on the book is welcome. Any error, though unintended, is the responsibility of the authors.

About BlueKraft Digital Foundation

BlueKraft Digital Foundation is a not-for-profit organization that is actively working in the realm of policy and governance matters. The Foundation brings together a wide spectrum of leading policy makers and citizens to debate, discuss, deliberate and formulate new ideas that will enrich India's development trajectory.

Our work is primarily focused on promoting the spirit of voluntary participation in sectors such as holistic education, women and child empowerment, farmer welfare, conservation of environment, digital and social media, and diaspora relations.

BlueKraft also works in the emerging discipline of data science.

The Foundation is privileged to have a youthful and vibrant team which is committed to public service and the cause of nation building.

Contents

PART II

PART I

Khadi for nation and Khadi for fashion. By purchasing Khadi, we are lighting the lamp of prosperity in the lives of lakhs of hardworking weavers.

—Narendra Modi

CHAPTER 1: Genesis

On an unusually bright and crisp winter afternoon in January 2015 two men were engrossed in deep discussion at Hyderabad House, in the heart of the Indian capital, New Delhi.

Once owned by one of pre-Independent India's most opulent and large royal households, the Nizam of Hyderabad, Hyderabad House is now the venue where the Government of India welcomes most foreign dignitaries. The grandeur of the building, the lush green lawns and the central location make it an ideal place to discuss politics, economics, trade, culture and other vital topics with visiting dignitaries.

The two men deliberating on diplomacy that January afternoon were President Barack Obama and Prime Minister Narendra Modi. After taking office in May 2014, Modi's innovative foreign policy became the topic of discussion both in India and globally. He surprised the world on a November evening when, he announced, through a Tweet that the chief guest for the 2015 Republic Day would be President Barack Obama. It was the first time that an American President was invited to grace the celebrations as the chief guest and it was also the first Republic Day parade with Narendra Modi as Prime Minister.

When President Obama arrived on 25th January 2015, the mood was upbeat. The talks in Hyderabad

House were productive and the joint press meet was a resounding success. As soon as the press meet ended, the two leaders were closeted in a room, leading to intense speculation outside—was there something left behind in the talks, is Modi discussing Pakistan with Obama, why have the two leaders gone into a room minus aides and top officials? The fact that the schedule of both leaders was delayed, was not missed either.

The scenario, however, was different in the room where PM Modi and President Obama were sitting. With their earphones on and a team of technicians guiding them, the two leaders commenced the recording of a special 'Mann Ki Baat' radio programme.

The next few minutes were devoted, not to serious diplomatic discussions, but light conversation—on the President's daughters visiting India, the men and women PM Modi idolizes, the rapid political and personal successes of both President Obama and Narendra Modi. Both leaders were at ease and answered all questions honestly and in a manner that would bring a smile on every face. The questions they answered were questions decided by the people, sent via post, on MyGov and through phone calls.

When the programme went on air on 27th January 2015, it was an instant hit. People from India and the United States tuned in, in large numbers. The honesty, the spontaneity and the chemistry between the two leaders couldn't be missed.

Thus ended another successful episode of 'Mann Ki Baat.'

An Unlikely Pair

Why would India's most tech-savvy politician seek to embrace a medium believed to be obsolete? Think of Narendra Modi using modern tools of communication, particularly in the virtual world and the picture that comes to mind is a Tweeting, Facebooking and an Instagramming leader who dominates the television and the Internet. In early 2009, when no leader had yet realised the importance of social media, he joined Twitter. At a time when Facebook was seen only as a medium of personal communication, he was out there, talking about development initiatives as the Chief Minister of Gujarat.

No wonder many found it surprising when, very early on during his tenure, the Prime Minister announced that he would do a monthly radio programme in which he proposed to share, as the name suggests, his 'Mann Ki Baat' or musings from the heart.

During a meeting with his aides on a rainy August evening in 2014, the Prime Minister expressed his desire to communicate with people through the medium of radio. He wanted to begin this programme in September 2014 itself. His team, a mixture of government officials and those he had brought along with him from Gujarat, began to work out the modalities of such a programme.

Then came the toughest part, that of deciding on a suitable name for the programme. How would it be branded? Inputs and options were sought through MyGov, the Government of India platform for public engagement and participation. Another set of questions persisted—how would people interpret the name? Would it connect with people across India? Meanwhile, a series of options for names ranging from 'PM Ke Saath Ru-Ba-Ru' to 'Vaarta Modi Ji Ke Saath' to even 'Modi Vani' started pouring in. It was now time to take a decision.

When his officials went back to him with the issue of the nomenclature, Narendra Modi exclaimed, "Arre isme kya kai? Kaho kuchh halki phulki mann ki baatein karoonga." The christening was done! They had finally found the name for the radio programme—it would simply be called 'Mann Ki Baat.'

There would be no mention of Narendra Modi or the office of the Prime Minister—it would have sounded very official or be seen as a means to achieve personal recognition. It was plain and simple 'Mann Ki Baat' or some musings from the mind, straight from the heart.

There was consensus on the frequency—monthly, but it was the time of broadcast that puzzled the Prime Minister's team. Should it be on a weekday, or on a weekend like Saturdays or Sundays? Should it be in the mornings or in the evenings?

Finally, it was decided that on Sundays at 11 A.M., once a month, would be a good time. After all, weekdays are out of the question and weekend evenings are not ideal for such a programme. Many people work on Saturdays, but Sundays at 11 A.M. is a perfect time. Thus, after the name, the time and frequency were also set.

Narendra Modi wanted to make the radio programme as interactive as possible. In the age of Internet and live television, conventional wisdom suggests that it is quite a task to make a radio programme interactive, but it was decided that the MyGov platform would be used to seek inputs, thoughts, suggestions and questions for the episodes. As time progressed, inputs started coming through letters, phone calls and the 'Narendra Modi Mobile App.'

Due to a packed September schedule, with the Chinese President visiting and the Prime Minister's own US trip, it was decided that the first episode would be aired on 3rd October, a day after Gandhi Jayanti and a day after the launch of the Swachh Bharat Abhiyaan, a flagship programme of the government for creating a 'Clean India'. Swachh Bharat Mission and 'Mann Ki Baat' started their journeys one day apart and also became very interconnected—there is no programme that has been talked about as regularly on 'Mann Ki Baat' as the Swachh Bharat Mission.

Let the Episodes Begin

Finally, on 3rd October on Vijaya Dashami at 11 A.M., the first episode of 'Mann Ki Baat' was on air. The Prime Minister touched upon a variety of issues, from eradicating social evils to urging people to wear Khadi, from cleanliness to issues relating to the specially-abled. He also named some selected people, who had asked questions on MyGov.

The ball was set rolling and there was no turning back. 'Mann Ki Baat' had begun and in style.

The next episode was broadcast on 2nd November and the Prime Minister shared that after his clarion call for wearing more Khadi, the sale of Khadi had shot up by a whopping 125 per cent. He spoke about the positive atmosphere created because of the Swachh Bharat Mission and about his visit to Siachen to show solidarity with the Army jawans.

Gradually, it became clear that behind these 'Mann Ki Baat' episodes was a message. Here was the Prime Minister, not talking about files, day-to-day government matters or government achievements and marketing the work of the government, even though he could have easily done that. He was going beyond all of this. This programme was about connecting with people from Kashmir to Kanyakumari, from Amreli to Agartala. It was purely about positivity. It had a message for youth: rise to the occasion and join the journey to make India a world power. It was about social change—in one episode devoted to the drug menace, the Prime Minister talked about the need to free youngsters from substance abuse. He spoke of how drugs adversely impact the social fabric of a family and affect national growth, and shared experiences from MyGov that would bring tears to the eye.

Some of the episodes had unique themes—he once asked people to share photos from various parts of India using *#IncredibleIndia*. This was a rage on social media. When he asked people to share a *#SelfieWithDaughter*, it became a trend worldwide. These things set the ground for a change—a larger sensitisation towards women or telling the world to come and discover the wonders of India. In June 2016 Narendra Modi called for popularising Yoga to overcome diabetes through *#YogaFightsDiabetes*. In some, he sought participation through mobile technology, thus showing another convergence of tradition and technology, where radio meets mobile.

Narendra Modi has made it a point to address students before their board exams. Never before had a PM directly engaged with school children on such an issue.

That 'Mann Ki Baat' is above partisan politics and never talks about the achievements of the government, has been evident whenever state assembly elections are taking place in some part of the country and the Model Code of Conduct is in place. During such times there is always some party that goes to the Election Commission (EC) with a request to monitor a 'Mann Ki Baat' episode or even stop it from being aired. During the Bihar election campaign, the Janata Dal (United) sent a high level delegation to the Election Commission on this issue. The EC has also released guidelines on areas the 'Mann Ki Baat' cannot cover. However, despite the scrutiny of political parties, there has been no instance where a 'Mann Ki Baat' programme has crossed the line drawn by the EC. In fact, in the September 2015 episode, Narendra Modi talked at length about the proactive efforts of the EC in enabling greater participation in elections as well as in cleaning poll related systems. There is always a dilemma when the Model Code of Conduct comes into force, but Narendra Modi has always steered clear of any controversy or any step that disrespects the authority of the EC and at the same time has continued his communication with the people through the radio.

On Sunday 26th April 2015, the Prime Minister addressed a sombre 'Mann Ki Baat.' Just the previous day, Nepal and parts of India had been affected by a severe earthquake. The trail of destruction was widespread. At such a time, the Prime Minister led the nation and gave a crystal clear message that the present government cares and that it is going to do everything possible to restore normalcy in the quake-affected Nepal.

Upfront and Behind the Scenes

This book is not only an authoritative compilation of all 'Mann Ki Baat' episodes, but also takes you behind the scenes, into the Prime Minister's residence, into the AIR building and to the people whose lives these 'Mann Ki Baat' episodes have touched.

It illustrates how these episodes have generated a social movement in people's lives. It brings out some not-so-open facets of every episode. Does the PM take one episode at a time or does he have a larger vision in doing these monthly radio programmes? The book answers this and many such questions. It is the story of an unlikely friendship between a tech-savvy leader and an otherwise ancient medium and how they have created magic month after month.

At a larger level, the 'Mann Ki Baat' exemplifies a new method of communication. It is direct, it is wide in its reach and it is soft in the nature of the message. It is in tune with the 'Modi way' of doing things—reaching out to the people without barriers. The most effective example of how brand 'Mann Ki Baat' has become a part of the mainstream is seen in how the opposition leaders use it to criticise Narendra Modi. In August 2015, the Congress President said, "The champion of 'Mann Ki Baat' has retreated into a '*maun vrat*' (vow of silence)." She was referring to the ongoing opposition pressure on the government to dismiss the External Affairs Minister, Sushma Swaraj and Rajasthan Chief Minister, Vasundhara Raje on perceived corruption charges. In both cases, the party and the government firmly backed their leaders. In September 2015, at a programme in Odisha, Rahul Gandhi pointed out that Narendra Modi only talks about his 'Mann Ki Baat' and ignores the 'Mann Ki Baat' of the rest of India. He compared the 'Mann Ki Baat' to mere lip service.

Even the ally of the Modi government, the Shiv Sena, uses 'Mann Ki Baat' to taunt the Prime Minister. Though an ally in both Delhi and Maharashtra, the Sena has always criticised the BJP and the Prime Minister on every possible occasion. Not to be left behind, MNS founder and Shiv Sena supremo Bal Thackeray's nephew Raj Thackeray termed it as 'Maun Ki Baat' at a rally in his home state.

There are also leaders who have sought to emulate the 'Mann Ki Baat' concept to connect with their people. Chhattisgarh Chief Minister Dr Raman Singh tried something in the form of 'Raman Ke Goth' in which he too used the radio to interact with people. There were reports that the Punjab Congress leader and former Chief Minister Captain Amarinder Singh would start his radio programme, 'Mann Di Gal', though that has not taken off yet.

Evidently, 'Mann Ki Baat' has become ingrained in public and political discourse. And, Narendra Modi has inverted the conventional wisdom of public discourse to brilliant effect: 'Mann Ki Baat' speaks to an individual instead of a crowd, even as it seeks to knit together a mass movement for change. The great theorist of modern communications, Marshall McLuhan, who popularised the concept of a 'global village', would have understood: the medium, radio, is also the message.

A Voice for Positivity

Through 'Mann Ki Baat', Narendra Modi did something unheard of—give the poor a voice and a medium to reach out to the government. Before every 'Mann Ki Baat', thousands of letters come to Akashvani and for the first time in September 2015, MyGov started a new facility, enabling people to call and share their thoughts. Now, the 'Narendra Modi Mobile App' has become popular among youth for innovative ideas. A large number of these letters and phone calls are not from the urban centres of Delhi, Mumbai, Bengaluru or Hyderabad, but from the small towns of Uttar Pradesh, Bihar and Madhya Pradesh. That the 'Mann Ki Baat' has connected with the Northeast is evident from the fact that so many letters are received from that region as well. Since May 2016, 'Mann Ki Baat' kiosks are being set up in various parts of the country, where people can go and record their messages and share their ideas. Kiosks were set up in places like Pune, Varanasi, Faridabad, Lucknow, Chandigarh, Shimla, Cuttack and Bhubaneswar in May and June 2016. The geographical spread is expected to increase with time.

An Overarching Theme

One theme has constantly emerged from the airwaves whenever Narendra Modi is speaking—that 'Mann Ki Baat' brings out the goodness and strength of society and reflects the changing mindsets in it. One would be surprised—an opportunity to directly reach out to the Prime Minister would be an attractive forum to vent grievances and complaints, but here people were instructing the Prime Minister to build dustbins, to talk about voter awareness and about the use of earthen lamps during festivals!

Narendra Modi is candid:

> *My experience in government tells me, India can be transformed and this is not due to Narendra Modi or any individual. This is due to the strength and skills of 125 crore Indians. Since we have assumed office, we have undertaken several initiatives and we are seeing how much people have trusted us. They have accepted these initiatives as theirs. I can see that the mindset of lack of trust and of sitting back and complaining is changing. People no longer feel this is not happening, that is not happening, they want to drive the change themselves and this is because they place immense faith in this government. This is precisely the faith that is reflected on the radio be it through letters, phone calls and the Mobile App.*

Elaborating more on this, Narendra Modi said:

> *Take the example of the 'Give it up' campaign. In passing I had urged people who can afford to do so, to give up their gas subsidies. As time progressed, we saw that the number of people giving up their subsidies kept increasing and these were not rich people. These were middle class, salaried individuals who rose to the occasion and selflessly gave up something for the sake of others. Today this number has crossed a crore. I talked about it during 'Mann Ki Baat' and I sensed that such an outreach is surely helping spread more awareness and helping people make the decision to give up their subsidies.*

Narendra Modi sees this as an indication of the people's trust in the government. After all, why would people give up their subsidies and give that amount to the government? Even in case of 'Give it up', 'Mann Ki Baat' was at the forefront of initiating a positive change that has touched so many lives and made a scheme like 'Ujjwala Yojana' a reality.

Warm Conversations, Not Cold Monologues

'Mann Ki Baat' has been a transformative national experience because it is a voice of caring from within the heart of governance that bridges distance. It is a warm conversation with citizens, rather than a cold diktat from authority. It is gentle persuasion anchored in the popular interest, shaped by the ethical impetus of shared introspection. It is a consistent call for a silent revolution in the quality of life, through change in a hundred small, but deeply significant ways.

Narendra Modi could have opted for any medium. He chose the radio for a reason. 'Mann Ki Baat' is not about votes or television optics. It is about behaviour, responsibility, hopes, dreams, struggle and achievement in everyday life. Narendra Modi gave a very logical explanation on the subject:

> *I have been a quintessential organisation man all my life. I know the difference the radio can make. American Presidents used it well. So many people heard Martin Luther King's 'I have a dream' speech on the radio. It has a transformative power like no other medium.*

On the radio, Narendra Modi explains, he coaxes; he never imposes. He looks at both sides of the argument. This is why he can confidently say in one broadcast, "I know I am choosing those topics which put the government in the dock." This is always more about conviction that politics.

The touch is gentle. The key is simplicity, a critical requirement of communication. The objective is change from any lingering or pervasive negativity to the positive horizon of our hopes. It is also invariably anecdotal. Real life examples, on drugs, road rage, and cleanliness form the crux of the programme. "I used to observe when we were out campaigning that people love anecdotes. They love hearing real life experiences. People relate to anecdotes", Narendra Modi once said. On 6th August 2016 Narendra Modi participated in the MyGov Town Hall programme where he individually met a large number of contributors, whose names have figured through the 'Mann Ki Baat' programmes. This was a remarkable gesture on the part of the Prime Minister and also very encouraging to others to contribute regularly and effectively for the 'Mann Ki Baat' programmes.

During President Barack Obama's landmark visit to India in January 2015, 'Mann Ki Baat' took on a plural dimension when both heads of government spoke from their heart, again peppering their speeches with interesting anecdotes. In that talk, Prime Minister Modi noted a similarity between Africa's Ubuntu philosophy and our own ancient vision distilled in a powerful truth: "The world is a family." The Ubuntu principle is equally evocative: "I am, because we are." That distils the essence of 'Mann Ki Baat.'

Narendra Modi has made radio cool once again and it will be interesting to see how he continues to use 'Mann Ki Baat' to talk of new things, share his perspective and engage with 125 crore people of India.

India's tourism potential is immense. Our nation is home to enchanting natural and historical wonders that can leave a lasting impression on the human mind. Tourism is also a great means of economic empowerment for the poor.

—Narendra Modi

CHAPTER 2: A Resurrection

On 13th August, 1965, a short and unassuming man was about to take his seat for what would prove to be one of the most important speeches (through the radio) of his life. He had been in politics for years, seen many challenges, witnessed history at close quarters, but the present situation was daunting to say the least. For months his country was at war with an immediate neighbour. He had been new to premiership, replacing the larger than life Pandit Jawaharlal Nehru only a year ago; the country's economic situation was not encouraging. The initial romanticism of Nehruvian socialism was fading and in the absence of a towering personality like Nehru, the internal machinations of the Congress Party were also heating up, threatening the stability of the government even during those challenging times.

The 1965 War was a herculean challenge for Lal Bahadur Shastri. He had to keep the morale of the nation and the troops high, and at the same time the reality was also sinking in that the war would be a disaster for the region in the long term; that while India was comfortably placed vis-à-vis Pakistan, the resource crunch in the long run and the strain on India's economy would be difficult to handle.

At such times, Shastriji turned to the radio. In a passionate speech he urged the people of India to rise to the occasion and shun partisanship. He also gave a very stern warning to Pakistan, saying that any design on their part to take away Indian territory would be wishful thinking and never would India allow mindless Pakistani aggression to succeed.

Prime Minister Shastri's radio address was the perfect antidote that the nation needed. The people of India paid heed to the Prime Minister's message in letter and spirit. The country stood like a rock behind Shastriji as he led the nation to victory in 1965, leaving Pakistan to lick its wounds.

Historical Overview

Unlike the West, where radio was an integral part of political communication, India began with a few inherent disadvantages. Due to colonial rule, the communication network remained under the control of the British and even after independence, the penetration of radio, or the lack of it made it impossible to have a 'radio only' strategy of political outreach.

The website of the All India Radio (AIR) does share a historical overview of the radio in India. It is mentioned on the site:

> *Broadcasting in India actually began about 13 years before AIR came into existence. In June 1923, the Radio Club of Bombay made the first ever broadcast in the country. This was followed by the setting up of the Calcutta Radio Club five months later. The Indian Broadcasting Company (IBC) came into being on July 23, 1927, only to face liquidation in less than three years.*
>
> *In April 1930, the Indian Broadcasting Service, under the Department of Industries and Labour, commenced its operations on an experimental basis. Lionel Fielden was appointed the first Controller of Broadcasting in August 1935. In the following month, Akashvani Mysore, a private radio station was set up. On June 8, 1936, the Indian State Broadcasting Service became All India Radio.*

The Central News Organisation (CNO) came into existence in August, 1937. In the same year, AIR came under the Department of Communications and four years later it came under the Department of Information and Broadcasting. When India attained independence, there were six radio stations in India, at Delhi, Bombay, Calcutta, Madras, Tiruchirapalli and Lucknow. There were three in Pakistan (Peshawar, Lahore and Dacca). AIR then had a coverage of just 2.5% of the area and 11% of the population. The following year, CNO was split up into two divisions, the News Services Division (NSD) and the External Services Division (ESD). In 1956, the name AKASHVANI was adopted for the National Broadcaster. The Vividh Bharati Service was launched in 1957 with popular film music as its main component.

Netaji and the Radio

Radio began to be extensively used by leading Indian figures through the 1940s and thereafter. Netaji Subhas Chandra Bose was a pioneer of sorts when he started the Azad Hind Radio in 1942 to shed light on the activities of the Indian National Army (INA) and generate a wider consciousness towards the Indian freedom struggle. There were weekly broadcasts in English, Hindi, Tamil, Bengali, Marathi, Punjabi, Pashtu and Urdu. An associate from Gujarat, MR Vyas, helped Subhas Bose to launch the channel.

In fact, if one were to look at Subhas Chandra Bose's speeches through the early 1940s, many of them were via the radio, including the Azad Hind Radio. On 11th March, 1942, Netaji addressed people through the Azad Hind Radio from a North German station, where he launched a sharp attack on the British. He termed the fall of Singapore as a, "prelude to the fall of the British Empire." He clearly affirmed in that address:

We are ready to cooperate with any nation that will help us in regaining our Independence. I hope that all my Indian brothers and sisters will help me in this war against the British. Even with her cunning, and underhand policy, Britain cannot fool India, neither can she stop Indians from cherishing their ideal of nationalism. India has decided to fight for her freedom. She will not only free herself, but will free Asia and even the whole world.

As a matter of fact, in a broadcast via Azad Hind Radio on 25th March, 1942, Subhas Chandra Bose spoke about rumours of his death (something that will interest those who are still working on the events in Netaji's life in the mid-1940s):

This is Subhas Chandra Bose, who is still alive, speaking to you over the 'Azad Hind' radio. British news agencies have spread all over the world the report that I had died in an aeroplane crash on my way to Tokyo to attend an important conference there. Ever since I left India last year, British propaganda agencies have from time to time given contradictory reports of my whereabouts, while newspapers in England have not hesitated to use uncomplimentary language about myself. The latest report about my death is perhaps an instance of wishful thinking. I can imagine that the British Government would, at this critical hour in India's history, like to see me dead since they are now trying their level best to win India over to their side for the purpose of their imperialistic war.

"This is Subhas Chandra Bose speaking to you over the Azad Hind Radio" became a line often repeated, each time he addressed people via the Azad Hind Radio. For him, the Azad Hind Radio became a means to directly reach out to the people, to boost the morale of his troops and periodically taunt India's colonial rulers about the war and their inability to grant freedom to India.

Bose's radio addresses continued and were at their peak between 1943 and 1945. Sometimes from Europe, sometimes from Singapore, Tokyo, Rangoon, Malaysia, his addresses were passionate and brought out the fighter in him. As the war began to take a turn for the worse and the Axis powers were heading towards a confirmed defeat, Subhas Chandra Bose raised the issue of ill-treatment meted out to those who served in the INA. At the same time, through his radio addresses, he continued to raise the morale of his troops. His radio broadcasts through June 1945, mention a rejection of the Wavell Offer and the need to carry on the struggle taken up by the INA. His passion and determination are clearly visible if one reads the transcripts of his radio broadcasts.

The Light has gone out

Mahatma Gandhi, a communicator par excellence himself is said to have given one of the best radio addresses on 12th November, 1947. That was the day he visited the AIR studios for the first (and perhaps the last) time to talk to people via the radio. The occasion was an address to the refugees from Pakistan who had made Kurukshetra their home. He did not speak much (around twenty minutes) but he shared the pain of those who were displaced thanks to a bitter partition and expressed solidarity with them. His address, which was delivered on Diwali day, was like that bright light bidding farewell to darkness and suffering.

On 30th January, 1948, when Mahatma Gandhi was assassinated, Pandit Jawaharlal Nehru turned to All India Radio to deliver one of his most emotional and emphatic speeches. Delivered extempore and with great sadness, Pandit Nehru lamented the loss of the 'light of our lives' leaving behind a trail of omnipresent darkness. He shared details of the funeral arrangements and urged the nation to remain united. In fact, the All India Radio

Headquarters located in Delhi has preserved the room, in which Pandit Nehru made that special broadcast.

Nehru continued to use the radio on occasions through his Prime Ministership. His radio address on 20th November, 1962, during the India-China faceoff is remembered, albeit for the wrong reasons. The people of the North-east felt wronged and betrayed by Pandit Nehru at a time when they needed him the most. An impression was created in the minds of the people that India's first Prime Minister, a towering leader in India and across the world, was insensitive to the aspirations and security needs of the North-east. It gave a message that Pandit Nehru had left the people of Assam to their fate when the Chinese came rather than do something more concrete about the worsening situation.

Banks, Privy Purses and the Emergency

After Nehru in 1962 and Shastri in 1965, the 'connection' between wars and radio continued in 1971 when Mrs Indira Gandhi used radio to address the nation and encourage the troops. Even in the 1970s, this was still the most extensive medium to send a message across the nation.

Mrs Indira Gandhi used the radio to communicate her Government's historic decision of nationalizing the banks. When the ordinance on bank nationalization was promulgated, she addressed the nation via All India Radio and offered explanations for the step. She made the case for state-run banks, which she saw as institutions that should touch the lives of millions of people, which would have a larger social purpose and thus be publically owned.

A similar situation arose in 1970. This time the context was the abolition of privy purses, which

Mrs Gandhi was championing. The Bill was passed in the Lok Sabha but fell by one vote in the Rajya Sabha (two-thirds was the number needed) and this led to Mrs Gandhi promulgating an ordinance, which President VV Giri approved. However, on 15th December, 1970, the Supreme Court declared the ordinance null and void, leading to a radio address by Mrs Gandhi in the evening of 27th December, 1970 during which she announced that she was dissolving the Lok Sabha and calling for fresh elections because those waiting for food, shelter and jobs were pressing for action. Her radio broadcast that evening made the case for her government's pro-poor and socialist agenda, leading to her emphatic win in the 1971 Lok Sabha elections.

The darkest moment in the history of independent India was also made public through the radio. In an unscheduled broadcast on 26th June, 1975, Prime Minister Indira Gandhi announced the imposition of Emergency. The next 21 months were the most difficult periods in the history of Indian democracy. Freedom of speech and expression were curbed. Media freedom was at an all-time low. All India Radio began to be referred to by many as 'All Indira Radio' as it was reduced to a propaganda machine for the Prime Minister and her party.

The next decade saw the advent of colour television in India. In 1982, for the first time, the people of India saw the Asiad Games telecast in colour. After years of radio or black and white television, the novelty of colour television was tremendous. The flipside of this was that of the radio losing popularity among leaders as the preferred mode of communication.

During the 1980s, Mrs Gandhi did use the radio to share with the nation her decision to call out the Army in Punjab in 1984. The rest, of course, is history, leading to Operation Blue Star, her own assassination and the Punjab problem that lasted through the 1980s and the early 1990s.

There is no major instance of Rajiv Gandhi placing the radio at the core of his communication strategy. Neither did subsequent Prime Ministers, VP Singh, Chandrashekhar, Deve Gowda and IK Gujral (who had short tenures) and PV Narasimha Rao (never known to be a communicator in the league of Nehru, Indira Gandhi, Vajpayee and Narendra Modi) use the radio substantively. By the time Prime Minister Vajpayee assumed office, India was a nation in transition, preparing to embrace the 21st century and the priorities of the nation were naturally being steered in that direction, leaving little scope for the radio to retain influence.

Therefore, when Narendra Modi's 'Mann Ki Baat' was broadcast on 3rd October 2014, it was after a very long hiatus that the radio was returning to the centre of public imagination and that too, at a frequency never seen in the past. Narendra Modi has created a strong mechanism for a Prime Minister to reach out to the nation at regular intervals, through a medium that is all-pervasive and in a format that can click with the people.

Where Modi is Different

From the above references, it is clear that while the radio was indeed used by Prime Ministers Nehru and Indira Gandhi post-1947, that usage was very different. Mrs Gandhi's radio broadcasts were often confrontational. Be it the broadcast on bank nationalisation, privy purses or the Emergency, these broadcasts were confrontationist in nature. In every broadcast, Mrs Gandhi was not only talking to the people, but also targeting her political opponents both inside and outside the party. In case of the Emergency, it obviously marked the start of a very shameful phase in India's history.

In contrast, Narendra Modi has used the radio for a very different purpose. He has shared things that common citizens can relate to, at regular periods to create an extraordinary impact. His radio broadcasts do not have a confrontationist tone. There is no reference to politics and no remarks on political opponents. Narendra Modi is the first Prime Minister for whom radio is not essentially a means of breaking news but a means of regularly communicating with people, on topics as wide as examinations, farmers' issues and giving water to birds during peak summers.

What was earlier used in times of special events, wars and tragedies, is now being used to reach out to citizens.

A New Paradigm

So, does 'Mann Ki Baat' mark the start of a revolutionary communication strategy that has marked a paradigm shift in how a leader communicates?

Did Narendra Modi adopt a brilliant strategy centred on a medium no one bothered to look at?

The man himself did not answer that question, but political commentator, journalist and someone who has seen Narendra Modi very closely, Ashok Malik had this to say:

> *Modi is an unusual communicator in that while he uses the media as an intermediary to propagate his message, he takes away the media's gatekeeper role, and curbs its ability to edit or censor him. He does this by creating events and hooks that the media cannot ignore, but where the media—and social media—play out his message in real time, without*

> *any lag or opportunity for filtering or interpretation. In that sense, he has turned the media's chief attribute—reporting compelling events—to, in effect, disempower it. The closest analogy I can draw is that with Franklin Delano Roosevelt and his 'Fireside Chats' as President of the United States in the 1930s. He spoke as an avuncular or brotherly figure to a nation and a people left confused by the Great Depression. He tried to talk up the national mood, and explained his policies and legislative changes in a broader framework, rather than make simply political and polemical speeches.*

Every elected government claims to rule by the Abraham Lincoln precept: *of the people, by the people and for the people*. The tricky part is "by the people". How do you come close to addressing that requirement without sending an invitation to confusion? Prime Minister Modi has found an answer: interaction, through the radio. It is not merely the Prime Minister who reaches out to the people, the people also find their way to the Prime Minister. Each episode of 'Mann Ki Baat' addresses personal and public concerns sent to the PM by Indians across the nation—a student's worry about examinations, or a parent's anguish about drug addiction in the family.

The Prime Minister speaks with compassion and anecdotal charm. He tells students that he is hardly the best person to offer advice on how to do well in examinations, because he was no more than an average student. Moreover, he adds, he had a terrible handwriting, and jokes that he probably passed because the examiner could not read what he had written. The message is unequivocal: don't stress. Poor marks are not the end of life (they certainly were not in his case). The PM recalls Swami Vivekananda's wisdom. Each one of us is a lamp, we are our own guide. He remembers that he used to once write poetry in Gujarati. "If successful," said one poem, "you get envy, and if a failure, ridicule. These are the cycles of life."

Historian Saradindu Mukherjee says:

> *In a country where an overwhelming majority of people, especially in rural areas are without a T.V. set and fewer still are reading newspapers, it is only proper that Narendra Modiji's reliance on the radio as the most effective means of communicating with people on matters of utmost concern to them is the best available option. Radio, in its smallest form, is a portable transistor, which neither costs much nor takes much space. It can be heard and unlike TV, serves without the necessity of being viewed. In that sense, both the medium and the message are really an effective idea even in the early 21st century. Modiji's choice of radio is thus a veritable symbol of his concern for the Aam Janta.*

This is how 'Mann Ki Baat' differs from any previous usage of the radio by leaders in India.

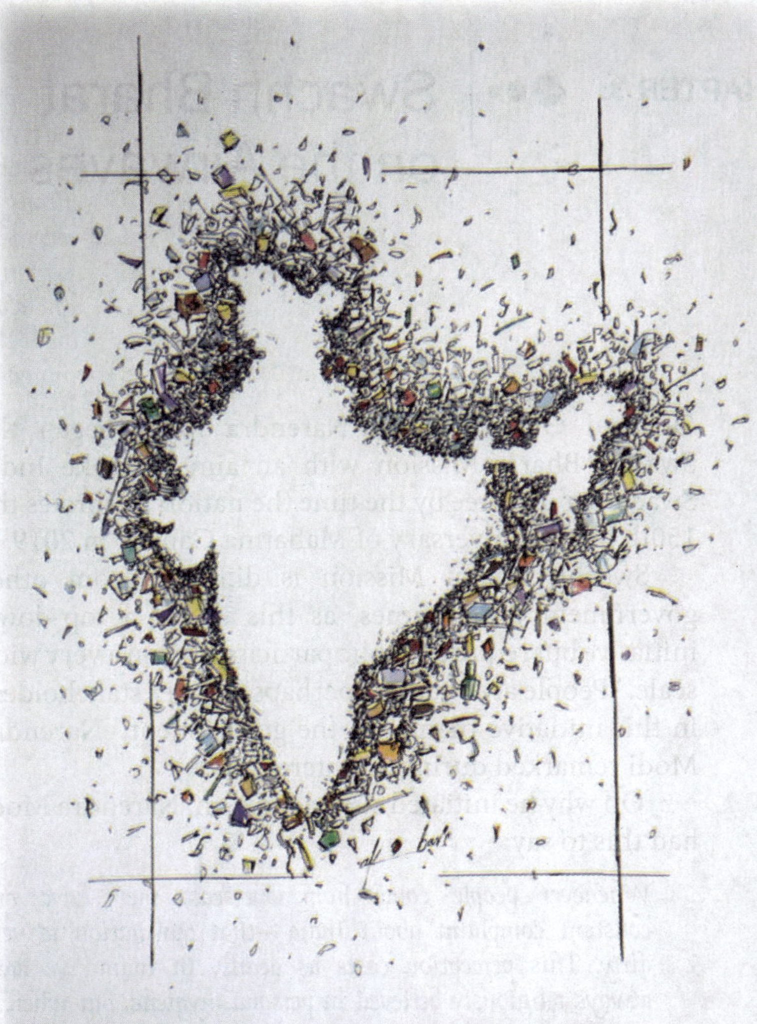

Swachh Bharat Abhiyaan is a mass movement aimed at making India free from dirt. A clean India is the strongest foundation for a prosperous India.

—Narendra Modi

CHAPTER 3: Swachh Bharat on the Airwaves

On 2nd October 2014, Narendra Modi began the Swachh Bharat Mission with an aim to make India Swachh or dirt free by the time the nation celebrates the 150th birth anniversary of Mahatma Gandhi in 2019.

Swachh Bharat Mission is different from other government programmes, as this is not a top-down initiative but requires public participation on a very wide scale. "People are equal, or perhaps, greater stakeholders in this initiative than even the government," Narendra Modi remarked during an interaction.

On why he initiated such a mission, Narendra Modi had this to say:

> *Whenever people come from overseas, they have one constant complaint about India—that our nation is very dirty. This perception costs us dearly. In India, we have always religiously believed in personal hygiene, but when it comes to societal hygiene, our commitment wavers. So many towns and villages are dirty and when there is a lack of proper hygiene, it is the poor who suffer the most. Illness becomes rampant and it hampers their productivity. I have always wanted to change this. When it comes to cleanliness, the most inspiring icon is Mahatma Gandhi and, therefore, we thought of giving a clarion call to make India dirt free by the 150th birthday of Mahatma Gandhi.*

The launch of Swachh Bharat Mission was met with unprecedented enthusiasm, even from unexpected quarters. Former Congress and Samajwadi Party leader, who served in the Rajya Sabha, Shahid Siddiqui, noted, "I can see another Gandhi in PM Modi. Mahatma [Gandhi] never separated social reforms from politics. [Narendra] Modi is also acting both as a reformer and a leader."

Gul Panag, who contested the 2014 Lok Sabha elections on an Aam Aadmi Party ticket, had this to say, "What a fantastic idea [Swachh Bharat Mission]. Can we please start being strict about checking littering? Don't litter and don't let anyone litter."

Businessperson Kiran Mazumdar Shaw opined, "Applaud PM Modi for making cleanliness a national mission. I have always felt despondent in the past as every effort to clean up failed."

Film actor Aamir Khan said, "This is a beautiful idea by our PM. We must all support this campaign."

Another actor, Priyanka Chopra, remarked, "This is an idea that is long overdue and there is no time like the present to begin the journey towards change."

The overall atmosphere was one of support and encouragement. Opposition politicians like Dr Shashi Tharoor took the lead in supporting the Mission. Tharoor, in fact was one of the nine people nominated by the Prime Minister to join the movement and further nominate nine more people to continue the chain and thus, integrate the entire nation in this quest for cleanliness.

Clean India on the Radio

The expectations from Swachh Bharat Mission are immense and the scrutiny under which it has been placed is equal if not more. Yet, not even the worst of his critics deny that this is for the first time that a Prime Minister has brought cleanliness to the fore and placed it at the centre of national discourse.

Tune in on Sundays for 'Mann Ki Baat' and it is not uncommon to hear the Prime Minister talking about cleanliness, again and again. Cleanliness has become the most talked about topic during 'Mann Ki Baat.'

In June 2016, Narendra Modi shared the touching story of Chandrakant Kulkarni, a retired government teacher who donated almost a third of his pension for 52 months through post-dated cheques for the Swachh Bharat Mission. For a retired teacher to donate Rs 5000 from his monthly pension of Rs 16,000 is no small thing. Narendra Modi met Chandrakant Kulkarni in Pune and even lauded him during the 'Mann Ki Baat' saying that people like him are an inspiration for the entire nation.

Chandrakant Kulkarni's life and the fact that someone no less than the Prime Minister himself mentioned it on the airwaves illustrated how the people of India have begun to connect themselves with the Swachh Bharat Mission.

Likewise, in August 2016, Narendra Modi shared stories from Chhattisgarh and Karnataka, where youngsters persisted with their parents for toilets. The anecdote he narrated in Karnataka was that of a girl in Koppal district who went on a Satyagraha for a toilet. It took the involvement of the local Gram Panchayat President, Mohammed Shafi to ensure that a toilet was built. In Chhattisgarh, a group of youngsters wrote letters seeking toilets, thus making a great difference for the local population.

The very first time Narendra Modi highlighted the issue of cleanliness was during the first episode of 'Mann Ki Baat' on 3rd October 2014. He made a passionate appeal to the people to support the Swachh Bharat Mission and make proactive efforts to create a clean India.

A month later, in November 2014, Narendra Modi shared:

> *Cleanliness... who could have imagined that this would become a mass movement? People's expectations are huge and rightfully so. People are seeing this issue in two ways—one is the issue of the dirt that is already there. There is an expectation that the government machinery at the central, state and local level, will now rise to the occasion and find a solution to this problem. The media has been positive too. The second and the satisfying part is that common citizens are thinking that we cannot let the country get dirty. Whatever has happened in the past has happened. We have to turn over a new leaf and we will keep our country clean. A lot of people who come to meet me from all walks of life talk about the Swachh Bharat Mission and cleanliness.*

From Waste to Wealth and Beyond

In another episode on 28th June 2015, Narendra Modi stressed on a different facet of cleanliness—that of recycling and waste management. He shared the mantra of 'Waste to Wealth' that seeks to tap into the utilitarian purposes of urban waste through proper systems and procedures.

On 30th August 2015, the Prime Minister spoke at length about the dengue menace that affected large parts of India, including the capital. The message was clear and direct—that there is a need to improve sanitation conditions, particularly in urban spaces. During dengue outbreaks, it is the poor who are affected, once again underscoring Narendra Modi's linkage between good sanitation, good health and why it matters to the poor.

Of Phone Calls and the Media

During the October 2015 episode of 'Mann Ki Baat', a few phone calls were included and one of them was about cleanliness. Narendra Modi shared on that day, "I got a call from Savita Rai of Mumbai. She laid emphasis on keeping one's surroundings clean and ensuring cleanliness even after the festivities are over." People have heard messages on keeping homes and surroundings clean before or during a festival, but here was Narendra Modi, through a caller from Mumbai, talking about giving importance to cleanliness after the celebrations had ended, when the potential for filth is at its peak.

In the same episode, Modi lauded the role played by the media in spreading the message of cleanliness. He took the name of several media houses that contributed towards a clean India and showcased the efforts of those working towards a clean India. Among those the PM lauded, was Ramoji Rao, the media doyen based in South India and leading English as well as Hindi channels. Narendra Modi recalled his visit to the 'Safaigiri Awards' organised by the India Today Group, where those working towards cleanliness were honoured.

The Prime Minister's encouragement and appreciation was acknowledged by leading journalists. Vikram Chandra of NDTV tweeted, "Thank you Narendra Modi for your kind words about NDTV and RB's Banega Swacch India campaign. Cleaning India remains a national priority." He described this initiative as "excellent" and praised the Prime Minister for this effort. Amitabh Bachchan, who was also a part of this campaign, tweeted, "PM acknowledges NDTV's Banega Swachh India campaign. We are encouraged to do more."

Dr Subhash Chandra of ZEE expressed joy on Twitter, "Thank you, Mr Narendra Modi ji, for your kind words expressed in Mann Ki Baat, about ZEE's support to Swachh Bharat Abhiyaan. As one family, espousing the belief of *Vasudhaiva Kutumbakam*, we shall continue our efforts in unifying the nation and the world!" Aroon Purie of India Today shared, "Very encouraged by PM Narendra Modi lauding India Today's efforts on Safaigiri in Mann Ki Baat."

The relationship between Narendra Modi and sections of the media is often described as frosty. However, when it comes to cleanliness, Narendra Modi has time and again lauded the role of the media in spreading the message and contributing towards a Swachh Bharat. They have, in his view, done so very objectively and with very sincere intentions.

When a Child 'Instructed' the Prime Minister

When Narendra Modi was sharing his 'Mann Ki Baat' on 20th September 2015, he received a phone call that he will always remember. The caller was a child. Nothing else is known about him, for he was too impatient to share his name or even his location. All that he said was, "Modi ji, now that you have taken up this movement towards a Clean India, you must put dustbins everywhere, on every street." When Modi heard this, his smile widened. He said, "Look at the power of our democracy. Here is a small child who forgot to share even his name. But, he had an order for the Prime Minister which I am sharing with you all."

This one phone call revealed a lot. It illustrated, on one hand, the herculean expectations from Narendra Modi and his team to deliver on the promise of a Swachh Bharat (and a whole lot of other things). On the other hand, it showed how involved people themselves have become with the Swachh Bharat Mission and the faith they have that their Prime Minister will listen to them. That a small child picked up the phone and ordered his Prime Minister to do something is a living example of this.

Anecdotes to Remember

On other occasions, Narendra Modi lauded initiatives taking place in the remotest parts of the country. On 26th July 2015, he shared an anecdote from Rajnandgaon in Chhattisgarh:

There is a small village in Chhattisgarh's Rajnandgaon district. The people of that village are making efforts to construct toilets. Today that village is open-defecation free. When this was achieved, the village celebrated that day like a grand festival. This is an ideal example of what I call 'Jan Man Badalna'.

In the same episode, he recounted an incident from neighbouring Madhya Pradesh:

In Harda, MP, the officials started an initiative that touched my heart and that is operation 'Mal Yuddha'. They added a new dimension to the Swachh Bharat Mission. They began a movement–'Brother Number One'–in which brothers gifted toilets to their sisters. See how the meaning of Raksha Bandhan changed!

Such instances generated a great deal of positivity. They also inspired others to take up the cause of a Swachh Bharat. During a conversation, Narendra Modi said:

I keep talking about Swachh Bharat, to the point of sounding repetitive because if we have to change mindsets, we will have to do it together and we will have to keep these memories fresh in the minds of the people. So many people write to me about their work, but due to shortage of time, I cannot share all of them. These stories make me very happy. From the Parliament to small children, everybody is now discussing cleanliness. Our critics want us to do more, but at least by critiquing us, they are discussing an issue like cleanliness which was ignored for years.

The emphasis on cleanliness does seem to have struck a chord with people. Suresh (@surnell on Twitter) pointed out,

"*#MannKiBaat*—Importance of cleanliness taken to new heights. Everyone is talking about it and most importantly 'doing' something about it." Amit Thadhani was happy that the Prime Minister highlighted the dengue menace. He opined, "PM talks about dengue and links it to water storage and Swachh Bharat. Very good to hear this." Ankit Bhuptani felt that the Prime Minister talking to the small child was worth remembering. He said, "The most heartening aspect [of today's 'Mann Ki Baat'] was to listen to the young boy, in his innocent voice, talk about Swachh Bharat."

The Chief Ministers of Chhattisgarh and Madhya Pradesh too expressed happiness on being mentioned by the Prime Minister for the work done by their states towards cleanliness. Dr Raman Singh observed:

> *It is a great occasion as PM Narendra Modi appreciated the efforts of the people of village Keshla for making it an open defecation free area. We thank the PM for his appreciation through 'Mann Ki Baat' and placing our Chhattisgarh on the national pedestal and also congratulate the people of Chhattisgarh.*

Mr Shivraj Singh Chouhan, the Chief Minister of Madhya Pradesh, also expressed his gratitude to PM Modi for appreciating the efforts in Harda to promote sanitation.

The Road Ahead

There are two choices before the nation—either to brood continuously about how unclean India is or to do something on the ground and bring about a positive change. The Swachh Bharat Mission is an effort towards the latter. Narendra Modi has kept this matter totally away from politics and has sought the support and co-operation of people from all walks of life. Opposition MP, Shashi Tharoor, who has both supported and criticised the Swachh Bharat Mission on multiple occasions, willingly participated in the movement after the Prime Minister invited him. Mata Amritanandamayi donated Rs 100 crore for cleaning the Ganga. Sports persons and film stars have also shown their support for this initiative. Most importantly, people on the ground have chipped in.

The Prime Minister has used the radio very well to showcase the importance which he attaches to cleanliness. His comments on cleanliness are not empty sermons. They are either stories or anecdotes. He has picked up the aspects of cleanliness that others tends to miss, such as dengue or post-festival cleanliness. His linking of the issue of cleanliness with the well-being of the poor has been instrumental in encouraging people to contribute to the Swachh Bharat Mission.

Bindeshwar Pathak is a well known name not only in India but across the world. He has devoted his life to building toilets and improving sanitation facilities and his selfless work through Sulabh has become a mass movement. He said:

> *The Prime Minister, Mr Narendra Modi has ignited the candle of cleanliness among Indians to make India clean. He has asked Indians to restore the culture of sanitation which Indians had during Harappan civilization. We should join hands with the Prime Minister with all our might and resources, to make India clean and free from defecation in the open. Be civilized, be cultured, be clean, make India clean and stand out in the row of civilized, cultured and clean nations.*

Yoga is becoming increasingly popular across the world. The first two yoga days were widely observed with record number of people taking part globally.

—Narendra Modi

CHAPTER 4:

'Mann Ki Baat' spurs a Mass Movement

Narendra Modi has always betted on the collective strength of the people. Those who have worked with him in Gujarat and Delhi say that few things excite him more than bringing people together to bring about a positive transformation. When he took over as the Chief Minister of Gujarat in 2001, the social indicators, particularly the state of education worried him, as it should have worried any Chief Minister. However, the way he tackled it was very different. Rather than sitting in air-conditioned rooms only making policies, Narendra Modi went to the villages of Gujarat in the peak of summer, with all the Cabinet Ministers as well as officials, and urged parents to educate their children, particularly their daughters, to enroll them in schools and reduce drop-out rates. The results were outstanding—enrolment in schools across Gujarat shot up, while drop-out rates decreased significantly. A state where children were known to stay home now saw record enrolment in schools. This is how a mass movement was born to transform the education sector in Gujarat.

Similarly, Gujarat's water problem worried Narendra Modi. He recounted:

> *Meeting after meeting, farmers and other people came to me to discuss the power situation. The perception is that once the power crisis is solved, development will happen. I told them, yes, I will look at the power woes but you focus on water conservation. You would be surprised that my repeated insistence led to a rise in the water table in Gujarat. And how did this happen? People took it up and made it a mass movement. Check dams were built. If you look at the Gujarat Government's Water and Sanitation Management Organisation (WASMO) initiative, the essence is public participation. The key to any initiative succeeding is to make it a mass movement, involve more and more people. The strength of our people is immense. They will ensure that it works.*

Similar initiatives were under taken to improve agriculture (Krishi Mela), to promote sports (Khel Mahakumbh) and initiatives like Gunotsav to create a stronger and more effective education system. All these initiatives were driven by the guiding principle that Jan Bhagidari or people's participation will lead to true development and empowerment of the poorest of the poor.

It is not surprising that through the radio, Narendra Modi raises issues that can create a larger awareness and togetherness so that the outcome of this collective strength benefits society at large. He picks up an issue and takes it directly to the people, and what is a better forum than 'Mann Ki Baat' to do so, to converse directly with the people and create a movement. In the final 'Mann Ki Baat' of 2015, on 27th December 2015, he gave a clarion call to people to interact with him through his 'Narendra Modi Mobile App' and enrich it with constructive ideas and inputs. In the same episode, he sought ideas on how to make the National Youth Festival 2016 a more effective platform for youngsters to showcase their strength and skills. This festival, an annual exercise, never received such prominence from the earlier Prime Ministers, but this was different. Seeking views on MyGov has also become a norm.

The radio has proven just the right medium for Narendra Modi to share his thoughts, particularly when it came to involving people and making what he called 'development into a mass movement.'

The reach of the radio is very wide, spanning across the length and breadth of India. It compliments beautifully what people see and hear on TV as well as social media. The impact was seen repeatedly when Narendra Modi would share instances of inspiring anecdotes, like an elderly person building toilets, or when local communities placed emphasis on cleanliness and sanitation.

Weaving the Right Yarn of Empowerment

Khadi has been a popular subject in 'Mann Ki Baat' from the first episode when the Prime Minister exhorted the citizens to re-adopt Khadi as a modern fashion statement, to the January 2016 episode where Modi again reiterated the benefits of adopting Khadi. In between, in the October 2015 episode, Narendra Modi reported back to the citizens on the growth in Khadi sales through retail sales counters and thanked them for responding to his call.

This spurt was a result of citizens, responding to his call. What was the government doing? This is where the follow-up mechanism works. The Ministry of Small and Medium Enterprises reports on a monthly basis on the implementation timelines of new ideas that keep on coming in. The introduction of Khadi denim designer-wear in June 2015, was a result of this process. In the regular deliberations that happen on how to further boost the adoption of Khadi and drive jobs growth through it, an idea that came through MyGov on institutional adoption of Khadi by government departments, was put across to all ministries for deliberation. Since March 2016, the entire cabin crew in Air India One, the official aircraft of the Prime Minister, are dressed in Khadi. The Railways have decided to adopt Khadi in a big way—from official uniforms to their beddings and toiletries in train compartments. Soon Air India followed suit. The private sector was not far behind. J.K. Cements joined the bandwagon next. The exhortation by the Prime Minister in his first episode, in October 2014, was being closely followed up and implementation was monitored one and a half years later.

Kalraj Mishra, the Union MSME Minister, under whose department this issue falls, said:

> *In the Prime Minister, we have got the best brand ambassador for Khadi. Back in the very first 'Mann Ki Baat' episode in October 2014 the PM called for using Khadi and the response was phenomenal. Individuals, organisations–both private and government–have added strength to this. I can say that Khadi is becoming cool once again and substantial credit goes to Modi ji. The medium of 'Mann Ki Baat' is notable because it reaches people across India and when a positive message is broadcast through such a medium it is bound to connect. My Ministry is trying all possible ways to make Khadi popular, particularly among youngsters. Khadi is stylish and economically empowering for weavers, which makes it a win-win situation.*

Through the radio, Narendra Modi exhorted people to use a product that was affordable, comfortable and very close to the heart of Mahatma Gandhi. He raised the pitch at a scale never seen before. He also put emphasis on 'Khadi for fashion' with an aim to appeal to the youth. Noted fashion designer Ritu Beri made a relevant observation by saying:

> *Our Prime Minister's call of 'Khadi for Nation and Khadi for Fashion' has resulted in the tremendous surge of global popularity of the traditional fabric. The demand for Khadi amongst retailers, promoters, designers and consumers has also escalated. As a sequel, there has also been a simultaneous restoration of the traditional fabric which has given the weavers a new lease of life.*

When Narendra Modi made the People of India and the World, Brand Ambassadors for 'Incredible India'

For a country that boasts of immense natural beauty, beautiful hills, the seas, pristine rivers, deserts and a cultural diversity that is perhaps unparalleled across the world, India's tourism sector has not reached its full potential. Facilities are seen to be lacking and there is a perception of a lack of cleanliness as well. Connectivity is another major problem. There is a perception that over and above what governments can do, people must also chip in and do their bit to make India more tourism-friendly.

During the 'Mann Ki Baat' episode on 31st May 2015, when Narendra Modi talked about the advent of the vacation season and invited people to share their photos of travel destinations in India using *#IncredibleIndia*, little did he know the impact it would have.

This 'simple' request from the PM flooded the Internet with breathtaking images of India, images that even citizens of India had never seen.

Just a few hours after the show was aired, Indians shared images of the country that showcased its beauty from all across. Some also shared their travel stories and the PM, later in the day, responded to some of the tweets, much to the delight of his fans, and even re-tweeted lots of such wonderful images.

The nature of images varied and was an eclectic mix, encapsulating India's enchanting beauty. Someone shared a beautiful view of the Teesta River, which originates from North Sikkim. Kaushal Inamdar shared an image of the Golden Temple in Amritsar, the holy shrine of the Sikhs. He also added that he was listening to the divine singers inside the temple. Yogesh shared pictures of magnificent Hampi in Karnataka and called his experience truly wonderful and blissful. Kaustubh Khare shared a beautiful image of the 17th century Sindhudurg Sea Fort in Konkan, which was once the pride of the Maratha navy.

This campaign caught the attention of people worldwide. Tahseen Shaukat, who was the Country Head of Ten Sports in Pakistan at that time, shared images of Udaipur in Rajasthan, a destination very popular among both Indian and foreign tourists. A Vietnamese youngster, whose Twitter handle goes by the name of @tienqueen, shared photos from all over India and expressed his admiration for India. Several photos made their way to an album created on Narendra Modi's Facebook page.

Chetan, a 27-year-old youngster from Khanna in Punjab, shared this: "I saw a photo of Pandharpur on Prime Minister's Facebook page. I had heard about the place but the photo tempted me to go visit and I actually visited it. Pandharpur is not a place that many people outside the local areas visit, but the *#IncredibleIndia* album did the trick."

#SelfieWithDaughter Campaign and 'Beti Bachao, Beti Padhao'

When Narendra Modi addressed the nation from the ramparts of the Red Fort in 2015, he had some tough words on the gender inequality prevailing in parts of

India. What started with the Independence Day speech soon turned into a pan-India movement in the form of 'Beti Bachao, Beti Padhao' Abhiyaan, with the entire nation coming together to raise awareness on saving the girl child and even ensuring that the girl child receives quality education.

In a small village of Bibipur in the state of Haryana, Sunil Jaglan, the village Sarpanch or headman, initiated a *#SelfieWithDaughter* campaign for giving an impetus to the movement for the empowerment of women. Haryana is one of the worst hit states in India when it comes to gender imbalance. So impressed was Narendra Modi by this innovative initiative that during the 'Mann Ki Baat' in June 2015 he said:

> *I am myself connected to you via the social media. I keep getting many new suggestions and new ideas and also good and bad information about our government. And, sometimes it so happens, that a small comment from an individual in some remote village in India conveys something that just touches our hearts. You are aware that the government has launched the 'Beti Bachao, Beti Padhao' programme. But you can't imagine the force that is lent to this programme when a village or a society adopts it. A few days back, a Sarpanch in a small remote village of Haryana, Mr Sunil Jaglan ji launched the 'Selfie with Daughter' campaign. Such an environment was created that every father wished to click a selfie of himself with his daughter and post it on the social media.*
>
> *I liked this idea and that too for a special reason. In Haryana, the number of girls in comparison to boys is dismally low. In around another 100 districts in the country, there is a similar dismal situation of skewed sex ratio. But it is the worst in Haryana. In that very same Haryana, if a Sarpanch of a small indistinct village lends this meaning to the 'Beti Bachao, Beti Padhao' programme, then I am certainly overwhelmed. It makes me so happy and it gives me a new hope and I do express my happiness. I request you all to take a selfie with your daughter and post it on #SelfieWithDaughter. And do not forget to post a tagline around the theme of 'Beti*

Bachao, Beti Padhao' with it, whatever be the language, it can be in Hindi, English or your mother tongue. And I promise to re-tweet the most inspirational tagline with you and your daughter's selfie. We can turn 'Beti Bachao, Beti Padhao' into a mass movement. I urge you all to take forward the programme launched by Mr Sunil in Bibipur village of Haryana. I request you all to post on #SelfieWithDaughter. Let us all enjoy the rising honour and prestige of our daughters, and see how joyful this entire experience of 'Beti Bachao, Beti Padhao' becomes. Let us all rid ourselves of this bad name that we have for not respecting our daughters.

This was enough to create a worldwide buzz! People from across the world took to Twitter and Facebook to share selfies. This campaign was universal in the true sense and did strike a chord with everyone who has a daughter.

People from all walks of life joined in. Maharashtra Chief Minister Devendra Fadnavis, Union Minister Nirmala Sitharaman, Karnataka MP Pratap Simha, Gujarat Minister Shankarbhai Chaudhary, former IPS officer and current Lt Governor of Puducherry Dr Kiran Bedi, film personality Shekhar Kapur, USA's Assistant Secretary of State Nisha Biswal, journalists Kanchan Gupta, Umesh Upadhyay and Richa Anirudh were among those who shared their selfies. Cricketer Shikhar Dhawan tweeted a picture with his two daughters which said—Daddy's Girls *#SelfieWithDaughter*.

Chitra Subramaniam, a well-known journalist, who shared a 'Selfie with Daughter' said:

I am an eternal optimist and remain very ambitious for India and Indians. I respect good wherever I see it and the Prime Minister's campaign to educate the girl child is one such campaign. I come from the world of media, policy analysis and communications and understand advocacy at the highest levels. In this particular instance, Mr Narendra Modi has framed the issue with a mix of reality and emotion, politics and activism. It is a data-driven call to focus on an issue that should be on top of India's priorities. The construction is creative. It is influenced and guided by the urgent need to get children in general, and girls, in particular, to live the life they deserve, so as to thrive and prosper. Experience has shown me that the radio is perhaps one of the most important forms of conveying a message and telling a comprehensive story. I say this with responsibility in times of Twitter and Facebook—the radio is not intrusive and the spoken word can have a wider impact than the written one. On that score, 'Mann Ki Baat' has done well. Speaking concretely about issues that are critical for Indian women—health, education and security—at this stage of our economic journey, the Prime Minister has enabled a very necessary policy dialogue. A nation that does not respect people who hold up half of its sky cannot grow with respect and dignity. The penny on this issue has dropped. 'Mann Ki Baat' must, now, bolster the advocacy by identifying resources, including financial resources, to make this pledge a reality. One reason why girls drop out of schools is the absence of toilets. By involving the private sector, the Prime Minister has succeeded in ensuring that India's development and growth become a shared responsibility. My tweet with my daughter was an attempt to speak to this reality.

Former Congress MP Naveen Jindal rose above the party lines and tweeted, "Love the *#SelfieWithDaughter* campaign. My selfie with my daughter Yashasvini @narendramodi" while sharing the selfie. Cricket legend Sachin Tendulkar too tweeted his selfie with his daughter Sara.

The excitement outside was equally remarkable. "*#SelfieWithDaughter*. Fathers are so important in a daughter's life. Thank you India for highlighting the importance," is what was tweeted by Bridgette Hemmerich. A Canada-based travel writer, Jim Byers (@JimByersTravel on Twitter) posted on Twitter, "Love India PM's concept of *#SelfieWithDaughter*. Very proud of my daughter, Kathleen. Photo @FourSeasons

Thailand!" Similar selfies were shared by the Editor-in-Chief of *The Street Magazine*, Janet Guyon, author Suzzie Welch and others. Nisha Biswal, one of the high ranking officials in the Obama administration, had great things to say about the initiative taken up by Narendra Modi and went on to share her selfies.

One must concede the final word on this to Kevin Philipp (@Kphilipp_ on Twitter), an American citizen who tweeted along with his selfie, "Whether in *#India* or *#America* or the world, nothing is more important than our daughters!"

The world's eyes were drawn to the nature of the problem and the fact that people from all walks of life joined and raised the chorus for ending any bias as far as the girl child was concerned. The radio, in this case, sowed the seeds of a larger movement that resonated globally.

Modi's 'Mann Ki Baat' for a Swachh Bharat

As seen in the previous chapter, 'Mann Ki Baat' and cleanliness have now become inseparable. If one were to do an analysis of all the topics covered in all the 'Mann Ki Baat' programmes till date, the most recurring topic will be none other than cleanliness.

By continuously reiterating his call for a Swachh Bharat, integrating many related stories and anecdotes in the programmes, Narendra Modi has attempted to use 'Mann Ki Baat' as one of the drivers to serve as a catalyst for a truly Swachh Bharat.

In context, on 2nd November 2014, Narendra Modi spoke about the impact of Swachh Bharat Abhiyaan on the psyche of the nation:

> *Cleanliness... Can anyone imagine that cleanliness will become such a huge public movement? The expectations are high and they should be so. I can see some good results;*

cleanliness can now be witnessed in two parts. One is those huge garbage piles which keep lying in the city; well the people in the government will work to remove those. It is a big challenge but you cannot run away from your responsibilities. All State governments and all municipalities will now have to take concrete actions due to the rising public pressure. The media is playing a very positive role in this. But there is the second aspect which gives me immense pleasure, happiness and a sense of satisfaction, which is that the general public has started feeling that no matter what happened in the past, now they will not dirty their surroundings. We will not add to the existing dirt.

Sharing anecdotes about people who have worked on cleanliness became very common during the 'Mann Ki Baat' programmes. These anecdotes were individual stories and contributions towards a Swachh Bharat and even comments by people on how Swachh Bharat has impacted their lives and society. Narendra Modi made it a point to appreciate the role of children in making the Swachh Bharat Abhiyaan popular. He said in November 2014:

What I am seeing is that this campaign has had a great influence on children. Many families mention that now whenever kids eat a chocolate, they themselves pick the wrapper and dispose it. I was seeing a message on the social media. Someone had posted a picture with the title 'My hero of the Day'. This picture was of a little kid, who picks up trash wherever he goes, even when going to school. He is himself motivated to do this. Just see, people now feel that it is their country and they will not make it dirty. We will not add to the existing dirt pile. And those who litter feel ashamed for someone is around to point it out to them. I consider all these to be good omens.

In November 2015, when Narendra Modi highlighted the proactive role played by the media in spreading the message of a Swachh Bharat and taking it to every household, this was another way to add momentum to an already building mass movement.

This is what Dr Subhas Chandra had to say on the Prime Minister's words for the media, "The role of the media is to be an effective agent of change, for the larger good of society. We, through Zee Media's multiple platforms, have always been proactive in furthering the cause of a Clean India. I was personally delighted, and so was my team when the Prime Minister lauded our efforts to further the message of cleanliness. We felt duty bound to be a means of conveying such a vital message of national relevance to our viewers. 'Mann Ki Baat' has played a positive role in making India cleaner and influencing mindsets, which will eventually help the nation."

When people hear the Prime Minister talking about things like lack of cleanliness, toilets and the importance of sanitation, it certainly motivates them to do their bit. 'Mann Ki Baat' has become a vital brand ambassador for the Swachh Bharat Movement and the positive impact is for everyone to see.

Yoga Goes Global

My dear countrymen, do you remember 21st June? In our part of the world, 21st June is important because it is the longest day of the year on this side of the world. Now this date has become famous for another reason. When I addressed the United Nations in September 2014, I proposed that 21st June be declared as the International Yoga Day. The entire world was amazed. You will also be amazed that within a hundred days, one hundred and seventy-seven countries from around the world supported this proposal. This is a landmark event in the history of the United Nations. This is also a moment of pride for all citizens of our nation.

Now we have the responsibility to make this a success. Did we ever think that yoga will become a medium for integrating mankind? Our ancestors gave the idea that 'the world is one family'. This is a moment of such pride for all of us. However, this movement will gain strength only when we join it in large numbers. We should adopt yoga in its true strength and aspects. Yoga joins the head and the heart, and is a medium of holistic health. It is also a medium for integrating the world.

Why should we not become yoga ambassadors? Why do we not nurture this legacy that will be beneficial for all mankind? Why should we not make it easily accessible? You must have relatives who live in different parts of the world. Call them and ask them to organise neighbourhood yoga meetings on 21st June. If they have no knowledge of yoga, ask them to get a book and organise book readings. Read a letter on yoga. I believe that all of us must take up the campaign to spread yoga across the world and for the welfare of mankind. We must do it for the benefit of suffering mankind, for those who have lost hope and are in need of new energy and hope.

I wish that all of you should take pride in the system of yoga, that has been accepted and received world-wide and is a gift of this nation to mankind. There are still three weeks left and I want that all of us should join together in this campaign. We should also attempt to integrate the world through this campaign.

These words during the 'Mann Ki Baat' programme in May 2015 reverberated across the world when on 21st June, lakhs of people joined the International Day of Yoga programmes and made it a historic occasion that the world will always remember. Yoga has existed for centuries with a very high degree of global popularity, but such institutional popularity and frenzy was not seen in the past. All of this was not only because an Indian Prime Minister spoke about yoga and the UN supported it. The groundswell of support was possible only because the people of India and the world embraced yoga and the concept of having an International Day of Yoga, with immense delight.

Through the efforts of the Government of India, driven by the deep personal interest of the Prime Minister, yoga received an unparalleled shot in the arm. On 21st June, it seemed that the world was engrossed in yoga. In Russia, yoga was done by several people across the length and breadth of the vast nation. From Japan, Australia, Central Asia to South America, it was as if one big global family had embraced yoga!

People in India did everything possible to make the first International Day of Yoga a success. Images of Rajpath on that day are now very popular. Entrepreneurs, film stars, sportspersons and political leaders, cutting across party lines, lent support. Narendra Modi's call to each and every Indian to become brand ambassadors of yoga, delivered on the radio paid rich dividends.

Baba Ramdev has said:

> *Yoga is the crown jewel in our glorious traditions. It is good for physical as well as mental health.*
>
> *In Narendra Modi, we have a leader who is not hesitant to showcase the power of Yoga to the world. He leads from the front.*
>
> *When Narendra Modi is talking about Yoga on the radio, he is not doing so as the Prime Minister. He is doing so as a fellow citizen, who is urging people to lead a healthier life. It is like a family elder guiding a person. It is great that Narendra Modi made Yoga popular across and outside India.*

Achieving Suraksha Bandhan

What is the best way to galvanise support for an initiative that will benefit a vast majority of 125 crore Indians? Narendra Modi surely thinks that radio is one of the best ways. On 31st May 2015, Narendra Modi used the radio to lay emphasis on giving a better future to India's poor. He said:

> *My heart is always yearning to do something for the poor people in our country. I always think of novel ideas and welcome suggestions from others in order to help the poor. Last month, we launched three key policies to provide social security to the people of our society, i.e., Prime Minister's Suraksha Bima*

Yojna, Prime Minister's Jeevan Jyoti Bima Yojna, and Atal Pension Yojna. It has been just twenty days since the launch of these policies, and I can proudly say that due to your trust in our nation, our government, our programmes and policies, the common citizens of our country have joined hands with us in such huge numbers. I am extremely happy in sharing the fact that within a short span of 20 days, more than eight crore and 52 lakh people have registered their names for these programmes. We have adopted important measures in the path of social security and it will act as a boon for the people in future years.

I would like to request those who have not yet received this information to acquire these benefits as soon as possible. No one could have imagined receiving Suraksha Bima Yojna by investing just one rupee per month or 12 rupees in a year. In order to get the benefits of Jeevan Jyoti Bima Yojna, you need to invest just 330 rupees in a year, which is less than a rupee per day. Therefore, by using these benefits, the poor will not be dependent on others for their living. The poor will become independent and self-confident. We are adopting different measures in this direction. I want to create an army of people, my army comprising poor people will fight against poverty and defeat it. Our nation has been burdened with poverty for years now, and we will take appropriate steps to try and eliminate poverty from our nation. We are sure we will succeed.

No government in the history of independent India thought of providing a social security cover to the poor. In terms of scale and logistics, this task was herculean. Getting the government apparatus to agree to such an idea was another challenge and, above all, the biggest challenge lay in how to make these schemes popular among people.

Narendra Modi said:

These schemes are aimed at giving our poor the dignity and security cover that they deserve. A lot of these people may or may not have access to television, but they surely have access to radio. I tried to talk about it during 'Mann Ki

Baat' and was very happy when several people wrote to me saying that they discovered about the schemes through the radio, after which they decided to get enrolled.

He went a step further during the 'Mann Ki Baat' episode on 28th June 2015 and reminded the citizens about Raksha Bandhan and Suraksha. He opined:

Last month, we had launched three insurance schemes. I had launched them from Kolkata and they received a commendable response in such a short span of time. There have been very few steps which have been taken from the perspective of social security but by way of these three schemes we are taking a big leap. In such a short time span, more than 10 crore people have become a part of these schemes, but we have to take it further. I have a thought which I want to put forth before you. Raksha Bandhan comes in the month of August. Can't we start a massive movement before this festival and make every woman, be they our mother or sister, a part of this, thereby giving benefit to them under this insurance programme? Be it a sister who is a domestic help in your home, or your own sister, why can't we gift them a Rs 12 or Rs 330 scheme on Raksha Bandhan for their entire life? This can be a big gift for a sister from her brother. Why can't we set the eve of Raksha Bandhan as a target and in a number of two crore, five crore, seven crore and 10 crore ... try to reach the sisters so that they can reap the benefit of this scheme? Let's come together and try to work towards the completion of this pledge.

Narendra Modi's 'Mann Ki Baat' created a mass movement of sorts on Raksha Bandhan on the 29th of August 2015, with several leaders taking it upon themselves to register women for these insurance schemes. The then Human Resources Development (HRD) Minister Smriti Irani was in Amethi to distribute the insurance coverage money to 25,000 women. Labeled as 'Suraksha Bandhan', the drive was especially aimed at women working as domestic helps and labourers. Put forward as the perfect gifts for sisters, it made available for brothers, three types of cheques which they could gift to their sisters and thereby give them security cover. The values of cheques were Rupees 201, Rupees 351 and Rupees 5,001.

Brothers from all parts of India gave their sisters the best Raksha Bandhan gift they could ever ask for, a gift that would protect them for life!

Those who took part in this conceded that the radio played the role of a catalyst in enabling more and more brothers to gift their sisters with something that would stay with them till the very end.

The Trend Continues

In December 2015, Narendra Modi shared a very unique proposition—he asked people to ensure that statues of great personalities remain in a clean condition all through the year.

This is, by all means, something to think about. Leaders are liberally erecting statues of historical personalities, but then neglect their upkeep and maintenance. The initial response to the Prime Minister's call has been encouraging, with some lawmakers showing the way. Meenakshi Lekhi, the BJP MP from New Delhi, a seat that houses the high and mighty of the nation, got several people together to clean a statue of Dr Babasaheb Ambedkar on his birth anniversary. MyGov launched a campaign, calling upon people to clean statues and share photos of the statue before and after it was cleaned.

A group of youngsters in Vidisha, Madhya Pradesh, cleaned the statue of the state's first Chief Minister, Ravishankar Shukla. Piyush Rout from Odisha shared two pictures on social media of a statue of Netaji Subhas Chandra Bose being cleaned. In the west, in Vadodara,

Gujarat, Pruthvi Desai cleaned the statue of Maharana Pratap. From Varanasi, Siliguri to Puducherry, people joined in large numbers to clean statues.

Supreme Faith in people

The reach of radio has advantages that no other medium offers. One message delivered properly can make a difference on an unimaginable scale. Narendra Modi realised this and has used radio time and again, to spread a message of positivity and to ignite the flame of public participation. This came from a conviction that together, the collective strength and wisdom of the people can do miracles. So, be it hard-selling India as an attractive tourist destination, or seeking to further awareness on cleanliness, or asking brothers to gift social security cover to their sisters, Narendra Modi placed his faith in the people and watched how one request through the airwaves could generate sparks, not only in India, but also across the world.

The 'Mann Ki Baat' with President Obama was special. The questions touched the heart. I am glad people from all over India got an opportunity to hear President Obama on various personal issues and shared memorable anecdotes.

—Narendra Modi

CHAPTER 5: 'Mann Ki Baat' Saath Saath: When President Obama and PM Modi shared their 'Mann Ki Baat'

Among the most popular 'Mann Ki Baat' episodes was the one on 27th January 2015, when Prime Minister Narendra Modi and US President Barack Obama jointly participated in the programme (parts of which have already been discussed at the start of the book). Unlike the programmes that come with a diplomatic visit and uncharacteristic of how two world leaders interact, Prime Minister Modi and President Obama opened up on several issues, ranging from the President's daughters visiting India, to an old picture of Prime Minister Modi standing outside the White House in the 1990s.

ABC News found the chemistry between the two leaders very natural, saying:

> *It is not surprising that the two leaders have immense mutual respect for each other. Both are self-made and first generation politicians who come from very humble background. President*

Obama worked as a community organiser while PM Modi worked for the BJP organisation for many years. These experiences are very valuable. Both won on the outsider plank, vowing to clean up Washington and Delhi and break the existing status quo. The 'Mann Ki Baat' during President Obama's visit was a phenomenal programme. It went beyond diplomacy and brought out a different side of the two leaders. It was personal and very warm.

Noted commentator Sadanand Dhume observed:

The decision to conduct a joint 'Mann Ki Baat' capped a successful summit between Prime Minister Narendra Modi and President Barack Obama. At the most basic level, it stood out as innovative: using radio to reach millions of listeners directly. At a deeper level, it signaled much more including Obama's personal warmth towards Modi and the values rooted in democracy shared by India and the United States. The joint 'Mann Ki Baat' was widely viewed by foreign policy experts who follow US-India relations as an innovation in public diplomacy. In my view, it intelligently highlighted India's great strengths as a democratic polity and open society. Nor was the symbolism of the two self-made men—each in his own way embodying a historic electoral mandate, addressing their people—lost on observers. All-in-all, a brilliantly conceptualised and expertly executed idea.

That heartfelt conversations can bridge historical differences and distance, was illustrated beautifully during the joint 'Mann Ki Baat' with Prime Minister Narendra Modi and President Barack Obama.

The Genesis of MKB

Narendra Modi mooted the idea of a radio programme, while planning for the Obama visit. The American side accepted and on 22nd January 2015, Narendra Modi posted a series of tweets that read:

I am eagerly looking forward to the special 'Mann Ki Baat' programme with President Barack Obama, which will be aired on 27th January. #AskObamaModi and be a part of this memorable 'Mann Ki Baat' programme, illustrating a special bond between India and the USA. 'Mann Ki Baat' with President Obama will not be complete without your participation! Send your Qs till the 25th, using #AskObamaModi.

Here again, public participation was the cornerstone. This would be a programme of Barack Obama, Narendra Modi and the people of the world's oldest and largest democracies. In no time *#AskObamaModi* became a trend and questions poured in. Akhilesh Mishra, then Director Content, MyGov, recalls:

We got an unprecedented response. People across India, many Indians living outside and indeed several Americans shared their questions and thoughts. These questions were not overtly political. A lot of people wanted to know stories from the growing-up years of these two leaders, their inspirations, and their motivation which drives them with such boundless energy and some anecdotes from their day-to-day lives.

Unlike other major speeches or events, where world leaders are present, there was no prior briefing for Narendra Modi. He made it clear that this was a heart-to-heart discussion with President Obama, beyond matters of diplomacy, politics and economics. It was a rare platform where the speakers took audience questions and answered them individually as well as jointly. The frank conversation thus reached everyone in the interiors of the country. The leaders were the hosts and the participants.

In fact, one of the most admired aspects of 'Mann Ki Baat' was the way both leaders conducted the programme themselves. Twitteratti and electronic media were abuzz with Narendra Modi's style of 'RJing.' Ravi Kant Mittal said on social media, "Narendra Modi giving RJs tough competition, conducting 'Mann Ki Baat' with Barack Obama very smartly."

Rahul Kanwal observed on social media:

> *Narendra Modi doing a fine job moderating the show with Barack Obama. Anchors will be out of business if Netas (leaders) interview each other.*

Fellow journalist Dibang was equally charitable and said:

> *Aaj Narendra Modi ne saabit kiya ke voh ek achchhe anchor bhee ban sakte hain. Sabhi anchors ke liye ghanti hai.*
>
> *(Today Narendra Modi has proven that he is also a good anchor. This is a warning bell for all anchors).*

Common Heritage of India and the US

The programme started by highlighting the similarities in the backgrounds of the two leaders and the heritage of both the nations. The fact that ancient African and Indian thoughts emphasise the universal unity of mankind through adages like, Ubuntu 'I am, because, we are' and *Vasudhaiva Kutumbakam* (the world is a family), shows how aligned we are across mankind. Over the years, people from India and the USA have built upon each other's ideologies. The famous American author and philosopher, Henry David Thoreau, expounded the concept of non-violence, which was further espoused across continents and practiced by the Father of our nation, Mahatma Gandhi. Thoreau's teachings came back to his own country when Martin Luther King Jr emulated Mahatma Gandhi's methods in the Civil Rights Movement. Mahatma Gandhi's vision is what inspired President Obama as well as Prime Minister Modi in their programmes of 'community organisation' and 'Swachh Bharat Mission'. President Obama had once said that, if ever there is one person from human history whom he could meet, it would surely be Mahatma Gandhi. While paying obeisance to the Mahatma at Raj Ghat, he wrote, 'The spirit of Gandhi is very much alive in India today. And it remains a great gift to the world.'

It is this common heritage and values like democracy, liberty, diversity and enterprise that prompted the then Prime Minister Atal Bihari Vajpayee to declare India and the USA as 'natural allies' in 2000. Prime Minister Modi and President Obama took it forward by declaring that India and USA can be 'best partners', working for shared prosperity and the well-being of their citizens.

An interesting aspect of their relationship was evident during 'Mann Ki Baat' when President Obama spoke about his appreciation for Prime Minister Modi's energy and his focus on solving India's burning issues like eliminating poverty, empowering women, ensuring availability of affordable electricity and clean energy, investments in infrastructure and education. He highlighted that even USA faces similar challenges and it is imperative for India and USA to collaborate and have a positive impact on the world.

The message of our shared responsibility to create a better and safer world by combating terrorist threats and keeping homelands and citizens safe from attacks, while responding expeditiously to humanitarian disasters and crises, first stated in the India–US Joint statement, was further reiterated in the radio broadcast.

Both leaders are passionate about ensuring that they leave a better and more sustainable planet for future generations. Prime Minister Modi had authored a book, *Convenient Action* on his experiences in countering climate change and sent it to President Obama in 2011. In his acknowledgement, President Obama wrote, "As our two nations work to address the new and complex challenges facing our world, I am hopeful about what our countries can accomplish together." This hope is now being fulfilled with Prime Minister Modi emphasising that countering climate change is an 'article of faith' for him and with President Obama sharing his concern.

It may be added that during the COP 21 Summit in Paris, in November 2015 Narendra Modi's other book on the issue, *Convenient Action-Continuity for Change* was launched by President Hollande and UN Secretary General Ban Ki-moon. This book builds on the topics touched upon in the previous book and espouses the idea of "climate justice".

The radio conversation showcased very rare facets of both Prime Minister Modi and President Obama. They discussed the fascination of President Obama's daughters with India and their strong interest in Mahatma Gandhi's non-violent strategies, which influenced the US Civil Rights movement. Prime Minister Modi linked President Obama's pride and affection towards his daughters with his own 'Beti Bachao, Beti Padhao' campaign. He emphasised how protecting and educating our daughters was not only a social, cultural and human duty, but was intrinsic to the Indian ethos.

The dialogue touched upon other areas like healthcare and education, where India and USA are working together to fulfill our commitment to deal with pandemics, while also creating opportunities for millions of children and youth. Both Prime Minister Modi and President Obama emphasised their desire to ensure that every person, even if from a humble background like theirs, should get equal access to such opportunities. It is a matter of pride and satisfaction that in our two great nations, even a tea seller or the son of a single mother could go on to lead the country.

Many experiences of the two, not widely known, were also revealed. Prime Minister Modi reminisced about his visit to Washington several years ago as a tourist, standing outside the White House. President Obama narrated a similar incident and both acknowledged that they never imagined that they would one day be inside the White House. Prime Minister Modi also spoke about his unforgettable experience of President Obama gifting him a compilation of Swami Vivekananda's speeches made at the World Congress of Religions held more than 120 years ago. President Obama had read the entire book and was proud of the fact that he came from Chicago, the venue of the World Congress.

Prime Minister Modi recalled the biography of Benjamin Franklin which he had read as a child and which had left a deep imprint on his life. A multi-dimensional personality, Franklin inspired Prime Minister Modi, who was impressed by his thoughts as a leading politician, thinker and social worker.

Both Narendra Modi and Barack Obama highlighted how technology had brought knowledge and information at everyone's fingertips and emphasised the importance of the government's continuous engagement and dialogue with today's global citizens. This resonates with how they have embraced social media and used it to connect with the public, particularly the youth.

People's Response

Those asking questions, ranged from a young girl from Ludhiana, Punjab, a chartered accountant from Mumbai, to a student from Jawaharlal Nehru University. Himani, a young professional working with an event management company, was casually surfing Twitter when she decided to try her luck and ask President Obama and PM Modi a question.

I was on the Internet and I thought, why not ask a question. I did not expect my question to be taken so I asked a simple

> *one—did Obama and Modi ever imagine they will occupy the positions they are in today. My question was not about GDP, exchange rates, economics, Syria or any such topic so I even forgot about it, convinced that my question would not be taken up. On the 27th I was at home when my friend called and broke the news. The calls and texts kept increasing. I finally heard it and was amazed at the humility of both leaders and the fact that an ordinary student like me can ask two most powerful leaders a question. This was an unforgettable experience.*

Pikashoo Mutha, a 32-year-old chartered accountant based in Mumbai, with almost no interest in politics, said:

> *I had little interest in politics. However, I wanted to know from the Prime Minister which American leader inspired him the most. Conventionally, the answer to this question would be Abraham Lincoln but somewhere deep within I knew Mr Modi would have a different answer and I was curious to know what it was. I was also very excited about the programme and got my friends to also tune in. When Narendra Modi took my name I was thrilled. His answer was also, as I had guessed, unique. The next day I went and bought a biography of Benjamin Franklin, parts of which I read and got inspired.*

However, there were many who were left without their questions featuring. A businessman from Mumbai, Vasant Chheda, asked the American President about his travel experiences across Asia as a youngster. He remarked:

> *I was really keen to know about President Obama's experiences because these experiences in one's youth shape a person's imagination. President Obama also has a connect with Asia and Africa. Like many others, I was hopeful my question would be answered but it wasn't. Naturally, there are time constraints. Having said that, the programme was captivating. The spread of questions and the intensity of the answers were superb. This was an out of the box idea, done in style.*

The 'Mann Ki Baat' with President Obama, naturally drew several reactions. Rajdeep Sardesai, who is often critical of the Prime Minister shared on Twitter:

> *Narendra Modi is the most artful political communicator in contemporary India. 'Mann Ki Baat' confirms his multi media event skills. Every channel covering #MannKiBaat and showing visuals of people from across India listening in rapt attention. Modi is a PR genius."*

Sagarika Ghose had this to say, "What a wonderful idea, *#MannKiBaat* with the Prime Minister and Barack Obama: incredibly communicative intimate tone! A lesson for all netas."

Shekhar Gupta took to Twitter to ask:

> *Do we have/had a better politician than Narendra Modi who connects with the people of his country so well? I doubt that. Anyone who grew up in the 1970s/80s in India: did you ever think you'd hear a US President and Indian PM do a joint radio show to an Indian audience?*

Noted Hindi journalist Akhilesh Sharma tweeted:

> *Listening 'Mann Ki Baat' between PM Modi and President Obama. Very interesting and a great concept. Important subjects discussed!*

A lot of people felt that 'Mann Ki Baat' was the highpoint of the Obama visit. The visit was truly a great success. The two sides were able to discuss issues as equal partners and finalise long pending issues like the nuclear deal, totalisation agreement, Defence Technology and Trade Initiative (DTTI) and massive creation of jobs through investments in clean energy and SMEs.

The India–US Declaration of Friendship of January 2015 built upon and expanded the Vision Statement of September 2014. The two statesmen further collaborated in using various communication channels for their outreach to the people of both countries—first a joint print editorial in the *Washington Post* and then a joint broadcast over the 'Mann Ki Baat–Saath Saath' became the preferred lever for deepening ties between the Chiefs and the two countries.

Prime Minister Modi and President Obama focused on re-energising their strategic partnership, and expanded the substantive underpinnings of our diversified bilateral relationship through consultations and stronger defence, security, and economic cooperation. They also expressed confidence that this continued bilateral collaboration would increase opportunities for investment, improve trade and investment ties and lead to the creation of jobs and prosperity in both economies.

As a symbol of India's growing strength and relevance in the comity of nations, President Obama reaffirmed that India's rise is also in the interest of the United States, regional and global stability, and global economic growth, while reiterating USA's readiness to partner with India in this transformation.

After reaching out together via radio, the two leaders continue to communicate with each other very closely. A hotline has now been established between Prime Minister Modi and President Obama and this was used for the first time just before Diwali in 2015, when President Obama called PM Modi and they talked about bilateral and global issues. India is the fourth country after Russia, Great Britain and China, to have a hotline with USA. For India, this is the first hotline at the level of Heads of State.

An article in the *New York Times* dated 10th March 2015 was titled, 'In relating to foreign leaders, Obama keeps it mostly business.' The article went on to illustrate how President Obama's diplomatic outreach was more business like as opposed to being overtly friendly. The article goes on to cite his interaction with various world leaders. However, the *NYT* writes, "White House officials say Mr Obama has established a personal connection with Prime Minister Narendra Modi of India..." During the 2016 Democratic Convention, the official video showcasing President Obama's legacy had prominent shots of Obama and Narendra Modi together.

Narendra Modi and Barack Obama have held bilateral meetings, joined Summits, addressed joint press statements but the 27th January 'Mann Ki Baat' stands out as a shining example of how two world leaders shaped the future of their nations and the world, while creating a deep personal bond with each other, and amongst the people of the largest and the oldest democracies in the world. Thus, the legacy of 'Mann Ki Baat' opening new channels of communication lives on.

Exams are a part of life. It is important not to get worked up before an exam. Have faith in your preparation and write the exam with a calm mind.

—Narendra Modi

CHAPTER 6: Youth's 'Mann Ki Baat'

Youngsters and 'Mann Ki Baat' have a very special relation. Narendra Modi once remarked, "India is a youthful nation. India's demographic dividend, if harnessed properly can take India to the pinnacle of global leadership in every sector. Almost two thirds of India is under the age of 35 but there is a lot more that can be done when it comes to fulfilling their dreams and aspirations."

Narendra Modi's connect with youth is spontaneous and pulsating. Those who have seen him closely, say that he is always eager to interact with youngsters. As Chief Minister of Gujarat, he initiated a first of its kind Chief Minister's Fellowship Programme to integrate youngsters in the working of the Government and enrich its functioning with their fresh perspective. His approach is not merely youth development, but also youth-led development.

He has also been a regular visitor to college campuses and a large number of people who come to his rallies and community programmes are youngsters. His interactions with youth have been different from conventional ways of interacting with youngsters. For one, he is very active on crowd sourcing and periodically seeks ideas and inputs from youth on what he should say. He has delivered memorable speeches on campuses.

At Delhi's prestigious Shri Ram College of Commerce (SRCC) in 2013, he talked at length about his comprehensive vision for youth-led development, which in the prevailing climate of mistrust and cynicism seemed like a whiff of fresh air. He has even addressed many convocation ceremonies. At the Benaras Hindu University (BHU) Convocation, he politely declined an honorary doctorate, leading to a massive round of applause from the predominantly young audience. He has also begun a practice of inviting students from Government schools to convocation ceremonies so that they are inspired by the sight of students in robes graduating with flying colours.

The youth of India were amongst the strongest supporters of Narendra Modi and the BJP in the 2014 elections and those who follow the Prime Minister closely are not surprised that it is so.

Enter the Radio

The advent of smart phones and jazzy mobile phones did, paradoxically, increase the popularity of FM radio among youth. It is not uncommon to see youngsters walking down the streets with their earphones plugged in, listening to the radio.

It is easy to spot a youth-centric flavour in 'Mann Ki Baat'. At a macro level, every topic can connect with youth, be it cleanliness, road rage, Yoga and so on. However, a closer scrutiny will suggest that Narendra Modi has both, picked the right topics, and has discussed exactly those issues that can keep youngsters motivated. The Prime Minister's words can have a deep impact and this is what Narendra Modi realised. He used 'Mann Ki Baat' to further strengthen the bond with youth.

So much is Happening and here is Modi talking to these children...

February is a busy month for any government, especially the last week or the last ten days. February 2016 was no exception. There were continuous Budget parleys, the General Budget, the Railway Budget, the President's address to both Houses of Parliament and the discussion that follows where the Prime Minister has to make an intervention were all in the offing. Narendra Modi addressed key farmer rallies in Odisha, Karnataka and Uttar Pradesh, where he elaborated on the government's measures for the welfare of farmers and agriculture.

Politically too, the Opposition upped the ante, following episodes at Hyderabad Central University (HCU) and the Jawaharlal Nehru University (JNU) in Delhi.

In the midst of all this, when Narendra Modi had to share his 'Mann Ki Baat' on 28th February, the air was full of speculation on what he would talk about, would he address the Budget and the Railway Budget related issues? Would he speak on the recent caste violence in Haryana, where one community was pitching for 'backward' status? Or would he take up the issues in JNU and HCU?

Narendra Modi, however, had a different idea. During a routine briefing of the January 2016 edition of 'Mann Ki Baat', he told his aides, "I had devoted a full episode to board exams and students last year. Many students, teachers and parents told me they enjoyed the episode. I will be doing a similar episode in February and this time I want to make it more innovative in structure and diverse in content."

Closer to the programme, Narendra Modi came up with another idea, that of inviting successful people, icons of success in their own right, to join the programme. In a meeting in February, to decide the flow of the programme, he said, "If a Sachin Tendulkar or a Viswanathan Anand also say something, the impact will be so powerful. Youngsters will get very motivated."

It was decided that an eclectic list of people would join Narendra Modi during 'Mann Ki Baat'- there would be Sachin Tendulkar, Viswanathan Anand, Professor CNR Rao and Morari Bapu.

Aides close to Narendra Modi point out how all these eminent personalities readily agreed to join the programme. Viswanathan Anand was overseas, but promptly called in and shared his thoughts. Professor CNR Rao said that while he does not carry a mobile phone, he would used a landline to share his words of encouragement with students.

Free from Tension and Full of Smiles: The Modi Way

In both the episodes in February 2015 and 2016 dedicated to students appearing for examinations, Narendra Modi had a clear message—he urged them to appear for exams in a tension-free atmosphere with a smile on their faces. The programme of February 2016, had a lot of other details—from what to do before the exams, to the day of the exam and even subsequent to the exams. Even minute details, which would otherwise seem trivial for a PM to speak about, like reading instructions carefully or meditating, talking to parents and friends, were all taken up by Narendra Modi. He even had things to say to parents and teachers, most notably urging them not to pressurise students for marks, but inspire them to work hard.

Each of the four celebrities who joined the programme on 28th February 2016 gave a very unique message. Tendulkar talked about setting one's own targets and achieving them, while Grandmaster Viswanathan Anand elaborated on why exams are like a game of chess that can be easily won. Professor CNR Rao highlighted the power of doggedness and tenacity, while Morari Bapu urged the students to keep calm and not fear anything, including failure.

Refreshing, Diverse and not Preachy

The pep talk to students, received uniform praise. Taking note of the diversity of the topics covered, Vraj Mehta, B. Tech., 2nd year student at Dhirubhai Ambani Institute of Information and Communication Technology, had this to say:

> *Even while speaking about examinations, Modi brought so many diverse aspects of exams to the fore. His central message of tension-free exams was like an umbrella under which there were points and anecdotes that made the programme very lively.*

Vaibhav Amit Patel from Dhirubhai Ambani Institute of Information and Communication Technology, found it refreshing. He said:

> *One does not have to be a student appearing for a board exam, a parent whose child or a teacher whose student is appearing for the exams to appreciate what the Prime Minister said. His thoughts came across like a breath of fresh air and with a very relevant message for the youth.*

Romila Rajul, who has just completed 12th from DPS, SAIL Township, Ranchi, CBSE board, made a pertinent point, saying:

> *Programmes on exams, what to do and what not to do run the risk of sounding extremely preachy and one-sided but Narendra Modi's 'Mann Ki Baat' was not like that: The interaction was two-way, as seen from the frequent names*

taken by the Prime Minister of people who contributed ideas and ancedotes on his Mobile App. It seemed as if the PM was sharing the 'Mann Ki Baat' of several people who expressed their thoughts on the subject.

Narendra Modi's message that 'one must do things, not to become something, but to make a difference in the society', connected very well with students and adults alike. In 2015, he cited the example of Sergey Bubka, to illustrate why it was essential to compete with one's own self and not mindlessly compete with others.

Attaining the Desired 'Results'

Students, parents and teachers who heard Narendra Modi, both, this year and the last, found it touching that a Prime Minister is connecting with the youth in this manner. Mukul and Alka Aggarwal are a couple based in Mumbai, whose son was appearing for his Class XII exams. He had already cleared his CA in his first attempt, but the pressure of the Boards increased as the exams came closer. Alka said, "Exam stress is very common and very disturbing. My child is no exception. We always told him to take it easy and not to get worried, but my son never listened. We all heard 'Mann Ki Baat' and the change was visible. Modi ji made my job easier."

There are many students and parents like this, who felt encouraged, when none other than the Prime Minister was addressing them directly.

Dialogue with the Youth

Examinee students are no vote bank. They are too young to vote and even for those who have come of age, the next elections are three years away. In a period where every statement, campus visit and programme is calculated in terms of votes and opportunities, Modi's 'Mann Ki Baat' could surely not have any political or electoral motives.

It would be fair to say that Narendra Modi rose to the occasion, going beyond what can be spoken about, either in Parliament or on any other platform.

The platform of 'Mann Ki Baat' is such that Modi could have spoken about anything. Considering the prevailing circumstances and the volatile situation in some parts, it is easy to succumb to the temptation of using a forum like 'Mann Ki Baat' to even settle political scores and make a point. From the beginning, Narendra Modi was clear that despite all that is happening, he will connect with students. There are other forums to address other issues.

Football Fever

Swami Vivekananda once said, that he "would rather want the youth to play football on the field, than read the Gita." In a nation where cricket is the most popular sport, Narendra Modi used the 'Mann Ki Baat' platform in March 2016, to speak of football, a sport that is gaining popularity particularly among the urban youth. The context was India hosting the 2017 U-17 FIFA World Cup.

Narendra Modi used the radio to convey, rather convincingly, why the U-17 World Cup is a very good opportunity for Indian youth. To begin with, the event would see a massive infrastructural upgradation of football facilities that would eventually help youngsters. A World Cup brings with it excellent sporting infrastructure that has the potential to create more interest in a sport.

At the same time with such a young population, India offers a great potential for football tournaments, for coaches and sporting companies to come and establish a base and make the game more popular.

Mega sporting events like the Olympics and the World Cup also bring more tourists to a nation. Sports lovers from across the world converge to catch a glimpse of the games and use the opportunity to travel to other places in the host-country. For instance, if a game is played in Delhi, foreign tourists would not miss a visit to the Taj Mahal, to Jaipur or to the hills. Narendra Modi observed during 'Mann Ki Baat' that the World Cup can also become an occasion to draw tourists to India and give economic opportunities to many youngsters.

The participative element was seen when he asked youngsters to share their ideas about the World Cup and how to make football more popular by sharing ideas on the Mobile App. Suggestions came in thousands and youth participation was laudatory.

The nature of comments was diverse. People were concerned about sports facilities and particularly facilities in sports other than cricket. There were several innovative suggestions on the branding of the tournament. A handful of comments expressed joy that since Narendra Modi was now the Prime Minister, the shame witnessed during the 2010 Commonwealth Games would not be repeated. Some ideas revolved around the need to take steps for facilitating the spread of football to all parts of the nation. After all, football is a cheaper game than others; all that is needed is a ball and a field. No bats, stumps, hockey sticks or golfing equipment that can be expensive!

Narendra Modi has promised to send these inputs to the relevant authorities and the chances are very high that the 2017 U-17 FIFA World Cup becomes a tournament powered by people's ideas off the field and great football on the field.

Deepening the Bond with Youth Organisations

Dilawar Singh, the Director General of Nehru Yuva Kendra, got a call for a meeting with the Prime Minister. At first he thought it may be a routine meeting on the working of the Nehru Yuva Kendra, but later he got to know that leading officials of all youth organisations had been called. "Such meetings are very rare, so I was not really sure what the agenda was."

Then, on Monday, 18th April 2016, the Prime Minister held a marathon meeting with authorities of leading youth bodies like the National Cadet Corps, National Service Scheme, Nehru Yuva Kendra, Bharat Scouts and Guides, Hindustan Scouts and Guides and Indian Red Cross Society. Dilawar Singh said of the meeting:

> *The meeting, which lasted for almost two hours was a first of sorts. Some of those present at the meeting do not recall any Prime Minister meeting these youth organisations in this manner and discussing ways in which these bodies can contribute to India's development. It has never happened before and is a very positive step.*

The Prime Minister heard every member present there and also shared his own thoughts on how these bodies can help in the Swachh Bharat Mission, creating open defecation-free clusters and other such means of ensuring societal change.

After the meeting was over, Narendra Modi remarked to an aide:

> *I am going to seek views on this from a larger canvas through my Mobile App and will also speak about it in Mann Ki Baat.*

Narendra Modi discussed the matter on the radio on 24th April 2016 when he answered a phone call on his meeting with youth organisations. He talked at length about the role these bodies have in the development of the nation and how these youth organisations need to be strengthened, even asking youngsters to share their views with him on his Mobile App.

A New Way of looking at Education

A question over the telephone by Mona Karnwal from Bijnor, during the 'Mann Ki Baat' programme on 24th April 2016 led to one of the most important statements made by Narendra Modi on education. His comments and answer to the question brought out his vision for education and youth-led development.

Mona spoke about the pitiable state of education in India and the need to look beyond education and focus on overall personality development.

Narendra Modi agreed with Mona Karnwal and spoke in detail on how the NDA Government was focusing on learning outcomes. He added that till now the focus was only on enrolment, but now the time has come to think of learning as compared with only schooling and think of outcomes as compared with outlays.

The statements suggested a brave shift from conventional policy-making. Clearly, the government is thinking about 'learning outcomes' as the main objective of school education. The government has taken steps to equip schools and teachers with resources that encourage learning, research and innovation, rather than perpetuating plain mugging up of facts.

In the past, governments would consider their job done if school enrolment was at a high. Narendra Modi, however, thought differently from the very beginning. In peak summers, he and his team went to the villages of Gujarat, asking parents to educate their children. At the same time, he also started the 'Gunotsav' that focused on evaluating the quality of education imparted.

It is indeed brave of a Prime Minister to challenge the *status quo*, especially on a subject as vital as education and offer a fresh perspective. That he did it through the radio, ensured the message amplified to all parts of the nation.

There are several other examples of the youth connect in 'Mann Ki Baat'. In February 2016, Narendra Modi recalled his experience at the 'Start-up India' launch and highlighted some of the interesting start-ups. He said:

> *India is a young nation and its youthful energy is a big source of inspiration. Any 'Mann Ki Baat' without a distinct youth related issue is incomplete. And, I don't have to work hard in deciding the topics. The number of letters, MyGov submissions, ideas on the Mobile App on youth-led development are so refreshing, insightful and engrossing that I rely heavily on them to make my point.*

When talking to or talking about youngsters, the message is not about what they are doing wrong or what they need to do right. It is instead about what can collectively be done to usher in an era where it is the youth of India who script their own future and create history by transforming India and take it to the pinnacle of global leadership.

Drugs are neither cool nor are they a style statement. We all have to work together to make India drugs free.

—Narendra Modi

CHAPTER 7: Social Transformation through the Airwaves

One noteworthy aspect of 'Mann Ki Baat' is that in episode after episode, the radio programme has covered topics that may not seem very 'consequential' or 'earth-shattering' on the face of it, but have played the role of a catalyst in furthering a positive spirit across society and inspiring people to work towards becoming agents of change.

'Mann Ki Baat' has struck a chord with the people of India because the radio programme has addressed very practical issues in our society. Issues that people can relate to. Instead of becoming a verbose commentary on what is good or bad, 'Mann Ki Baat' has stimulated debate and discussion, leading to ground level initiatives by scores of people who are working towards nation-building.

Take for instance something like placing water on window ledges for birds during summer. As shown later in this chapter, one call from the Prime Minister was enough to galvanise countless youngsters across India to do the same and urge others to do it as well.

As mentioned before, while addressing such issues, Narendra Modi is neither excessively empirical nor is he extremely vague or overtly philosophical. For instance, when he spoke about drugs, he did not get into minute details like the number of people affected by substance abuse or the number of deaths it causes. Anybody interested in that could have consulted an encyclopedia. Similarly, a stoic monologue on why drugs are 'bad' would amount to stating the obvious and not draw the attention of a listener. Beyond being 'preachy' or 'holier than thou' and beyond an overkill of empirical data, Narendra Modi used public participative forums like letters, MyGov and later his Mobile App to express the voice and views of people, giving it a personal touch and describing the realities of and solutions to a flaw prevalent in our society.

Be it mitigating the menace of drugs, preventing road rage or overcoming diabetes, the 'Mann Ki Baat' way of doing things has always been that of a catalyst to ignite the collective power and wisdom of society. That the power of *Jan Bhagidari* or people's participation will always be greater than every other means is a core belief.

Health is Wealth

During the 'Mann Ki Baat' programme on 27th March 2016, Narendra Modi raised the issue of two diseases that have affected several lives in India and across the world—diabetes and tuberculosis (TB). Conventional wisdom would suggest that it is rather 'trivial' for a Prime Minister to spend time on discussing illnesses that are not uncommon, but Narendra Modi thought differently.

The crux of his argument during that episode by 'Mann Ki Baat' was simple—it is very important to lead a healthy and balanced life and that lifestyle diseases, like diabetes, can be prevented by self-corrective measures.

On why he decided to pick these two issues, Narendra Modi shared:

> *I was reading about World Health Day and how the theme for 2016 was to beat diabetes. It is quite common to find people suffering from diabetes and part of their problems is their own lifestyle. So I decided to speak about diabetes. But, then I also read somewhere that 24th March is observed as TB day and when I got to know some facts, I was startled. India consists of 1/6th of the world's population but 24% of the world's TB cases are in India. There is a massive problem of timely detection and on many occasions people do not even know they are suffering from TB. And, the most important part is that in both these cases we can prevent and treat the disease. Keeping this in mind, I felt I should address the topic and appeal to the people of India.*

Narendra Modi approached the subjects logically. On diabetes he made a passionate appeal to the people to alter their lifestyles, wherever possible. During the discussion Narendra Modi remarked:

> *It surprises me that earlier children would go outdoors and play. Due to this they would sweat it out, imbibe values of teamwork and this would be good for the overall personality. Now a child plays cricket, tennis or football on the computer or playstation. This is extremely bad for the health and the growth of the self. Moreover, this is where foundations of a sedentary lifestyle are laid.*

He emphasised on why there has to be a change in the way we look at diabetes. Instead of perpetually treating diabetes with injections and medication, why not ensure that it never sets in?

On TB, he stressed on the need for a correct and complete treatment. The latter is vital because a lot of people leave their TB treatment halfway thinking that the worst is over, but this is a great disservice to the body. Incomplete treatment of TB can cause drug resistant TB which can be dangerous.

Narendra Modi appealed to people to get themselves checked for TB if there was even a slight apprehension. This is because the symptoms of TB can often be ignored as an occurrence of a common cold or a temporary illness. He spoke of the efforts of the Government to combat TB, like the setting up of 13,500 microscopy centres around India, over 4 lakh DOTS providers and state-of-the-art advanced laboratories.

By referring to diabetes and TB, Narendra Modi's message was loud and clear. He sought to shift the discourse from treatment to prevention. In very clear terms he called for a lifestyle change where there is enough physical exercise. In case of TB, he affirmed that through complete and correct treatment, India can overcome TB.

In this context, Union Minister for Health and Family Welfare, JP Nadda says:

> *In the case of TB, public knowledge is limited, in the sense, that people tend to be unaware that complete and timely treatment can cure the disease. When Shri Modi posited this information on 'Mann Ki Baat' platform, we saw increased curiosity towards TB related issues. I see this as a very positive sign for the nation that the highest elected office of the country is in direct contact with every citizen.*

Prof MC Misra, AIIMS Director, says:

> *We have experienced significantly increased awareness and questions about benefits of yoga and lifestyle modifications for the control of diabetes, high blood pressure and TB cure after the Prime Minister highlighted it during 'Mann Ki Baat.' A healthier India can be a reality when all stakeholders join the quest with equal passion. On that count, the PM's radio programmes are hugely popular and a major source of mobilization, bringing attitudinal change, focus and impact that will definitely yield better short and longer term results towards improving health of India's large population.*

Tackling road rage

A few days before the 'Mann Ki Baat' programme of 26th July 2015, Narendra Modi was surfing the television. It was one of those rare days when the Prime Minister got some time to catch a glimpse of what's happening in the world of TV. That is when he saw a horrific road accident on one of the news channels. What was even more horrific was the neglect of the victim, who lay injured on the road for a good ten minutes, unattended.

Sharing his sadness, Narendra Modi said:

> *The victim was on a scooter. He was hit and he was lying unattended. These are two wrongs at the same time—the first, the sheer carelessness with which people drive on our roads and the second, our lack of sensitivity to the injury of others, even if it is in front of you.*

No sooner had he seen this news, than he decided that he will talk about it on the radio. He called for facts relating to road accidents in India and the numbers proved his worst fears right, that India fares very poorly as far as road safety is concerned. The frequency of road accidents, in one part of the country or another, was very high.

When he did speak on 26th July on the radio, Narendra Modi did not deliver a sermon loaded with only advice and criticism. He began by talking about what the Government can do and then went on to expand on what citizens can do to minimize road mishaps. He urged parents to speak more often at home about road safety and create the right atmosphere to make our roads safer. He observed that if the atmosphere at home is one of awareness towards road safety, accidents can be avoided.

He also stressed on the need to provide adequate emergency care to those affected by road accidents. Once an accident takes place, it is vital that the victim gets access to timely medical attention that can be potentially life-saving.

Importantly, however, he made it a point to talk of the need to be aware of such accidents. Subtly yet firmly he conveyed the message that while road rage was wrong, apathy to human suffering was worse. This change, he pointed, could only come from within and be collectively initiated as a society.

The response to Narendra Modi's message was encouraging. Veteran journalist Milind Khandekar shared on social media, his personal experience of how his father lost his life on a Delhi roads due to lack of timely help. He expressed hope that things would change after the Prime Minister raised the issue during 'Mann Ki Baat'. Om Prakash Gupta welcomed Narendra Modi's words, recalling his own tragedy of losing his 22-year-old son to a road accident.

Narendra Modi's idea of 'cashless treatment' for accident victims and examples of places where it has been implemented (Gurgaon, Jaipur, Vadodara to Mumbai, Ranchi, Rangaon and Mundiya National Highway) was widely applauded. This initiative prevents one from worrying about the lack of money for the first fifty hours of the accident. A toll free number 1033 for providing information relating to accidents and ambulance services was shared. Yet, Narendra Modi put a caveat, "...these services are for post accidents. One must strive to avoid accidents in the first place, and it is also important for us to understand this from the perspective that each and every soul, each and every life is precious."

The onus is on us to prevent accidents and God forbid, if they do happen, ensure that we provide the fastest and the most effective treatment to the injured.

Drug Free India

During one episode of 'Mann Ki Baat', Narendra Modi recalled:

> *When I had first given the address for people to write to me, I noticed that several letters were coming in on the drug menace. I asked officials for more details and was told that in addition to the letters I was reading, there was substantial opinion being expressed on the drug problem. I was also convinced that 'Mann Ki Baat' could be the ideal platform to speak about the menace and initiate a mass movement to make India drugs free.*

During the 'Mann Ki Baat' episode in November 2014, Narendra Modi remarked that the next episode would cover issues pertaining to the drug problem and asked parents, teachers, and those who have been prone to substance abuse and others in general to share their experiences. "I did not want it to be a monologue. Yes, everybody knows drugs are bad, so merely repeating that would not have made much of a difference. Sharing real life experiences is what would make a real impact."

The crux of Narendra Modi's 'Mann Ki Baat' on 14th December 2014 was, 'we as a society have to tackle this menace and we have to tackle it together'.

In a pertinent observation, Narendra Modi urged the society to go beyond just blaming those involved in substance abuse. He added that these are mainly youngsters, but they are not bad; it is the drugs that are bad and the addiction that is wrong. Blaming youngsters will only deepen their addiction, and not get them out of it.

While sharing the pain of parents and friends of those addicted to drugs, he urged them to share their problems with the police and made an appeal to the police to help these families by offering workable solutions.

Another theme in Narendra Modi's message on drugs was that everybody must have a dream, which they must pursue. A dreamer pursuing his or her dreams will not have the time or energy to fall prey to substance abuse. He cited the example of sportspersons, who train hard and devote their lives to sporting excellence, imbibing values of discipline and determination.

During the radio programme, Narendra Modi systemically demolished this perception gaining currency among sections of our youth that drugs are 'cool.' He categorically affirmed that drugs are not cool. Very often children, particularly in bigger cities, consider drugs as a mark of being in sync with modern times, but instead they end up affecting their own lives and careers. This argument was forcefully put forward by Narendra Modi.

As far as drugs are concerned, a substantial part of the issue is the disjointed family structure in India. The pressures of life, heavy workload and the need to maintain a reasonable standard of living puts great burden on parents. In such circumstances, parents are unable to devote time to their children. Narendra Modi urged parents to maintain a healthy balance between personal and professional lives, whereby professional ambitions are fulfilled and personal life does not suffer. This balance can play a great role in keeping children away from drugs.

After sharing success stories on how people overcame their drug problems, Narendra Modi called for wider debate and discussion on the subject. He asked people to use *#DrugFreeIndia* and talk about the issue. *#DrugFreeIndia* was not only a top trend, but also saw several people coming out and sharing their personal experiences.

Former MP Shahid Siddiqui summed it up wonderfully when he shared on Twitter, "Modi's Bhashan on drugs is excellent. Impressed. A good leader doesn't want power but also acts as a guide, friend and philosopher for (the) nation." Raju Narisetti, another well-known commentator, noted that Narendra Modi is the first ever Prime Minister to acknowledge the drug problem. National Award winning journalist and documentary maker, Vinod Kapri, who has also been critical of Narendra Modi, appreciated this initiative on social media and congratulated the Prime Minister. People saw Narendra Modi's address as refreshing, one that connected with the youth and keeping in mind Modi's vision for 'Mann Ki Baat', was far from being preachy.

Recalling his experience, Narendra Modi said:

> *Before the programme I got so many letters; when the programme happened, the response to #DrugFreeIndia was overwhelming and even after the programme the correspondence continued. People wrote to me appreciating the fact that this topic was taken up in such a direct manner.*

Water for Men and Birds

This instance may seem rather 'trivial', but offers a rich insight into how 'Mann Ki Baat' has attempted to usher in small changes with arguably a strong impact.

In May 2015, Narendra Modi made a rather unusual request during the 'Mann Ki Baat' programme. He urged people to keep a bowl of water on their balconies, corridors and windows sills, so that birds could quench their thirst from it during peak summer.

Why would a Prime Minister speak of providing water for birds, during a radio programme being broadcast all over, was a question several people asked. However, a lot of people attempted to do that and wrote back saying it was indeed quite a good idea. Many also shared on social media the images of a bowl of water on their windows.

A year later, in March 2016, a small child, Abhi Chaturvedi from Gurugram, called Narendra Modi and reminded him to convey the same message for the upcoming summer. That youngster's message was broadcast on the airwaves along with a letter from Mysuru's Shilpa. Shilpa urged the Prime Minister to ask people through 'Mann Ki Baat' to offer water to their milkmen, postmen, hawkers, vegetable sellers and such people who frequent their homes during the day in peak summer. Instantly sold to the idea, Narendra Modi narrated Shilpa's message and urged people to do the same, linking it not only with compassion, but also with dignity of labour.

This may be a very inconsequential thing, but, if done across the board, can lead to a massive change in mindset vis-à-vis how we treat fellow humans and birds, particularly when temperatures are soaring.

For Equal Access and Opportunity

There is a lot more that can be done as far as creating better opportunities for persons with disabilities is concerned. Even now, a large number of public places are not accessible to persons with disabilities. The number of avenues of growth available to them also leaves a lot to be desired.

It is in this context that one must look at the fact that Narendra Modi spoke about persons with disabilities in the very first episode of 'Mann Ki Baat' on 3rd October 2014. He read out a suggestion by one Gautam Pal, who wrote about greater civic participation for persons with disabilities. In the address, the Prime Minister recalled his interaction with specially-abled athletes as Chief Minister, which inspired him to involve them in Gujarat's sports extravaganza, 'Khel Mahakumbh' and create separate sporting events for persons with disabilities. He added that when it comes to persons with disabilities, it is the responsibility of the entire nation to ensure a change in mindset and that they are not denied the opportunities that they deserve.

Narendra Modi raised the issue of persons with disabilities again in the second 'Mann Ki Baat' episode on

2nd November 2014. This time he narrated steps taken by the HRD Ministry for providing assistance to persons with disabilities who want to pursue technical education. Another initiative of the HRD Ministry, of making Kendriya Vidyalayas and Central Universities accessible to the physically challenged, was also shared by Narendra Modi. Evidently, the wheels to a positive change had been put into motion from the very beginning.

A Collective Transformation

'Mann Ki Baat' has provided an ideal forum to speak about issues affecting our society, day-to-day issues that are otherwise forgotten in the rough and tumble of our daily lives.

Narendra Modi has shared his views and those of the people and stressed on issues and topics that can have a long lasting impact on our society. This is because the matters dealt with affect so many people and at the same time make the individual think about where things are headed and whether there is a scope to change them.

So, the next time when someone places a bowl of water on their windows sills; offers water to their postmen; offers help to an accident victim and becomes more sensitive to the needs and aspirations of a specially-abled person, there are great chances that he or she may have been inspired by 'Mann Ki Baat', not merely the voice of the Prime Minister but the voices of fellow citizens who enrich the radio programme with their views and speak through no less than the Prime Minister of India.

Human life is precious. Let us not cheapen it by showing disregard to road safety rules. Make our roads safe and secure, and every journey memorable.

—Narendra Modi

CHAPTER 8: ●•• 'Mann Ki Baat' and Participative Governance: Mails, MyGov, Mobile and Missed Calls

It is the last Sunday of July 2015 and Dr Suchitra Raghavachari is up early so that she can finish her household duties and be free for an important 'appointment' at 11 A.M. This has now become a routine for this practising radiologist from Chennai, where, unlike other weekends which are slightly more conventional, the morning half of one Sunday of every month is reserved for this special purpose.

Little did Dr Suchitra know that this particular Sunday, in the rainy month of July 2015, would have a pleasant surprise in store for her. Even as she was just settling down on the sofa at the stipulated time, with a cup of tea, she sat up again, startled, at what she had just heard. For a moment she could not believe it. Was the name mentioned in the programme hers? Had her name actually been mentioned in front of a live audience of millions? That too by none other than the Prime Minister of India!

What Dr Suchitra heard next amazed her even further. Narendra Modi had not only acknowledged her suggestions, but had gone a step further and announced a historic new initiative. For the first time in the history of independent India, the Prime Minister's 15th August speech, from the ramparts of Red Fort, would be crowd-sourced. This would be done through the citizen engagement platform MyGov and this, like a lot of other things, was first shared on the radio.

There are many like Dr Suchitra, who have been mentioned during the various 'Mann Ki Baat' episodes. The people mentioned by the Prime Minister have been from small towns in Uttar Pradesh, from hinterlands of Bihar and the urban landscape of Bengaluru. Their thoughts have been on issues ranging from start-ups, farmer issues and the menace of drugs.

During most 'Mann Ki Baat' episodes, Narendra Modi makes it a point to invite ideas on a particular topic from people. In January 2016, he urged parents, teachers and students to share their exam experiences, keeping in mind the exam season commencing in February.

Broadly speaking, there are Four 'M's that have emerged as the primary means of sharing thoughts and ideas for the 'Mann Ki Baat' programmes. They are—Mail, MyGov, Mobile and Missed Call.

Postal Connect

Even in this era of emails, WhatsApp and Facebook, the Indian postal network still remains one of the largest, strongest and widely used networks in the country. It is not uncommon for people to send and receive letters by Speed Post in this day and age. It is also true that a large number of Indians are not very mail-savvy and rely on postal services to communicate with near and dear ones.

During the first few 'Mann Ki Baat' programmes, the ideas and inputs that came were through the citizen engagement platform, MyGov. That is when the Prime Minister realised that a lot more can be done to diversify the nature of views. In a meeting with aides, the officials from All India Radio (AIR/Akashvani) and MyGov officials, Narendra Modi asked:

> *Can we think of enabling people to write letters to us which can be taken up in every episode? Letters will increase the reach and make 'Mann Ki Baat' more popular across rural India. People will feel—yes, I can also write to the Prime Minister and convey my views.*

The rural connect is worth noting here. There cannot be a better means to connect with rural India than the postal network. Being fully aware of this, Narendra Modi stressed on creating an opportunity for people to write letters and be a part of 'Mann Ki Baat'.

It was decided that all letters could be sent to the All India Radio Headquarters (Broadcasting House, Parliament Street, New Delhi–110 001) in the heart of the capital. The iconic building in Lutyens' Delhi's Parliament Street is an intrinsic part of India's colonial and post-independence history. (The iconic building is Broadcasting House. However, AIR headquarters are located in the newer building down the street–Akashvani Bhawan).

Narendra Modi himself popularised the address by mentioning it on air, programme after programme, so that people could make a note of it and send their letters.

Officials at AIR agree that with the Prime Minister sharing the address there has been a quantum jump in the number of letters being received.

When Narendra Modi devoted an entire programme to the Land Bill in March 2015, so many farmers wrote to him with their ideas and views. Contrary to conventional wisdom, the nature of letters received was not sceptical, but articulated ideas on how to ensure faster agrarian growth and industrialisation.

About the Land Bill programme and the letters received, Fayyaz Sheheryar, Director General of All India Radio had this to say:

> *The number of letters shot up as soon as the Prime Minister broadcast the postal address. The letters are very diverse. We were afraid this would become primarily a means of grievance redressal but it was not so. People were sharing thoughts, their suggestions and so much more. The communication was very informal. Even when the Land Bill episode was taking place, the letters were not on predicted lines. People were not just complaining, cribbing, quarrelling. They had a lot of constructive suggestions. Most of the letters are from villages, indicating the popularity of the programme in rural areas.*

In fact, the AIR Headquarters also has a 'Mann Ki Baat' room where all letters are stored.

When this was discussed with Narendra Modi, he had casually remarked:

> *I have always said—some people find it fashionable to hard sell a narrative that everything around us is negative. But I want you to see the letters I get for 'Mann Ki Baat'. People are not complaining. Yes, some of them share their grievances, but by and large they are talking about things you cannot even imagine. People share their memorable stories with me, someone who has built toilets in villages, somebody who is teaching poor children…there are start-up experiences. These letters show the inherent positivity in the people of India and the letters are a reflection of India's strength.*

When Narendra Modi was asked whether he gets time to read all the letters, he said:

> *Most certainly not. The volume is too much for me to do so. But the letters I read, I read word to word and even if I do not talk about them in the programme, I ensure that people's issues are addressed or their thoughts are given active consideration.*

So, if not Narendra Modi, then who scans the letters? A preliminary scan is done by the AIR team itself. Every letter is read and a short list is made which is then sent to the Prime Minister. The choice of letters to be taken up in the final programme lies with Narendra Modi himself. AIR officials add that any letter that is political in nature or uses any abusive language (which is rare though) is not entertained at all. This is in sync with Narendra Modi's philosophy of keeping 'Mann Ki Baat' apart from the daily rough and tumble of politics.

While talking about the letters being received for 'Mann Ki Baat', Narendra Modi noted:

> *Even in this age of mails and technology, the joy of a letter is very special. I think the medium is very personal. Receiving a handwritten letter has a very different feeling. A few years ago I had urged people to share Diwali greetings through handwritten letters and people responded very well.*

Thus, there is no doubt that letters brought the people closer to 'Mann Ki Baat' and widened the range of people participating in 'Mann Ki Baat'.

MyGov-Our Voice

'Mann Ki Baat' and 'MyGov' have a very special relationship. They complement each other and are central to Narendra Modi's vision of participative governance.

MyGov was among the first initiatives that Narendra Modi conceived, soon after assuming the office of the Prime Minister of India. Here was a platform that could help realise his dream of participatory governance or *Jan-Bhagidari*. It was launched on 26 July 2014, the day the Modi Government completed two months in office. The aim of the platform was to achieve the following purposes:

Pro-active citizen participation in policy making;
Citizen participation in governance tasks; and
Volunteer participation to achieve synergy in the ideas and discussions in online world, with action on the ground.

One of the carefully considered decisions taken at the stage of conception was that MyGov must retain all the strengths and flavours of social media—it should be free and fair, open and accessible to all without discrimination and that each idea must be considered on its merit alone. Indeed, MyGov should become a hub of ideas, where suggestions would compete based on their merit alone. However, one other decision was taken that would give MyGov the winning edge—there would be no activity on MyGov without a prior buy-in by a relevant department or ministry of the Government of India.

This was done to ensure that all discussions and tasks on MyGov would have a defined closure point and therefore, the valuable time that citizens spent on it would be tied up with a clearly defined proposed action of the government. This way, MyGov would evolve as a useful platform for citizens, while retaining the flavour of a free flowing online general discussion forum, and avoiding the trap of being reduced to a discussion forum and instead, becoming a platform for enforcing action. This conceptual clarity at the level of the head of government, with a clearly defined mandate asking ministries and departments to factor-in citizen suggestions in discussions and tasks they have initiated on MyGov, and in the eventual policy, programme or schemes they frame, has resulted in MyGov acquiring the credible reputation that it has.

MyGov, not surprisingly, was the first source of people's thoughts and inputs for 'Mann Ki Baat'. In fact, in the very first episode, the names that Narendra Modi took were from MyGov itself.

Ameya Joshi, an aviation professional based in Pune, was travelling in his car on 26 July 2015, when his phone rang. He ignored the call as he was driving, but the phone would simply not stop ringing. Within seconds of one call ending, another would start. Ameya finally pulled his car to the side and picked up his phone, but he was unprepared for what he heard next—the Prime Minister had just mentioned his name in his radio address. Even as he was processing the information, in a flash he remembered the suggestion that he had contributed in the open forum on MyGov, where each month, citizen ideas are solicited in the weeks preceding that month's episode of 'Mann Ki Baat'. In between taking congratulatory calls all day and week, and helping other friends and family members sign up for MyGov, Ameya did not miss noticing one unique standout feature of interacting through MyGov and observed:

> *A lot of people write letters to government departments or even newspapers or give suggestions at various forums and sites, but they can never be sure whether they are even being read or not. With the digital platform of MyGov, we are now assured that every suggestion is being carefully read. And when the suggestion was seen and recognised in the name of the contributor, more number of friends and family would start contributing with their own individual ideas, thereby building a multiplying chain.*

Akhilesh Bajpai, although hailing from Kanpur, lives in the National Capital Region of Delhi. A few years ago, this diploma engineer in electronics, met with an accident and injured his hand, resulting in disability. Sometime later, while trying to book a ticket for himself through the IRCTC web portal, he realised something peculiar. The IRCTC web portal, while allowing for booking tickets under various quotas, like the quota for senior citizens, had no provision for booking a ticket under the physically disabled quota. The only option to get such tickets booked was from the ticketing counter at the railway stations, which presented its own set of challenges.

This was a simple provision that could be worked out in the IRCTC portal, which had probably earlier escaped the attention of the railway management. When the Ministry of Railways launched its consultation on MyGov, Akhilesh found it an opportune forum to put forward his suggestion. Within a month of the suggestions, the Ministry of Railways issued a notification incorporating this provision in the IRCTC website. When the Prime Minister later mentioned this in his 'Mann Ki Baat', as one of the most effective yet simple way in which MyGov could be used, it evoked in Akhilesh a sense of belonging, there was at least one forum through which one could get heard. He now has some additional suggestions as well, to further simplify the processes and is again counting on MyGov to put his ideas into action.

From September 2015, MyGov introduced a novel feature to further enhance the participatory nature of 'Mann Ki Baat'. Citizens could now call up a MyGov Toll Free Number (1800-11-7800) and record their suggestions for the Prime Minister's consideration. The premise was simple—if you had a unique idea or a suggestion, then not only could that idea reach up to the level of the Prime Minister, but the entire nation would hear of it in your own voice through what was the most heard broadcast in the country. This new feature caught the imagination of the people and was a runaway success. Each month, when the toll free line would be opened three to four days in the lead up to the scheduled broadcast of 'Mann Ki Baat' that month, thousands of citizens would call up to record their suggestions. From a young school boy in Punjab 'ordering' the Prime Minister of India on Swachh Bharat, to a young entrepreneur in Gorakhpur wanting to know more about the Mudra Scheme, from a young girl in Pune requesting the Prime Minister to exhort the youth to register as voters, to a compassionate man from Alwar requesting that we all use clay diyas for Diwali and thereby promote employment, the ideas were wide and varied in scope and thought, and yet all had a common thread running through them—a desire to become a part of, or contribute to the process of nation-building.

The Process

Every month, the 'Mann Ki Baat' open forum is launched on MyGov, about ten days before the scheduled broadcast for the month. Some episodes of 'Mann Ki Baat' are dedicated to pre-defined topics, while in most episodes, Narendra Modi has relied on a wide range of inputs and then decided the themes and ideas that he would speak on. Based on that particular month's agenda or even otherwise, the content team is briefed on the guidelines for the first round of the screening process to be followed for that month.

Some guidelines remain consistent across episodes. Like in case of letters, general comments shorn of any specific ideas or suggestions are not shortlisted. Political comments, either in favour or against any person or party, are never shortlisted, nor are personal grievances, which do not have a broader policy implication.

Suggestions to improve existing programmes are best encouraged on discussions forums specific to the ministry running those programmes and therefore, such suggestions on 'Mann Ki Baat' forum are generally not taken up, unless the contributors have a very unique suggestion to make. Thoughts on topics already covered by the Prime Minister in previous episodes are generally not shortlisted, unless some entirely new perspective is presented.

While screening the comments, the content team looks at the uniqueness of the idea, any innovative thought or suggestion, a personal anecdote which can help narrate a larger goal and examples and experiences, which, when narrated to a wider national audience, can motivate them to do something similar in their lives.

The committee is aware of seasonal interest in topics and that there may be a genuine need of picking some comments in a particular month. For the episode of June 2015, for example a lot of contributors requested the Prime Minister to speak on water conservation, just as the monsoon season was starting. The screening committee was aware that such suggestions have a saliency for that month and therefore, those comments could not be missed.

To make the selection process truly reflect the voices of the people, it was important that all subconscious bias be completely eliminated. Therefore, from the very first episode of 'Mann Ki Baat', the selection committee was formed in a way that it would together, in its diversity and composition, eliminate the subconscious bias. The core team of five people, who do the first round of screening, between them represent the regional and cultural diversity of India and bring in varied professional competence, from engineering graduates to masters in journalism to MBAs in rural management, to masters in mass communication. The second and third round of screening is done by the Director (Content) and the CEO of MyGov respectively. This ensures an adequate representation of the current aspirations of people while also weighing in the experience of a career bureaucrat who has worked across the system. In its entirety, this team adequately reflects the present demographic profile of India while also being representative of the kind of people who are the most prominent users of MyGov, both in diversity and mindset.

Every few days, usually every third day, a list of comments received till then is taken and is screened. Although the team members divide the comments equally between them and then start going through their respective pool of comments one by one, they do so sitting together in a screening room so that the team can take a collective view on a comment in case there is a doubt about its relevance or utility.

Once the team has shortlisted the comments, they are sent to the Content Director of MyGov, who undertakes a second round of screening. In this round, the comments selected in the first round are organised in buckets of similar topics and a representative comment, reflecting that topic most accurately is then picked up. A second, smaller, representative short list is then prepared. Both these shortlists—the complete short list of comments prepared by the core team and the smaller representative shortlist—is then, in consultation with the CEO of MyGov, sent to the Prime Minister's Office. However, the entire dump of comments for each episode is also sent to the Prime Minister's office, in case they want to include any suggestions that may have not been shortlisted. This process of sending shortlisted suggestions is repeated every few days, up until two days before the scheduled broadcast of the episode.

This process, put in place for the MyGov Open Forum for 'Mann Ki Baat', has also been replicated for screening the audio calls on the toll free number. The essential message of each audio call is transcribed with the help of the MyGov team and a team of dedicated MyGov volunteers across the country. The transcribed calls are then screened following a similar process as for the MyGov messages in the open forum. A shortlist of the transcribed messages is then sent to the Prime Minister's Office. The actual audio recordings of those calls that have been approved for inclusion in the final script of that month's 'Mann Ki Baat' are then made available.

Akhilesh Mishra, then Content Director, MyGov says:

> *The numbers and the variety of topics covered in the comments are such that the process has to be elaborate. It is not about how many suggestions the Prime Minister actually takes, it is about giving the complete and correct picture of what the people feel and want to share with the Prime Minister. We are always conscious of the fact that we have to merely transmit what the people are actually conveying, without in any way editorialising from our end.*

One limitation that MyGov has is that it is an internet driven medium. The number of people connected to the internet, through various devices, is about 350 million and though this is very large in absolute numbers, it is still relatively small when compared to the total population of India. How then does MyGov reach the internet dark regions of the country? As the Digital India revolution makes internet access more broad-based in the years to come, these issues would resolve themselves automatically, but what could be the solution in the interim? This is a work in progress and various options have been explored, including the option of enabling the access of MyGov through a mobile phone dial-in, the penetration of which is now almost a billion.

The symbiotic relationship that MyGov has with 'Mann Ki Baat', made it an obvious choice to be the first activity on MyGov, where people without internet access could also use MyGov by dialing in from the phones. This is how the concept of a toll free number (1800-11-7800) for 'Mann Ki Baat' evolved. This was an important expansion of horizons for *Jan Bhagidari* and would be truly mass-based, if it gave equal opportunity to all.

According to Akhilesh Mishra:

> *The bulk of the comments is such that the process has to be elaborate. It is not about how many suggestions the Prime Minister actually takes, it is about giving the complete and correct picture of what the people feel and want to share with the Prime Minister.*

Mobile First

There are many people who never write a letter or for various reasons are not regular on MyGov. For them a third channel of interaction has been established in the form of the 'Narendra Modi Mobile App'. The App has emerged as a critical medium of interaction between the people and the Prime Minister. On repeated occasions, Narendra Modi has talked about how the Mobile App helps him connect with people, particularly the youth of India and read their pulse on the happenings across the nation and the world.

On being asked about the App with reference to MyGov, Narendra Modi said:

> *The App directly connects me to citizens. People feel they are writing to the PM directly and are in communication with him. For a citizen sitting in any corner of the nation, to directly write to the Prime Minister through a mobile, without any officials, any delay, is very empowering and this is what our democracy should be about—empowering people to directly reach out to those in high office.*

The Mobile App was integrated with the 'Mann Ki Baat' process very early on. Those who use it, say that the Mobile App is the easiest way to connect and communicate with Narendra Modi. There is no need to go all the way to a local post office, buy stamps and post. Neither does it require a MyGov profile. All it takes is a mobile phone and some free time. Convenience is the hallmark of using the App to share ideas and thoughts for 'Mann Ki Baat'.

It was through the App that the Prime Minister shared stories of start-ups across India and encouraged them. Similarly, the February 2016 episode on students' exams had considerable content sourced from the Mobile App.

Akhilesh Mishra, added:

> *The energy levels seen on the Mobile App have to be seen to be believed. But what is really striking is the level of positivity across the entire spectrum of users. Young men are sharing their entrepreneurial dreams, women are talking about new ventures they have started by taking the Mudra loan, students are taking out time to share their success mantras with other fellow students.*

The MyGov team monitors the comments received on the App as well. Here, Akhilesh made a remark that is not surprising:

> *When it comes to the App, the Prime Minister is seeing it daily so there have been times when he has said, 'there is a good comment on the App, I want to speak about it!'*

As of now, the numbers on the App are steadily and significantly rising and that day is not far when the App will become the single largest source of inputs for the Prime Minister.

A Missed Call to Hear It All

'Mann Ki Baat' is a missed call away and that too in your own language. In January 2016, Narendra Modi shared on Twitter that 'Mann Ki Baat' can be heard in one's own language by giving a Missed Call on 1922. A number that can be easily remembered was chosen for this purpose.

Initially, the programme could only be heard in English and Hindi. During the February 2016 programme, Narendra Modi announced that the programme can also be heard in one's own language from now on.

While unlike the earlier three mediums, 'Missed Calls' do not allow citizens to share their inputs; they are a vital key to expand the reach of the programme and a major source of inspiration for people to write in to Narendra Modi and be a part of the programme.

In a unique coincidence, the last Sunday in July 2015 happened to be on the 26th. 26 July, happens to be the Kargil Vijay Diwas, and is also the founding day of the citizen engagement platform MyGov. In the 'Mann Ki Baat' episode broadcast on this day, after paying his respects to the brave soldiers who gave India a proud victory in the Kargil war, Prime Minister talked at length about MyGov and its one-year journey. It is in this episode that he announced his intention to crowd source his Independence Day speech. From the ramparts of Red Fort, Modi thus became the first Prime Minister to talk of *Jan-Bhagidari*. MyGov, letters to All India Radio and the monthly 'Mann Ki Baat' are all helping to erect the edifice of participatory governance. Dr Suchitra from Chennai summed it up very well:

> *For the first time in 30 years we have a majority government under the dynamic leadership of Prime Minister Modi. Without people's voice I do not think a majority government would have been formed. It is our government which we voted for. It would succeed the way we want it to, only with people's participation. We have to work together as equal partners.*

The foundation has been laid. The vision that Narendra Modi has nurtured, is on the path to fruition.

The numbers are impressive. Even as of 1st September 2014, almost a lakh comments had been posted on the MyGov Open Forum. Almost 3.85 lakhs phone calls and suggestions have been shared and total number of missed calls using 1922 stands at 4.52 crore. Hearing 'Mann Ki Baat' in one's own language adds to the increasing reach of the programme and gets more people to join the bandwagon. The average duration of each call is18 to 20 minutes. This means, people are hearing a substantial part of the programme (most of the programmes are around 25 minutes) on their mobiles.

Mails, MyGov, the Mobile and the Missed Call have become the bridge through which every Indian's 'Mann Ki Baat' can become the Indian government's 'Mann Ki Baat' and vice versa, heralding a phase of truly participative democracy and responsive leadership.

Public participation is at the core of every 'Mann Ki Baat'. The programme is an expression of the views and aspirations of 125 crore Indians.

—Narendra Modi

CHAPTER 9: Post Box 111 and more: Harnessing the Ideas of 125 crore Indians

Due to obvious time constraints, Narendra Modi cannot possibly take up all the inputs he receives before every 'Mann Ki Baat' programme. Thus, it is natural to ask what happens to those comments that were not taken up or those comments that required follow up and possible action from various Government departments?

When this question was put to Narendra Modi himself by the authors, he said, "This always played on my mind. 'Mann Ki Baat' is never about the few people who get mentioned on air; it is about the lakhs of people who write to me, with a hope that here is someone who can share their joys and sorrows. It is important that their ideas and at times grievances are looked into."

While 'Mann Ki Baat' is not an avenue for grievance redressal, there are times when people share with Narendra Modi certain grievances that they want him to look into. Likewise, many innovative ideas are also shared but which Narendra Modi may not have taken up during the episode, but surely merit the attention of the relevant authorities.

As discussed earlier in this book, 'Mann Ki Baat' is never about one way communication. It is not a monologue by a Prime Minister, but a dialogue of equals between Narendra Modi, the person and the people of India.

From the very beginning, there were efforts to put in place a system which would be robust and structured, to act upon the suggestions after each broadcast.

Ideas which are Part of 'Mann Ki Baat'

After a 'Mann Ki Baat' programme is broadcast on the scheduled Sunday, the team handling MyGov, in close coordination with the PMO, immediately prepares a set of actionables that emanate from the episode. These actionables are then grouped under relevant ministries and departments. If they can be dovetailed with a flagship programme of the government already in place then that is done. Otherwise, the concerned ministry is identified and listed. Typically, there is a list of about a dozen actionables every episode.

This list is then vetted and sent to the respective ministries within a few hours of the episode being broadcast. In addition to the idea being explained and the suggested action to be taken being delineated, a status report is sought on the existing programmes and schemes, if any, being implemented and centered on the suggested idea. In case there is something similar being already implemented, then proposals are sought from the ministry on how the new suggestion being given can be included in the framework. In case it is a new thought, then proposals are invited on the feasibility of the idea. Some ministries are more pro-active in responding, while others have to be prodded. However, within a week, the first set of responses with a proposed action plan is on the table.

Follow-up Mechanism for Ideas not Part of Broadcast

What happens to ideas that have made it through the selection process, but could not be included in the broadcast? In this context, be it known that the two principal organisations through which suggestions come—the All India Radio and MyGov interfaces. Each has set up its own defined systems to create a follow up mechanism.

All India Radio

Episode after episode, the number of letters coming to AIR shoots up dramatically. The team handling the operational aspects—Manohar Singh Rawat, Programme Executive for 'Mann Ki Baat', Laxmi Shankar Bajpai, DDG (Programme), AIR Delhi and Rajeev Kumar Shukla, DDG-Policy & Sports DG:AIR, immediately realised that the volumes of letters coming would overwhelm their current systems. As they deliberated on what to do next, the first thing they agreed that needed to be done was to create a separate identity within the AIR system, for inviting suggestions through letters. Rawat suggested speaking to the Chief Post Master General for creating a separate Post Box, dedicated exclusively to 'Mann Ki Baat.' That is how the address—*Mann Ki Baat, Post Box 111, Akashvani Bhavan*, came into existence. But then came the next issue—addressing the letters that are worthy of consideration, but are not part of the broadcast. The team deliberated this with Fayyaz Sheheryar, Director General of AIR, who, based on just the single interaction the team had with the Prime Minister while recording the first episode stuck on the idea of seeking advice on this from the Prime Minister himself. This opportunity arose during the November 2014 episode. The Prime Minister heard them out and thus was born 'Post Box 111' as a regular programme on AIR. It was launched rather quickly, in the third week of December 2014.

'Post Box 111' is broadcast every Sunday on the same time slot as 'Mann Ki Baat', i.e. 11 A.M., except on that Sunday when 'Mann Ki Baat' is broadcast. It goes on air on the Indraprastha Channel of the AIR, Delhi and the entire FM Rainbow Network of the AIR. AIR FM Rainbow is also available on free dish, Doordarshan DTH service and is live-streamed on the Internet and on AIR's mobile app, thus reaching all corners of the globe.

Soon 'Post Box 111' became an extension of 'Mann Ki Baat'. While each episode of the latter comprises the Prime Minister's thoughts and views on a number of issues, 'Post Box 111' focuses on each issue separately, one by one, episode by episode. To discuss issues, the invited experts come from myriad fields ranging from art, culture, psychology, sociology, governance, journalism, youth affairs and sports, women's issues, science and technology, defence forces, agriculture, health, social security, innovation, et. al.

On the suggestion of Narendra Modi himself, it was decided that each episode of Post Box 111 should have renowned experts from the domains discussed in that episode. This would lend critical credibility to the ideas and suggestions being discussed. Experts who have been part of 'Post Box 111', include noted psychiatrist Dr Nimesh Desai, renowned danseuse Shovana Narayan, well known activist Dr Kiran Bedi, noted academic Prof. Pushpesh Pant, Former Secretary-General of Rajya Sabha Dr Yogendra Narain, Chairman of Sulabh International Dr Bindeshwar Pathak, veteran sportsperson Zafar Iqbal, eminent litterateur Chitra Mudgal, journalists Shri Alok Mehta and Rahul Dev, the Sarpanch of village Bibipur, Haryana, Sunil Jaglan (who first started the #SelfieWithDaughter campaign), Director of Save Life Foundation, Piyush Tiwari and a host of other eminent people. In one episode of 'Post Box 111' noted Islamic scholar Prof. Javed Jameel was invited and he eloquently analyzed Sufism and Islam.

Follow up Mechanism on MyGov

MyGov is both, the initiator of many of the ideas and suggestions that are eventually voiced through 'Mann Ki Baat', as well as the executing mechanism through which many of the ideas are implemented. Be it the Ek Bharat Shrestha Bharat Contest, the Duties of a Citizen Contest or the *#StatueCleaning* activity, the seeds of these ideas germinate through many of the suggestions that come through MyGov. These are then executed through MyGov as well. So how does MyGov handle the follow up mechanism?

Akhilesh Mishra, then Content Director, MyGov explains, "After each episode, we identify the ideas that were part of the shortlist but were not included in the eventual broadcast. They are then bracketed according to ministries and departments for being eventually sent to the concerned department for their consideration." After a periodic interval, when sufficient suggestions on a range of issues concerning a ministry have been collated, they are then sent to the respective ministries for their consideration while keeping the Prime Minister's Office in the loop. Gaurav Dwivedi, CEO MyGov, explains the rationale of this approach:

> *MyGov has not been conceived as an implementation agency of the government, but as one single, common interface between the citizens and the government. Our job is to collate suggestions from citizens, and then send them in an intelligible format to the respective ministry.*

When asked whether MyGov has a mechanism to track the progress in implementation of the suggestions that are sent, Dwivedi replied:

> *Yes we do. We are in constant touch with the designated nodal officers for MyGov that each ministry has identified - for not only continuously identifying new activities for MyGov, but also for following up on status updates for suggestions that have been sent by MyGov.*

Sometimes, however, MyGov also becomes the implementation platform for the ideas discussed in 'Mann Ki Baat'. The Prime Minister talked about his vision for Ek Bharat Shreshtha Bharat during his address on the occasion of the birth anniversary of Sardar Patel on 31st October 2015 and invited citizens to draw up the charter of the scheme themselves. A contest was launched on MyGov on 5th November 2015 to facilitate this. During the Mann Ki Baat broadcast that month, Prime Minister again explained his vision in detail and sought ideas from the citizens. As Akhilesh Mishra says:

> *The Ek Bharat Shreshtha Bharat Contest was an eye-opener for us. The breadth of new ideas envisioned and the detail through which many of these ideas had been fleshed out was really striking. We formed an inter-departmental jury to select the winners and in the process over 30 unique, implementable ideas were also identified.*

These ideas were then compiled and a detailed proposal was then sent to the Prime Minister's office.

Many a time ideas on MyGov, which could not be included in a particular episode, have actually triggered a chain of reactions beyond 'Mann Ki Baat'. The specially-abled have been among the most prominent contributors on MyGov, both through the Open Forum as well as through the Toll Free audio calls. This constant communication with a range of suggestions is a major contributing factor in shaping and rolling out of the Accessible India Campaign. The identification of 50 most used public buildings in 50 most prominent cities of the country was done through MyGov. Seetharam Bhat sent in this suggestion for the August 2015 episode of Mann Ki Baat:

> *Namaste Modiji, I am a physically challenged person wheelchair bound. There are immense and insurmountable challenges that we face in our daily life trying to earn a living. It would be of great help if you can address this section of society during the International day of the Physically Challenged on December 3rd or during one of the Mann Ki Baat addresses. This section of society is neglected by government, society and family. Kindly address our challenges and concerns.*

This suggestion did not form part of the broadcast in the August episode of Mann Ki Baat. But the suggestion was noted, the ministry notified and programmes were drawn up with timelines. The Prime Minister himself committed to attend the launch of Accessible India Campaign on 3rd December 2015. Unfortunately, because of the rains that flooded Chennai, and his pre-occupation with that emergency which neccessitated a visit to the city, the Prime Minister could not attend the launch on 3rd December. The 'Mann Ki Baat' connection did not end though. In the 'Mann Ki Baat' later that month, the Prime Minister dedicated a significant portion of the episode to directly communicate with the specially-abled, discussed in some detail the new announcements for them and explained the concept of "Divyang", the new expression coined by him.

M-Feedback

In recent months, the 'Narendra Modi Mobile App' is buzzing with ideas and suggestions, many of which are very valuable for government departments. These suggestions are carefully studied by the MyGov team and a similar process of documentation and classification ensures that each suggestion finds its way to the concerned department and ministry for their information.

The ideas shared on the Mobile App have been found to be very practical and insightful. Because it is most convenient to use a mobile phone, people comment on it on the move, in between their travels, thus boosting the activity on the mobile. It has been seen that the Mobile App is very popular among youth as well.

Participation with a Difference

When someone writes a letter, it is with an expectation; an expectation that Narendra Modi will hear him or her. It would be unfair to lakhs of people writing in, if their views are discarded simply because they were not broadcast in one episode. Over the months, a robust feedback mechanism has evolved and it not only enables views to be shared easily, but also routes the thoughts of people to respective departments, so that their views can positively impact policy. The process of screening, collecting, forwarding and then following up may seem very bureaucratic, but episode after episode it has been practiced with efficiency and systemic flaws are being regularly corrected.

'Mann Ki Baat' is based on the core premise that every idea merits a thought and wherever possible, merits action. This again is in sync with Narendra Modi's idea of *Jan Bhagidari*, of filling the system with fresh ideas and inputs from the 125 crore people of India.

The bond of humanity is the greatest of all. Time and again, when the world has faced mindless destruction, India has risen to the occasion to help the world and ensure that things return to normal.

—Narendra Modi

CHAPTER 10: What the Numbers tell us

While the rest of the chapters have been focussed on a qualitative study of 'Mann Ki Baat' covering the key themes of the programme, this chapter looks at 'Mann Ki Baat' from a quantitative point of view.

A study was undertaken of the 'Mann Ki Baat' episodes from October 2014 till January 2017 (a total of around 783 minutes) in order to ascertain the core ideas and themes that emerge when looked at from a macro level.

The study was done by preparing a dictionary corpus, a standard reference of all phrases, words, laws, programs, policies and other government phraseology.

Some of the findings are very interesting.

The chart overleaf reveals which sector is spoken about most often during every episode. The sector that is mentioned the highest number of times is skill development and education (31%), followed by matters relating to the welfare of women and children as well as social upliftment and social transformation (20%). Topics relating to the economy and digital India come third (17%), followed by farmer issues (14%) and governance (13%).

Some topics recur seasonally. For example, the early parts of the year, most notably January, February and March 2015, 2016 (and January 2017) show a huge spike in skill and education sector being talked about. This is understandable considering that this is the peak board exam season.

The months of May, June, July and August have consistently seen more discussions on the health sector with Yoga being a common topic in 2015 and 2016.

Women and child empowerment, though not taking up considerable space during any particular episode, have been consistently mentioned during most of the episodes. Either an anecdote, a phone call, a letter or a topic is discussed that is concerned with women and child development.

Trends of Key Themes
October 2014-January 2017

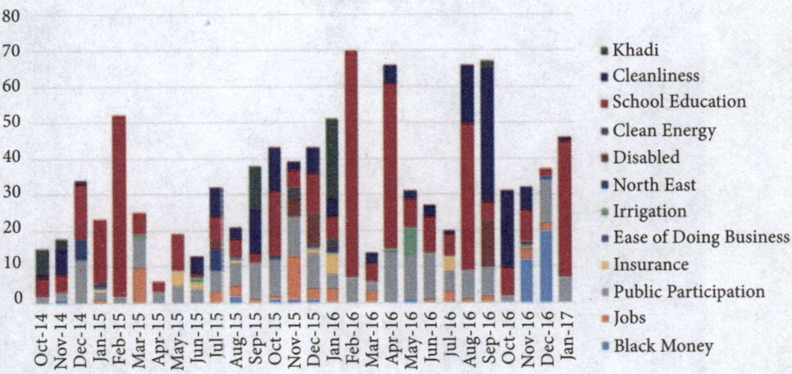

Khadi promotion took significant time in October 2014 and 2015, November 2014, September 2015 and January 2016. These coincide with the birth and death anniversaries of Mahatma Gandhi.

The Government's fight against black money takes up key space during the episodes towards the end of the year, specially November 2014, October 2015, November 2015, December 2015 and the last two episodes of 2016, when demonetisation was the lead subject.

This recurrence is however only thematic. Once you go into details, you will see how the issues raised by the

Prime Minister always vary. Each issue is presented in a different way, supplemented with anecdotes or a phone call.

Swachh Bharat Mission, Swachhta, Cleanliness, Hygiene, Toilets, Defecation, and Sanitation have been focussed on consistently across 'Mann Ki Baat' and data shows that except in a few early episodes of 2015, they have been discussed extensively all the time. The discussion on cleanliness through the end of 2016 has been increasing. This can be attributed to the Swachh Bharat Mission completing two years and there being concrete outcomes to show the efforts under the Mission.

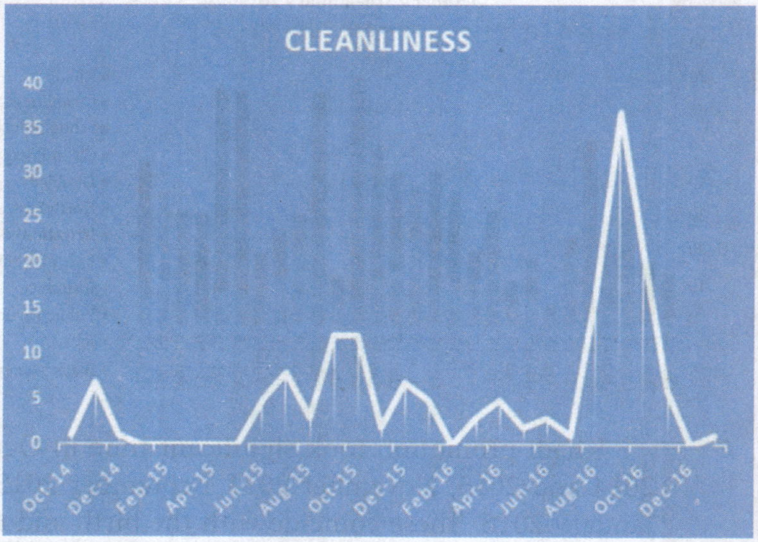

One constant theme of 'Mann Ki Baat' is volunteering and contribution from the people. As Narendra Modi says, he is the medium, the voice is that of the people of India. He seeks ideas from people before every episode and he asks for feedback on a variety of themes during every episode. Words like–invite, suggestions, invited, public participation, volunteer, get involved, ideas, people's participation, share, encourage, urge, awareness, spread, contribute–find considerable mention in 'Mann Ki Baat' as shown in the chart below.

Many 'Mann Ki Baat' episodes have a distinct call to action–it can be an appeal to the youth to further cashless transactions, an appeal to further 'Beti Bachao, Beti Padhao', a call to share photos of 'Incredible India' to get more tourists into the country and awareness to prevent road accidents. Public participation remains the USP of 'Mann Ki Baat.'

That politics is a no-no is evident by the fact that words like 'BJP', 'Congress' or references to any political leaders are absent in any of the episodes. In no episode has the 'BJP' been mentioned. The Congress has been mentioned once in the context of Congress Governments implementing land bills in their states. Besides that, there has been no mention of the Congress either. These findings reaffirm the fact that 'Mann Ki Baat' has gone above politics rather than being constrained by it.

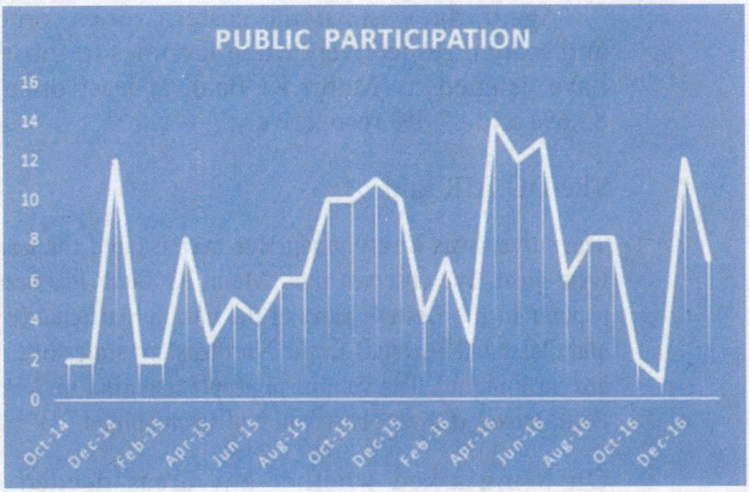

In October 2016, the All India Radio conducted a survey on 'Mann Ki Baat' and its reach across the nation. The aim of the survey was to gauge the strengths and overcome any limitation, wherever noticed.

The survey, which was carried out across 22 states and 2 Union Territories, revealed some very interesting points:

About 92% of the people had heard of 'Mann Ki Baat' and about 80% of them had heard it once in their lives.

States where the awareness levels were particularly high were Manipur (95.5%), Madhya Pradesh (92.5%), Gujarat (92.5%), Assam (90%) and Goa (90%).

As far as zones were concerned, awareness in the Western Zone was highest (96.7%), followed by the Eastern Zone (88.5%).

In the list of states where the audience had heard 'Mann Ki Baat' at least once, Madhya Pradesh and Gujarat emerged on top with almost 85%, followed by Bihar (78.5%), and then Maharashtra and Goa (around 70%).

Again, the western and eastern zones come first and second respectively when it comes to those who have listened to 'Mann Ki Baat' at least once with 85.6% and 82.4% respectively.

The DG AIR said:

The survey was a very productive exercise and the learnings were great. We observed that 'Mann Ki Baat' has been very popular in the Eastern parts of the nation, particularly Bihar and Odisha. The trends in the Northeastern states like Assam are encouraging. The volume of people listening to 'Mann Ki Baat' makes it a very powerful and strong brand.

On being asked whether any areas needed extra attention, DG AIR said:

It was noticed that the audience in southern India was not matching the numbers in the eastern, western and northern parts. When we did more study on this, we found out that there was an issue of language. The regional broadcast used to take place at 8 PM on the evening of the 'Mann Ki Baat' but we decided to broadcast it immediately after the programme in the morning. We saw that due to this, numbers improved substantially. The numbers from the South after October (when the survey was conducted) are a lot better.

As far as the duration of every 'Mann Ki Baat' is concerned, the shortest programme was the first episode, lasting almost 13 minutes and the longest one has been the episode on 27th November 2016, lasting almost 37 minutes. This was the episode in which the Prime Minister talked at length about demonetisation.

Over time, the duration of each programme has got longer. In 2014 and 2015, only 3 episodes were longer than 30 minutes; whereas through 2016 and 2017, only 3 were below 30 minutes (out of which one was of 29 minutes 48 seconds).

The numbers tell a story–that of an all-encompassing and unprecedented outreach by Narendra Modi through a medium conventionally believed to be obsolete and past its prime.

'Mann Ki Baat' has resonated from the hills of Kashmir to the coasts of Kanyakumari. It has been heard in the deserts of Kutch and Rajasthan, in the forests of Chhattisgarh and Jharkhand, as well as in the Northeast.

Narendra Modi used every medium to popularize 'Mann Ki Baat.' Every episode is shown live on his website, on his Mobile App, and the episode is immediately available on Sound Cloud. The episodes of December 2016 and January 2017 were live on Narendra Modi's Facebook page as well. Every 'Mann Ki Baat' programme is available in 23 different languages. Besides this, 'Mann Ki Baat' is shown live on several television channels and radio stations.

Every episode is clearly moulded to sync with the Prime Minister's emphasis on public participation. There are few parallels of any leader interacting so extensively with citizens on topics that further the spirit of debate, discussion and thereafter, transformation powered by the people.

Mann Ki Baat – Joint radio address by PM Narendra Modi and President Obama

PM Narendra Modi during Mann Ki Baat

PM Narendra Modi meets Shri Chandrakant Kulkarni who gave 52 post-dated cheques towards Swachh Bharat

PM Narendra Modi initiating the Swachh Bharat drive in New Delhi

PM Narendra Modi meets top contributors of Mann Ki Baat

PM Narendra Modi with the AIR team

PART II

CHAPTER 1: October 2014

My dear countrymen,

Today is the holy festival of Vijaya Dashami. My heartiest greetings on the occasion of Vijaya Dashami to one and all.

Through the medium of radio, I would like to share a few heartfelt thoughts with you today. And, I hope that not only today, but this cycle of conversation may be carried out regularly in the future. I will try my best, to take out time twice a month or even once, to speak with you. I have also decided that whenever I speak to you in the future, it will be on a Sunday morning at 11 A.M. It will be convenient for you too and I will be content to have shared my thoughts with you.

Vijaya Dashami—A Symbol of Victory of Good over Evil

We are celebrating the festival of Vijaya Dashami today, which is a symbol of the victory of good over evil. A gentleman named Ganesh Venkatadari, from Mumbai, has written to me that we must take a vow to eliminate ten bad habits from within ourselves on the occasion of Vijaya Dashami. I express my gratitude to him for this suggestion. As individuals, all of us must strive to put an end to our bad habits and vanquish them. For the sake of our nation, I believe that all of us should come together and take a vow to rid our country of dirt and filth. On the occasion of Vijaya Dashami, we must take such a vow.

Swacch Bharat Movement

Yesterday, on 2nd October on the eve of Mahatma Gandhi's birth anniversary, of our 125 crore countrymen have started the 'Swachh Bharat' movement. I trust that all of you will take this forward. I had shared a thought yesterday, which is that I will nominate nine people and they need to upload their videos of cleaning the country on social media websites, and nominate nine more people to do the same. I want you all to join me, clean up the nation, and nominate nine more people in this drive. Ask your friends, you don't need to go too far, and they will also nominate nine more people. Eventually, the entire nation will be filled with this atmosphere. I strongly believe that all of you will join hands with me to carry this movement forward.

Khaadi Revolution

Whenever we think of Mahatma Gandhi, we are reminded of Khaadi. You may be wearing a variety of clothes, made of different fabrics and company brands. Is it not possible to include Khaadi too? I am not telling you to use only Khaadi products. I am just requesting you to use at least one Khaadi product, like a handkerchief, or a bath towel, a bed sheet, a pillow cover, a curtain or anything of that kind. If you have an inclination to use various types of fabrics and clothes in your family, you can also buy Khaadi products on a regular basis. I am saying this because when you buy Khaadi products, it helps poor people light lamps on Diwali, so please buy a product or two. Also, you can avail a special discount on Khaadi products from 2nd October for a month. It is a very small thing, but has a very big impact which connects you to the poor and you will see this as a success. When I speak of 125 crore countrymen and assess the outcome, we assume that the government will take care of everything and as individuals, we stand nowhere. But we have seen that if we intend to move ahead, we need to identify our potential, understand our strengths and I can vouch that we as a people, as a country are incomparable in this world. You all know that our own scientists have been successful in reaching Mars, with the least expenditure. We do not lack in strength, but have forgotten our forte. We have forgotten ourselves. We have become devoid of hope. My dear brothers and sisters, I cannot let this happen. I always remember one of the sayings of Swami Vivekananda how, he always laid emphasis on one thought, and he might have, possibly, shared this thought with many others.

A New Awakening

Swami Vivekananda used to recount how, once a lioness was carrying her two cubs and came upon a flock of sheep. She had a desire of preying upon them and started running towards the flock. Seeing her running, one of the cubs too, joined her. The other cub was left behind and the lioness after preying upon the flock moved on. One of the cubs went with the lioness, but the other cub was left behind, and was brought up by a mother sheep. He grew among the sheep, started speaking their language and adapted to their ways of life. He used to sit, laugh and enjoy with them. The cub, who went with the lioness, had grown-up now by now. Once, he happened to meet his brother and was shocked to see him. He thought "He is a lion and is playing with sheeps, talking like sheep. What is wrong with him?" He felt that his ego was at stake and went to talk to his brother. He said, "What are you doing, brother? You are a lion." His brother replied, "No, I am a sheep. I grew up with them. They have brought me up. Listen to my voice and the way I talk." he then said, "Come", I will show you who you really are." He took his brother to a well and told him to look at his own reflection in the water, and asked him, if both of them had similar faces. "I am a lion, you, too, are a lion." His brother's self-esteem got awakened; he attained his self-realization through this and even a lion brought up among sheep started roaring like a lion. His inner soul was awakened. My countrymen, 125 crore Indians have infinite strength and capabilities. We need to recognise ourselves. We need to identify our inner strengths and like Swami ji used to always say, we need to carry our self-respect, identity ourselves and move forward in life and be successful. This will, in turn, make us a winning and successful country. I believe, all our countrymen, a population of 125 crores, are efficient, strong and can stand against any odds with confidence.

Responsibility of Society Towards Specially-abled

These days, I have been receiving many letters through social media websites, like Facebook, and from friends. One of them, Mr Gautam Pal, has addressed the issue regarding specially-abled children. He has floated the idea of planning some schemes for them and extending moral support by separate Municipalities, Municipal Corporations or Councils to them. I liked his suggestion. I have experienced this during my tenure as the Chief Minister of Gujarat. A Special Olympics was held in Athens in 2011. After the Olympics, I invited all the participants and winners of specially-abled category from Gujarat at home. I spent two hours with them, and it was the most emotional and inspiring incident of my life. I believe that a specially-abled child is not the responsibility of parents alone in a family, she/he is the responsibility of the entire society. God has chosen this family to support a specially-abled child, but a child is the responsibility of the entire nation. After this interaction, I got so emotionally attached with them, that I started organizing separate Olympics for them in Gujarat. Thousands of children, with their parents, used to come and attend, I, too, used to attend the Olympics. There was an atmosphere of trust and, this is the reason, I liked the suggestion given by Mr Gautam Pal and felt like sharing it with you.

Journeys and Destinations

It reminds me of another story. Once a traveller was sitting by the side of a road, and was asking everyone the way to a specific place. He kept on asking for the route from several people. A man sitting beside him was observing this. The traveller eventually stood up and started asking the passers-by again. The man observing him finally said, "The way to your destination is from here." The traveller replied "Brother, you were sitting next to me for so long, and saw me asking the route from everyone. If you knew the route, why didn't you tell me before?" The man answered, "I was waiting to verify whether you really intended to reach your destination or whether you were asking people just for your knowledge. But, when you stood up, I was assured that you truly wish to reach your destination, and decided to confirm the address."

My countrymen, till the time we do not decide to walk, stand on our own; we will not receive guidance from others in our journey. We will not find people to hold our hands and help us in walking. We need to take the initiative in walking and I trust that all 125 crore Indians, are capable of walking on their own and will keep on moving ahead.

Sharing of New Ideas

For the past few days, I have been receiving very interesting suggestions from people. I know, when to adopt these suggestions. But, I want everyone to actively participate in these suggestions since we all belong to our nation; and the nation does not only belong to any government. We are the citizens of our nation and we need to all unite without any exceptions. Some of you have suggested simplifying the registration process for small scale industries. I will definitely put this under the government's notice. Some of you have written to me for incorporating skill development courses in the school curriculum from the 5th standard onwards as this will help students learn various skills and crafts. I loved this idea. It has also been suggested that even the youth should compulsorily participate in skills development courses along with their studies. One of the suggestions given was to keep a dustbin at every 100 meters for the purpose of putting in place a cleaning system. Some of you have also written to me to abolish the use of plastic bags.

I am receiving numerous suggestions from people. I have always been telling you to write to me and narrate a true incident, which is positive and inspiring for me and our countrymen, along with the supporting evidence.

If you do this, I promise to share all those thoughts or suggestions with everyone, through 'Mann Ki Baat'.

I have only one intention in speaking with you all—Come, let us serve our Mother India. Let us all take our nation to new heights. Let us all take a step forward. If you take one step, our nation takes 125 crore steps to move forward, and for this purpose, on this auspicious occasion of Vijaya Dashami, we need to defeat our inner evils and pledge to do something good for the nation. A beginning has been made today. I will be sharing my thoughts with all of you in the future also. Today, I have shared all spontaneously thoughts from my heart. I will meet you all next at 11 A.M. on Sundays, but I trust our journey shall never end and I hope to continue receiving love and suggestions from you.

After listening to my thoughts, please do not hesitate in sharing your thoughts or in advising me. I will appreciate it if your suggestions keep coming in. I am glad to have been able to talk with you through this simple medium of radio, which reaches each and every corner of the nation. I can reach the poorest homes, as my and my nation's strength lies within the huts of the poor, within the villages; my nation's strength lies with the mothers, sisters and with the youth; my nation's strength lies with the farmers. Our nation will progress only if you believe in it. I am expressing my trust in the nation. I believe in your strength, hence, I believe in our nation's future.

I would once again like to thank one and all for taking time out and listening to me. Thank you all!

For listening to the audio, please log on to http://www.narendramodi.in/mann-ki-baat or scan the given QR code.

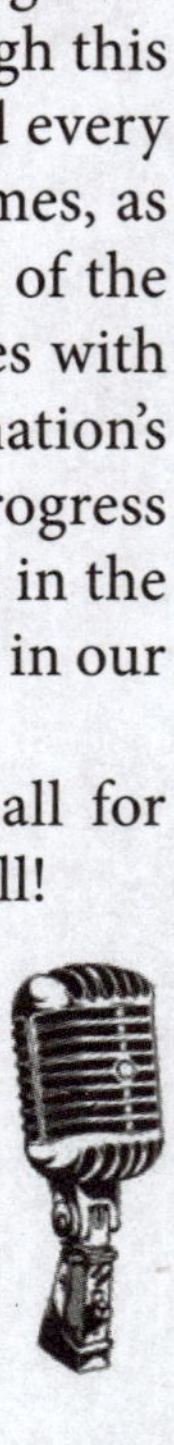

CHAPTER 2: November 2014

My dear countrymen,

I am here with you again today, after almost a month, and a month is quite a long time. A variety of things keep happening around us, all the time. All of you must have recently celebrated Diwali, with great fervour and joy. It is these festivals which keep bringing in happiness in our daily lives. Be it the rich or the poor, villagers or urban dwellers, festivals hold a very varied significance in everyone's lives. And since, this is my first conversation with you all post Diwali, I convey my warm wishes to everyone.

Last time, we had a general conversation. But then, I had certain new realisations. We believe at times that nothing is going to ever change, every citizen of the country is nonchalant about things that plague our society and that no one would do anything about it. Since my last conversation on 'Mann Ki Baat', to this conversation, I have wanted you to change this mindset.

Neither is our country like this, nor are our people, indifferent. Sometimes I feel, the nation is way ahead and it is the government that is lagging behind. And, from my personal experience, I can say that governments too need to change their mindset. And I say this because I can see a tremendous sense of commitment in Indian youth today. They are eager to do their bit and are looking for an opportunity, where they can help bring in change, while making essential efforts at their end. The last time I had asked them to buy at least one Khadi outfit and not to be a *Khadidhari*. But the feedback I got from Khadi stores was that in a week's time, the sales of this cloth had jumped up by 125%. In this way, as compared to last year, the sales for this year were more than double in the week following the 2nd of October.

Cleanliness

Cleanliness... Could anyone have imagined that cleanliness would become such a huge public movement? The expectations are high and so they should be. I can see some good results and 'cleanliness' can now be witnessed in two parts. One is the huge garbage piles which keep lying around the city, which the government will work to remove. Cleanliness is a big challenge, but one cannot run away from one's responsibilities. All state governments and all municipalities will now have to take concrete actions due to rising public pressure. The media is playing a very positive role in all this, but there is also the second aspect. This second aspect gives me immense pleasure, happiness and a sense of satisfaction, it is that the people in general have started to feel that whatever has happened in the past should be left behind and moving ahead they should not dirty their surroundings or add to the already existing dirt.

A gentleman, Mr Bharat Gupta from Satna in Madhya Pradesh, has sent me a mail on MyGov.in where he has shared his personal experience while travelling by the Indian Railways. He says that people eat on trains and usually litter around. While touring for so many years, it is only this time that he noticed no one was littering and were rather looking for dustbins to throw their trash. When people did not see any arrangements for this, they collected all their litter in a corner instead. He says that it was a very gratifying experience for him. I thank Bharat ji for sharing this experience with me.

What I am seeing around is that this campaign has had a great influence on kids. Many families mention that now whenever kids eat chocolate, they themselves pick up the wrapper and dispose it off. I also saw a message on social media, where someone had posted a picture with the title, "My hero of the day". The picture was that of a little kid who picks up trash wherever he goes, even while going to school. He is himself motivated to do this. See how people now feel that it is their own country and they will not dirty it and add to the existing piles of garbage. And those who litter feel ashamed of doing so, as someone is always around to point it out to them. I consider all these to be good omens.

Raising Awareness of Social Issues

Another thing is that many people come to meet me from various sections of society, be it government officers, people from the film world, sports world, industrialists, scientists... All of them, whenever they interact with me, about four to five minutes of a ten-minute discussion, deals with social issues. Someone talks about cleanliness; some others talk about education, while others talk about social reforms. There are also some people who discuss the running of family life. I used to initially think, if a businessman comes, he will definitely talk only about things of his personal interest. I am seeing a major change, people talk less about their own interests and more about taking on some social responsibility.

When I add up all these small incidents, I see a larger picture and I realise that we are moving in the right direction. It is true that unhealthy environment leads to diseases and sickness, but where does sickness strike first. It first strikes the poor household. When we work towards cleanliness, we make a major effort in the direction of helping the poor. If the poor families are saved from diseases, then they will be saved from a lot of added financial problems. If a person is healthy, then he works hard, earns for the family and helps in running the family smoothly. And so, this cleanliness drive is directly related to the health and welfare of my poor brethren. We may not be able to do something to help the poor, but by keeping the environment clean, we help the poor in a big way. Let us view it from this perspective and it will be very beneficial.

I receive different kinds of letters. The last time I had mentioned about our specially-abled children, whom God has given some kind of deficiencies. I had expressed my feelings regarding such people. I see that people who work in this field are sending me their success stories. But I also got to know about two things from my people in the government. People from the HRD Ministry, after hearing my talk, felt the need to do something and the officers came together to work out an action plan.

Action Plan for Specially-abled

This is an example of how changes are coming about in the country's governance. Firstly, they have decided that those who are specially-abled and who want to pursue technical education, a thousand of them who are good, will be selected for special scholarships, and a plan has been made for this. I congratulate the officials who have thought on those lines. Another important decision is that all the Kendriya Vidyalayas and all central universities will have a special infrastructure for specially-abled individuals, for example, to help them climb stairs, there will be a provision of ramps to facilitate their movement by wheel chairs. They need different kinds of toilets and the HRD Ministry has decided to allocate additional one lakh rupees to the Kendriya Vidyalayas and the central universities for this purpose. This fund will be used by these institutions to create infrastructure for the specially-abled. This is an auspicious beginning and these things will lead us to change.

Diwali in Siachen with Jawans

I had the chance to visit Siachen a few days back. I spent Diwali with our jawans who are ready to lay down their lives for the nation. When the nation was celebrating Diwali, I was there at Siachen. It is because of these bravehearts that we were able to celebrate Diwali and so I wanted to be with them. I experienced the difficulties in which they spend their time there. I salute all my jawans. I want to share another matter of great pride with you. Our jawans work in the field of security. In calamities, they risk their lives to save our lives. They also fetch medals for us in sporting events. You will be glad to know that these jawans have won a gold medal in a very prestigious event in Britain called the Cambrian Patrol, defeating contestants from 140 nations. I offer them my heartiest congratulations.

I also got an opportunity to meet the young and dynamic students, both boys and girls over tea, who had won medals in Sports. They gave me renewed energy. I saw their zeal and enthusiasm. The facilities in our country are quite less as compared to other nations, but instead of complaining, they were just sharing their joy and excitement. For me, this tea programme with these players was very inspiring, and I really felt good.

Black Money

I would like to tell you something more and that too from my heart. I truly believe that people of my country trust my words and my intentions. But today, once again, I want to reiterate my commitment. As far as black money is concerned, my people, please trust your Prime Servant, for me this is an Article of Faith. This is my commitment that the hard-earned money of the poor people that is stashed abroad, every penny of that should be brought back. The ways and means to be followed can be however different. And this is very obvious in a democratic country, but on the basis of what I understand and know, I assure you that we are on the right track. Today, nobody, neither me, nor the government, nor you, nor even the previous government, knows how much money is stashed abroad. Everyone gives an estimate calculated in his/her own way. I don't want to get lost in some such figures and estimates and believe that it is my commitment that, even if it is 2 Rupees or 5 Rupees, or millions or even billions, this is the hard-earned money of the poor people of my country and it has to come back. And I assure you that I will keep trying for this till the end. No efforts will be spared. I want your blessings to be with me always and I assure you that I will always do whatever is required to be done for you. I give my commitment to you.

Menace of Drug Addiction

I have received a letter. It has been sent by Mr Abhishek Parikh. The same sentiments were expressed to me by many mothers and sisters when I was not even the Prime Minister. Some doctor friends had also expressed their concern and I too have expressed my views on this issue a number of times in the past. Mr Parikh has drawn my attention towards the increase of drug addiction that is fast catching up with our young generation. He has asked me to discuss this topic in 'Mann Ki Baat'. I agree with his concern and I will definitely include this topic in my next edition of 'Mann Ki Baat'. I will discuss the topic of drugs, drug addiction and the drug mafia and how they are a threat to our country's youth. If you have some experience, any information in this regard, if you have ever rescued any child from such drug addiction, if you know of any ways and means to help, if any government official has played a good role, if you give me any such information, I will convey such efforts to the public and together we will try to create an environment in each family where no child ever thinks of choosing this vice out of sheer frustration. I will definitely discuss this in detail in the upcoming edition of 'Mann Ki Baat'.

I know I am choosing topics which will put the government in the dock. But how long can we keep hiding such issues? How long will we brush these important concerns under the carpet? Some day or the other we need to take a call, follow our instincts. For fulfilling grand intentions, tough calls are equally important. I am mustering up the courage to do so because your love inspires me to undertake such steps. And I will continue to do such things because of your love.

Some people told me, "Modi ji, you have asked us to send you suggestions on Facebook, Twitter and through email. But a large section of the social class does not have access to these facilities, so what can they do?"

Your point is very valid. Everyone does not have this facility. Well then, if you have something to say relating to 'Mann Ki Baat', which you hear on the radio even in the villages, then do write in to me on the following address:

'Mann Ki Baat',
Akashvani,
Sansad Marg,
New Delhi.

Even if you send in some suggestions through letters, they will definitely reach me. And I will take them seriously, because active citizens are the biggest asset for development. Even if you write one letter, it indicates that you are very active. When you give your opinion, it means that you are concerned with national issues and this is the strength of the nation. I welcome you.

For my 'Mann Ki Baat', your 'Mann Ki Baat' should also reach me. I will try and interact with you again next month. I will make an effort that whenever I talk, it is a Sunday, and around 11 A.M. So I get closer to you.

The weather is changing and winters are slowly setting in. This is a good month for health. Some find it a good season for eating. Some find it good for wearing nice clothes. Besides food and clothes, it is a good season for your health, so don't let it go waste and make the most of it.

Thank you.

For listening to the audio, please log on to http://www.narendramodi.in/mann-ki-baat or scan the given QR code.

CHAPTER 3: December 2014

My dear fellow countrymen,

Today, I have this great opportunity of interacting with you again. You must be wondering why a Prime Minister should be interacting the way I am. Well, first and foremost, I am less of your Prime Minister and more of a Pradhan Sewak (principal servitor). Since childhood, I have been hearing that by sharing, the intensity of our pain becomes less, while the intensity of our joy grows manifold. Well, I think, this is the guiding thought behind 'Mann Ki Baat'. It is an opportunity for me to sometimes share my concerns and sometimes my joys. Sharing my deepest concerns with you makes me feel light-hearted and sharing my joy multiplies my happiness.

Drug Trap

Last time, I had mentioned my concern about the youth of the country. It is not because you chose me as the Prime Minister, but because I feel concerned as an individual. Sons and daughters of many families are caught in the trap of drugs. It does not destroy just the person involved, but affects the entire family, the society and the nation at large. Drug is such a grave menace that it destroys the most powerful individuals.

While serving as the Chief Minister of Gujarat, my officers with good records would often come to ask for leave. Initially they would hesitate to spell out the reasons, however on insisting they revealed that their child had fallen into the drug trap and they now needed to spend time with their kids and rehabilitate them. I could see the bravest of my officers struggling to control their tears. I met suffering mothers too. In Punjab, I had the chance to meet some mothers who were very angry and yet concerned about their children who had fallen into the trap of drugs.

We have to work together as a society to tackle this menace. I understand that the youth who fall into this drug trap are often blamed. We blame these youth for being careless and irresponsible. We perceive that the victims are bad, but the fact is that it is the drugs that are bad. The youth are not wrong; it is this addiction which is wrong. Let us not blame and wrong our children. Let us get then rid of this habit of addiction and not victimize them. Blaming the children would push them further into addiction. This is, in fact, a psycho-socio-medical issue and let us treat it as such a problem. This menace needs to be handled carefully as its solution is not limited to medical intervention only. The individual concerned, his family, friends, the society, the government and the legal system, all have to work in tandem to tackle this menace. Each one of us has to contribute to get rid of this menace.

A few days ago, I had organised a DGP level conference in Assam. I expressed my concern over this issue and my displeasure at the non-serious attitude of the people concerned. I have asked the police department to seriously discuss this issue and come out with relevant solutions. I have made a suggestion that the department should launch a toll-free helpline as the families often feel ashamed to come out in the open about the addiction problem of their children. They have no one to confide in. Parents from any part, any corner of the country, can freely approach the police if their children have fallen a victim to addiction. The department has taken this suggestion seriously and is working towards its fulfilment.

The Three Ds

The drug menace brings about the three Ds. These three Ds are not the ones related to entertainment, but the three Ds related to drugs.

First D is Darkness, the second D is Destruction and the third D is Devastation.

Drugs lead a person to a blind path of destruction. There is nothing left in its trail but devastation. This is a topic of great concern and demands total attention.

I had mentioned this topic in my last address in 'Mann Ki Baat'. We have received more than 7,000 letters on our Akashvani address. Some letters were received in the government offices. We also received responses on the government portal, MyGov.in, online and through e-mails. Lakhs of comments were received on twitter and facebook. Hence, a deeprooted concern in the society's psyche has found a voice.

I am especially thankful to the media of our country for highlighting this concern. Many channels conducted special hour long programmes. These programmes were not just meant to criticize the government, instead, they were forums for open discussion, showing concern, and an effort to come out with workable solutions. These initiatives created a background for healthy discussions. The government was also sensitized to its responsibilities in this direction, and it can no longer remain neutral to these concerns.

There is a question I want to ask the youth caught in the drug trap. I want to ask these youth that when for three or four hours they are in a state of intoxication, they might be feeling free of all concerns, free of all tensions and in a different world altogether. But have they ever thought over the question of where does the money used for buying drugs go? Have they ever thought about it? Just make a guess. What if this drug money goes to terrorists? What if this money is spent by terrorists to procure weapons? And with these weapons, the very same terrorists might be pumping bullets in the heart of our soldiers. The soldier of our country gets martyred. Have you ever thought about our soldiers—a soldier who is so dear to his mother, the treasured son of Mother India, the brave son of the soil, is hit by a bullet probably funded by the money spent on purchasing drugs. I know and firmly believe that you too love your motherland and have tremendous respect for our soldiers. Then how can you support a habit which funds the drug mafia and terrorists.

Some people feel that when a person is in despair, faces failures and when he is directionless, he is an easy prey to drugs. But I feel that people who lack ambition, who do not have any set goals and targets, who have a deep vacuum in their lives, are the ones who will try to get access to drugs. If you want to avoid drugs and save your children from this menace, then foster ambition in them, make them dreamers, and make them individuals with a desire to achieve something in life. Then you will see that they will not be easily distracted. Their aim then will be to achieve something in life.

Have you ever followed a sportsman's life? A sportsman is motivated forever. In bleak winters, everyone feels like sleeping in the warmth of a quilt, but a sportsman will still rise at 4 A.M. or 5 A.M. and go for his workout: Why? Because the goal is set. Similarly, if your child is aimless, there are chances of him/her falling prey to a menace like drugs.

Take a Thought, Make it your Life

I remember the words of Vivekananda. These words are very apt for all young people. I am sure you will keep repeating this thought over and over again. "Take a thought, make it your life. Ponder on it and dream about it. Make it an integral part of your dreams. Make it a part of your mind, veins and each and every part of your body and forget everything else."

This thought of Vivekananda is apt for every young person, and that is why I say that each person should have an ambition in life. Having an ambition does not allow your focus to shift to unnecessary things.

Some take drugs under peer pressure because it looks 'cool', some consider it a style statement. So sometimes, in an attempt at one-upmanship, the youth inadvertently fall into this serious trap due to their wrong mental perception. Addiction is neither cool nor a style statement. In reality, it is a precursor to destruction. So whenever your friends boast about their drug habits, do not applaud and enjoy such conversations. Do not be a mute spectator to such absurdities. Have the courage to stand against such conversations and say 'No'. Have the guts to deride such a conversation, reject such a conversation and have the guts to tell the person that he is wrong.

Importance of Time

I would like to share some views with the parents too. These days none of us have time, all of us are running against time to earn our livelihood. We are racing against time to improve the quality of our lives. But in this blind race, do we have time to spare for our kids. Do we ever work for our childrens' spiritual progress and discuss it with them, instead we discuss only material progress. How are they doing in their studies, what has been their progress in exams, what to eat and what not to eat, where to go and where not to go—mostly these topics form the core of our entire interactions. Do we share such a relationship that our children can bare their hearts to us? I request all of you to do this. If your children share a frank relationship, then you can very well know what is going on in their life. Children do not take to bad habits suddenly. It happens gradually and it also impacts the home. Observe the changes that are happening in your home. If you observe closely, I believe that you may be successful in detecting the problem at the very beginning. Be aware of your child's friend circle and don't focus your conversations on material progress alone. Your concern should extend to their inner thoughts, their logic, their books, their friends and their mobiles—how and where are they spending their time. These need to be taken care of. I believe that no one else can do what parents can for their kids. Our ancestors have left us certain pearls of wisdom and that is why they are known as statesmen. A saying goes like this:

Paanch Varsh Laaw Lijiye
Dass Laaw Tadan dei
Paanch Varsh Laaw Lijiye
Dass Laaw Tadan dei
Sut Hi Solah Varsh Mein
Mitra Sarij Gani Dei
Sut Hi Solah Varsh Mein
Mitra Sarij Gani Dei

This means that till the age of 5, a child should grow in the loving and tender care of his parents, and by the time he is 10, the values of discipline should be inculcated in him. Sometimes we see that an intelligent mother gets angry and does not speak with her child throughout the day. This is a big punishment for the child. Actually, the mother punishes herself, but the child too gets punished in turn. The mother just has to say that she will not talk and the 10 year old will remain worried for the whole day, and change his habits. By the time the child is 16 years old, the relation should be one of friendship. There should be an open conversation with him. This is a brilliant advice which has been passed on by our ancestors. I would like to see this inculcated in our family life.

Another thing brought to our notice is the role of the pharmacists. Some of the medicines lead to addiction. So, such medicines should not be distributed without a doctor's prescription. Sometimes a simple thing like a cough syrup can trigger addiction. It becomes the starting point of addiction. There are quite a few things that I would not like to raise on this platform. But we will have to follow and accept this discipline.

Role of the Society

These days many children from villages go to city for higher education and start living in a hostel or a boarding school. I have heard that sometimes these avenues become the entry point of such addiction. For this, the education system, society and the security forces will have to be vigilant. Each one will have to fulfil their roles and responsibilities. The government will fulfil the responsibilities on its end. We should constantly strive to fulfil our obligations.

I would also like to mention about the letters we have received. Some of them are interesting, some are filled with grief and some are inspiring. I cannot mention all, but I would like to mention one. There was a certain Mr Dutt. He was deep into addiction. He was also jailed, where he had several restrictions. Later, his life changed. He studied in jail and gradually, his life was transformed. His story is very famous. He was in Yerawada Jail. There might be many such inspiring stories. Many people have emerged victorious in their fight against addiction. We too, can come out of such habits and so, we should definitely try. We should make efforts for de-addiction and rehabilitation. I would also ask celebrities to be a part of this initiative—be it from the field of cinema, sports or someone in public life, be it the cultural or spiritual world, we should use every possible platform to create awareness. There should be constant messages in public interest. They will certainly have an effect. To those who are active on the social media, I would request them to start a continuous online movement using *#DrugsFreeIndia*. This will be more relevant because most of the addicted youth are a part of social media. If we take this *#DrugsFreeIndia* movement forward, then we will do a great service towards public awareness and education.

I want to take this concern forward. I would request all those who have successfully come out of this addiction to share their stories. I touched this topic because, like I said in the beginning, grief lessens though sharing. This is a topic of national concern and I am not here to sermonize. And neither am I entitled to preach. I am just sharing my grief with you. I also want to share the pain of the families who are suffering from this menace. I want to create a responsible environment. There can be difference of opinions, but let us make a beginning somewhere.

World Cup Win for the Blind Cricket Team

Like I mentioned before, I want to share happiness as well. Last week I had the opportunity to meet the Blind

Cricket Team. They had won the World Cup. They were exuding joy, excitement, and great self-confidence. God has given us everything, eyes, hands, legs i.e. we are totally capable, yet we lack this kind of determination and passion which I could see in the blind cricketers. What zeal and enthusiasm, really it was contagious. I felt super charged after meeting them. Such incidents bring great pleasure in life.

In the past few days, there was yet another noteworthy event. The cricket team from Kashmir defeated Mumbai on their home ground. I do not view it as one's victory and another's loss. I view it differently. All the stadiums in Kashmir have been inundated after the floods. Kashmir is passing through a tough phase. The circumstances have been extremely grim with these boys not standing any chance to practice. Yet the team spirit shown by these boys, their conviction and determination, is inspiring. These boys have shown us that we can overcome the most trying and testing circumstances if we remain focused on our goals. This news gave me immense pleasure and I take this opportunity to congratulate all these players on their victory.

International Yoga Day

Two days back, the United Nations has decided to celebrate June 21st as International Yoga Day. It is a matter of great pride and honour for India. Our ancestors developed this beautiful tradition and today, the entire world is associated with it. It does not merely benefit one personally but it has the potential to bring all the people together globally. The entire world came together on the issue of yoga in the UN and a unanimous resolution was passed just two days back (11th December 2014). 177

countries became the co-sponsors. In the past, when it was decided to celebrate the birthday of Mr Nelson Mandela, 165 countries became co-sponsors. Before that, efforts were on for International Toilet Day and 122 nations became co-sponsors of that initiative. For celebrating 2nd October as the Non-Violence Day, 140 countries became co-sponsors. But 177 countries co-sponsoring yoga is a world record of sorts. I am thankful to all the countries which have come forward in support and have honoured the sentiments of Indians and decided to observe World Yoga Day. It is now our duty that yoga reaches out to the masses in its true essence.

Retreat with Chief Ministers of State

Last week, I had the chance to have a meeting with the Chief Ministers of all the states. This tradition has been going on for the past 50-60 years. This time it was organized at the Prime Minister's residence. We started it as a retreat program with no papers, no files and no officers. It was a simple interaction where the Prime Minister and Chief Ministers were all the same, seated together like friends. For more than two hours, matters of national concern were seriously discussed in a friendly atmosphere. Everyone just poured their hearts out. There was no political agenda involved. This too, was a memorable experience that I wanted to share with you.

Rejuvenating North-East

Recently I had the chance to travel to the North-East. I was there for three days. Many a times, youth express their desire to see the Taj Mahal, Singapore or Dubai, but I would urge all nature lovers, all those who want to experience the divinity in nature, to visit the North-East. I had gone earlier too. This time, when I went as the Prime Minister, I tried to explore its potential. Our North-East has tremendous potential and possibilities. It is a land of beautiful people and beautiful surroundings. I was filled with immense joy after visiting the place. Sometimes people ask "Modi ji, don't you get tired?" I want to say that whatever little fatigue I had, the North-East took it away, and I am thoroughly rejuvenated. Such is the pleasure that I derived from that visit. The love and respect accorded by the people there, is something that will stay with me forever. The kinship and affinity showed by the people of the North-East touched me deeply. I will also tell you, it is not a joy only for me to enjoy, it is there for you to enjoy too. So, do travel to the North-East and enjoy.

Broadcast of MKB in Regional Languages

The next edition of 'Mann Ki Baat' will happen in 2015. This is probably my last programme in 2014. I wish you all a Merry Christmas. I would like to wish all the very best for the New Year in advance. It gives me immense pleasure to know that this programme 'Mann Ki Baat' is broadcast in regional languages by the local radio stations the same night at 8 P.M. And it is surprising to know that some of the regional voice-over artists also speak in a voice very similar to mine. I am surprised at the brilliant work being done by the artists associated with Akashvani and I would like to congratulate them. I consider this as an effective medium to connect to the masses. We have had a tremendous response. Seeing the response, Akashvani has devised a new method for your convenience. They have taken a new Post Box number.

So now if you wish to write to me, you can write on this Post Box number.

'Mann Ki Baat'

Post Box no. 111, Akashvani

New Delhi.

I will be waiting for your letters. You may not realize, but your letters become my inspiration. Some suggestions penned down can do good for the entire nation. I am thankful to you all. We will meet next in 2015 and on some Sunday morning, we will again have our own 'Mann Ki Baat'.

Thank you very much.

For listening to the audio, please log on to http://www.narendramodi.in/mann-ki-baat or scan the given QR code.

CHAPTER 4: January 2015

Today, Mr Barack Obama, the President of the United States, joins us in a special programme of 'Mann Ki Baat'. For the last few months, I have been sharing my 'Mann Ki Baat' with you. But today, people from various parts of our country, have asked questions.

But most of the questions are connected to politics, foreign policy, and economic policy. However, some questions touch the heart. And I believe, if we touch upon those questions today, we shall be able to reach out to the common man in the different parts of the country. And therefore, the questions asked in press conferences, or discussed in meetings—instead of those—if we discuss what comes from the heart, and repeat it, hum it, we get a new energy. And therefore, in my opinion, those questions are more important. Some people wonder, what does 'Barack' mean? I was searching for the meaning of 'Barack'. In Swahili language, which is spoken in parts of Africa, the word 'Barack' means, 'one who is blessed'. I believe alongwith a name, his family has given him a big gift.

The African countries have lived by the ancient idea of 'Ubuntu', which alludes to the 'oneness in humanity'. They say, "I am, because we are". Despite the gap in centuries and borders, there is still the same spirit of *Vasudhaiva Kutumbakam*, which we speak of in India. This is the great shared heritage of humanity. This unites us. When we discuss Mahatma Gandhi, we remember Henry Thoreau, from whom Mahatma Gandhi learnt disobedience. When we talk about Martin Luther King or Barack Obama, we hear from them, respect for Mahatma Gandhi. Such are the things that unite the world.

Today, Barack Obama is with us. I will first request him to share his thoughts. Then, I and Barack will both answer questions that have been addressed to us.

I request President Barack Obama to say a few words.

Mr Barack Obama:

Namaste! Thank you, Prime Minister Modi, for your kind words and for the incredible hospitality you have shown me and my wife Michelle on this visit and let me tell the people of India, how honoured I am to be the first American President to join you for Republic Day; and I am told that this is also the first ever Radio address by an Indian Prime Minister and an American President together, so we're making a lot of history in a short period of time.

Now, to the people of India, who are listening from all across this great nation, it's wonderful to be able to speak to you directly. We are just back from a discussion in which we affirmed that India and the United States are natural partners, because we have so much in common. We are two great democracies, two innovative economies, two diverse societies, dedicated to empowering individuals. We are linked together by millions of proud Indian-Americans, who still have families and carry on traditions from India. And I want to say to the Prime Minister, how much I appreciate your strong personal commitment to strengthening the relationship between these two countries.

People are very excited in the United States about the energy that Prime Minister Modi is bringing to the efforts in this country, to reduce extreme poverty and lift people up, to empower women, to provide access to electricity and clean energy and invest in infrastructure, and the education system. And on all these issues, we want to be partners. There are many efforts that I am promoting in the United States, to ensure that the young people get the best education possible, to make sure that the ordinary people are properly compensated for their labour, and paid fair wages, and have job security and health care. These are the same kinds of issues that Prime Minister Modi, I know cares so deeply about in here. And I think there's a common theme in these issues. It gives us a chance to reaffirm, what Gandhi ji reminded us, should be a central aim of our lives. And that is, we should endeavour to seek God through service of humanity because God is in everyone. So these shared values, these convictions, are a large part of why I am so committed to this relationship. I believe that if the United States and India join together on the world stage around these values, then not only will our people be better off, but I think the world will be more prosperous and more peaceful and more secure in the coming future. So thank you so much Mr Prime Minister, for giving me this opportunity to be with you here today.

Mr Narendra Modi:

Barack, the first question comes from Raj from Mumbai. His question is that, the whole world knows about your love for your daughters. How will you tell your daughters about your experience of India? Do you plan to do some shopping for them?

Mr Barack Obama:

Well, first of all, they very much wanted to come here. They are fascinated by India, however, unfortunately each time that I have taken a trip here, they have had school and they couldn't leave school. And in fact, Malia, my older daughter, had just recently had exams.

They are fascinated by the culture, and the history of India, in part because of my influence, I think. They are deeply moved by India's movement to Independence, and the role that Gandhi played in not only the non-violent strategies here in India, but how those ended up influencing the non-violent Civil Rights Movement in the United States.

So when I go back, I am going to tell them that India is as magnificent as they imagined. And I am quite sure that they are going to insist that I bring them the next time I visit here. It may not be during my Presidency, but afterwards, they will definitely want to come and visit.

And I will definitely do some shopping for them. Although I can't go to the stores myself, so I have to have my team do the shopping for me. And I'll get some advice from Michelle, because she probably has a better sense of what they would like.

Mr Narendra Modi:

Barack said he will come with his daughters. I extend an invitation to you. Whether you come as the President, or thereafter, India looks forward to welcoming you and your daughters.

Sanika Diwan from Pune, Maharashtra, has asked me a question. She asks me, whether I have sought assistance from President Obama for the 'Beti Bachao, Beti Padhao Mission'?

Sanika you have asked a good question. There is a lot of concern over the sex ratio in India. For every 1000 boys, the number of girls is less. And the main reason for this is the problem in our attitudes towards boys and girls.

Whether or not I seek help from President Obama, his life is in itself an inspiration. The way he has brought up his daughters, and the way he is proud of them.

In our country too, I meet many families who have only daughters. And they bring up their daughters with such pride, give them such respect, that is the biggest inspiration. I believe that inspiration is our strength. And in response to your question, I would like to say that, to save the girl child, and to educate the girl child is our social duty, cultural duty and a humanitarian responsibility. We should honour it.

Barack, there is a question for you. The second question for President Obama comes through e-mail. Dr Kamlesh Upadhyay, a doctor from Ahmedabad, Gujarat asks:

Your wife is doing extensive work on tackling modern health challenges like obesity and diabetes. These are increasingly being faced in India as well. Would you and the First Lady like to return to India to work on these issues after your Presidency, just like Bill and Melinda Gates?

Mr Barack Obama:

Well, we really do look forward to partnering with organisations and the government and non-governmental organisations here in India, around broader Public Health issues including the issue of obesity. I am very proud of the work that Michelle has done on this issue. We're seeing a world-wide epidemic of obesity, in many cases, even starting at a very young age. And a part of it has to do with an increase in processed foods, not naturally prepared. Part of it is a lack of activity for too many children. And once they are on this path, it can lead to a lifetime of health challenges. This is an issue that we would like to work on internationally, including here in India. And it is a part of a broader set of issues around global health that we need to address. The Prime Minister and I have discussed, for example, on how we can do a better job in dealing with issues like pandemic. Making sure that we have good alert systems, so that, if a disease like Ebola, a deadly flu virus or Polio appears, it is quickly detected and treated immediately making sure that it doesn't spread. The public health infrastructure around the world needs to be improved. I think the Prime Minister is doing a great job in focusing on these issues here in India. And India has a lot to teach many other countries who may not be advancing as rapidly in improving this public health sector. But it has an impact on everything, because if children are sick, they can't concentrate in school and they fall behind. It has a huge economic impact on the countries involved and so we think that there is a lot of progress to be made here and I am very excited about the possibilities of considering this work even after I leave office.

Mr Narendra Modi:

Mr Arjun asks me a question. An interesting question. He says he has seen an old photo of me as a tourist outside the White House. He asks me what touched me when I went there last September.

"It is true that when I first went to America, I was not lucky enough to visit the White House. There is an iron fence far from the White House. We stood outside the fence and took a photograph. White House is visible in the background. Now that I have become the Prime Minister, that photo too has become popular. But at that time, I had never thought that sometime in my life, I would get a chance to visit the White House. But when I visited it, one thing touched my heart and I can never forget that. Barack gave me a book that he had located after considerable effort. That book had become famous in 1894. Swami Vivekananda, the inspiration of my life, had gone to Chicago to participate in the World Religions Conference. And this book was a compilation of the speeches delivered at the World Religions Conference. That touched my heart. And not just this. He turned the pages of the book, and showed me what was written there. He had gone through the entire book! And he told me with pride, that, 'I come from the Chicago where Swami Vivekananda had come.' These words touched my heart a lot. And I will treasure this throughout my life. So from once standing far from the White House and taking a photo, to visiting the White House and receiving a book on someone whom I respect... You can imagine how it would have touched my heart."

Barack there is a question for you from Himani from Ludhiana in Punjab.

Well the question is: Did you both imagine you would reach the positions that you've reached today?

Mr Barack Obama:

And it is interesting, Mr Prime Minister, you're talking about the first time you visited White House and being outside that iron fence. The same is true for me. When I first went to the White House, I stood outside that same fence, and looked in, and I certainly did not imagine that I would ever be visiting there, much less living there. You know, I think both of us have been blessed with an extraordinary opportunity, coming from relatively humble beginnings. And when I think about what's best in America and what's best in India, the notion that a tea seller or somebody who's born to a single mother like me, could end up leading our countries, is an extraordinary example of the opportunities that exist within our countries. Now I think, a part of what motivates both you and me, is the belief that there are millions of children out there who have the same potential, but may not have the same education, may not be getting exposed to opportunities in the same way; and so a part of our job, a part of the government's job is that young people who have talent, and who have the drive and are willing to work for, it are able to succeed. And that's why we are emphasising school and higher education. Making sure that children are healthy and making sure those opportunities are available to children of all backgrounds, girls and boys, people of all religious faiths and of all races in the United States, which is so important. Because you never know who might be the next Prime Minister of India, or who might be the next President of the United States. They might not always look the part, right off the bat. And they might just surprise you if you give them the chance.

Mr Narendra Modi:

Thank you Barack. Himani from Ludhiana has also asked me this question, 'Did I ever imagine I would reach this high office?'

No. I never imagined it. Because, as Barack said, I come from a very ordinary family. But for a long time, I have been telling everyone–never dream of becoming something; if you wish to dream, dream of doing something. When we do something, we get satisfaction, and also get inspiration to do something new. If we only dream of becoming something, and cannot fulfil the dream, then we only get disappointed. And therefore, I never dreamt of becoming something. Even today, I have no dream of becoming something. But I do dream of doing something. Serving Mother India, serving 125 crore Indians, there can be no greater dream than this. That is what I have to do.

I am thankful to Himani.

There is a question for Barack from Om Prakash, who is studying Sanskrit at JNU. He belongs to Jhunjhunu, Rajasthan. Om Prakash is the convener of special centre for Sanskrit Studies in JNU.

Well this is a very interesting question. His question is: The youth of the new generation is a global citizen. He is not limited by time or boundaries. In such a situation what should be the approach by our leadership, governments as well as the societies at large?

Mr Barack Obama:

I think this is a very important question. When I look at this generation that is coming up, they are exposed to the world in ways that you and I could hardly imagine. They have the world at their fingertips, literally. They can, using their mobile phone, get information and images from all around the world and that's extraordinarily powerful. And what that means, I think is that governments and leaders cannot simply try to govern, or rule, by a top-down strategy. But rather, have to reach out to people in an inclusive, open and a transparent way. And engage in a dialogue with citizens, about the direction of their country. And one of the great things about India and the United States is that we are both open societies. And we have confidence and faith that when citizens have information, and there is a vigorous debate, that over time, even though sometimes democracy is frustrating, the best decisions and the most stable societies emerge and the most prosperous societies emerge. And new ideas are constantly being exchanged. And technology today I think facilitates not just within countries, but across countries. And so, I have much greater faith in India and the United States, countries that are open information societies, in being able to succeed and thrive in this New Information Age, than the closed societies that try to control the information that citizens receive. This is because ultimately that's no longer possible. Information will flow inevitably, one way or the other, and we want to make sure we are fostering a healthy debate and a good conversation between all people.

Mr Narendra Modi:

Om Prakash wants me to answer the question as well, that has been asked to Barack.

Barack has given a very good answer. It is inspiring. I will only say that once upon a time there were people inspired primarily by the Communist ideology. They gave a call,– 'Workers of the world, Unite'. This slogan lasted for several decades. I believe, looking at the strength and the reach of today's youth, I would instead say, 'Youth, Unite the world'. I believe they have the strength and they can do it.

The next question is from CA Pikashoo Mutha from Mumbai, and he asks me, which American leader has inspired me?

When I was young, I used to see Kennedy's pictures in the Indian newspapers. His personality was very impressive. But your question is as to who has inspired me. I liked reading as a child and got an opportunity to read the biography of Benjamin Franklin, who lived in the eighteenth century. He was not an American

President, but his biography is so inspiring. It teaches us how a person can intelligently try to change his life.

If we feel excessively sleepy, how can we reduce that?

If we feel like eating too much, how can we work towards eating less?

If people get upset with you for something, that does not meet their expectation or because of the pressure of work, then how to solve this problem?

He has addressed such issues in his biography. And I tell everyone to read Benjamin Franklin's biography. It inspires me even today.

Benjamin Franklin had a multi-dimensional personality. He was a politician, a political scientist, a social worker and a diplomat. He came from an ordinary family and was even unable to successfully complete his education. But till today, his thoughts have an impact on the American life. I find his life truly inspiring. And I will tell you as well, if you read his biography, you will find ways to transform your life too. He has talked about simple things. So I feel you will be inspired as much as I have been.

There is a question for Barack from Monika Bhatia.

Well the question is: As leaders of two major economies, what inspires you and makes you smile at the end of a bad day at work?

Mr Barack Obama:

And that is a very good question. I say sometimes, that the only problems that come to my desk are the ones that nobody else solves. If there were easy questions, then somebody else would have solved them before they reached me. So there are days when it's tough and frustrating. And that's true in Foreign Affairs. That is true in Domestic Affairs. But I tell you what inspires me, and I don't know Mr Prime Minister if you share this view, almost every day I meet somebody who tells me, "You made a difference in my life."

So they'll say, "The Health-Care Law that you passed, saved my child who didn't have health insurance." And they were able to get an examination from a Physician, and they caught an early tumour, and now he is doing fine.

Or they will say, "You helped me save my home during the economic crisis."

Or they'll say, "I couldn't afford college, and the programme you set up has allowed me to go to the university."

And sometimes they are thanking you for things that you did four or five years ago. Sometimes they are thanking you for things you don't even remember, or you're not thinking about that day. But it is a reminder of what you said earlier, which is, if you focus on getting things done, as opposed to just occupying an office or maintaining power, then the satisfaction that you get is unmatched. And the good thing about service is that anybody can do it. If you are helping somebody else, the satisfaction that you can get from that, I think, exceeds anything else that you can do. And that's usually what makes me inspired to do more, and helps to get me through the challenges and difficulties that we all have, since, obviously we are not the only people with bad days at work. I think everybody knows what it is like to have a bad day at work. You just have to keep on working through it and eventually you make a difference.

Mr Narendra Modi:

Indeed Barack has spoken words from the heart ('Mann Ki Baat'). Whatever position we may hold, we are human too. Simple things can inspire us. I also wish to narrate an experience. For many years, I was like an ascetic. I got food at other people's homes. Whoever invited me, used to feed me as well. Once a family invited me over for a meal repeatedly and I did not want to go, because I felt they were too poor. I felt that if I go to eat at their place, I will become a burden on them. But eventually, I had to bow to their request and love and I went to eat a meal at their home. It was a small hut where we sat down to eat. They offered me roti made of *bajra* (millet), and milk. Their young child was looking at the milk and this gave me a feeling that the child had never even seen milk before. So I gave that small bowl of milk to the child and he drank it within seconds. They had probably bought milk so that I could have a good meal. This incident inspired me a lot. A poor person living in a hut could think so much about my well-being. So I should devote my life in their service. So these are the things that serve as an inspiration and Barack has also spoken about what can touch the heart.

I am thankful to Barack for giving me so much time. And I am thankful to my countrymen for listening to 'Mann Ki Baat'. I know radio reaches every home and every lane of India. And this 'Mann Ki Baat', this special 'Mann Ki Baat', will resonate forever.

I have an idea. I'll share it with you. There should be an e-book made of the talk between Barack and me today. I hope the organisers of 'Mann Ki Baat' will release this e-book. And to you all, who have listened to 'Mann Ki Baat', I also say, do participate in this. And the best hundred thoughts that emerge out of this will also be added to this e-book. I want you to write to us on Twitter, on Facebook or online by using the hashtag *#YesWeCan.*

- *Eliminate poverty—#YesWeCan*
- *Quality healthcare to all—#YesWeCan*

- *Youth empowered with education—#YesWeCan*
- *Jobs for all—#YesWeCan*
- *End to terrorism—#YesWeCan*
- *Global peace and progress—#YesWeCan*

I want you to send your thoughts, experiences and feelings after listening to 'Mann Ki Baat'. From them, we will select the best hundred, and we will add them to the book containing the talk that Barack and I have had today. And I believe, this will truly become the 'Mann Ki Baat' of us all.

Once again, a big thank you to Barack and to all of you. Barack's visit to India on this sacred occasion 26th January is a matter of pride for me and for the country.

Thank you very much.

For listening to the audio, please log on to http://www.narendramodi.in/mann-ki-baat or scan the given QR code.

CHAPTER 5: February 2015

Hello, my young friends. The entire day today, you must have probably been preoccupied with the ongoing cricket match. On the one hand, you have your exams and on the other, this World Cup. You might also be asking your younger sister to tell you the score of the match from time-to-time. Sometimes you must be elated about the fact that Holi is just around the corner and then suddenly you may get disappointed that even your Holi festivities will go for a toss. Why? Because exams are approaching and I am sure you must be tense. But friends, I am there with you at this important juncture in your life. This is an important occasion for you and hence, I am here to motivate you.

Exam Pressure

You have been studying hard and must be tired. Your mother and father scold you and so do your teachers. Only God knows all that you have to hear, day in and day out. Whether it is Class 10th or 12th, the whole year you must be hearing things like—"get off the phone, switch off the TV, you are glued to the computer the whole day..." And you might be sincerely wishing that the sooner the exams finish, the better it will be, isn't it? I understand your mental condition and hence, I am here to share my views through 'Mann Ki Baat' with you. But this topic is a little difficult.

As far as today's topic is concerned, I really don't know who will benefit from my conversation, as parents might wish that I touch upon those issues that they cannot discuss with their children. The teachers, on the other hand, may be thinking that I should say certain right things to the children while the students on the other hand might be entirely wishing that I say things which might ease off the pressure at home. I don't know who will primarily benefit from this, but I will have the satisfaction to know that I was there, with my young friends, on the most important occasion of their life and that I was sharing my inner feelings with them. This is my idea behind the conversations.

I do not have the right to guide you on how to write a paper or how to pass the exams well or what tricks should be used to obtain better marks because, I consider myself as an average student on such issues. I myself never scored well in any exams in my life. I was a very average student and on top of that, I had a very bad handwriting. So I think that most of the time, I passed the exams since the teachers could not comprehend my handwriting! Well, so much for the light talks.

The Right Approach

But today, I want to definitely tell you something important. Your approach to exams goes a long way in deciding the results of your exams itself. There are many people I have seen who view this as the most important challenge of their lives and they believe that a failure here, means a failure for life.

But friends, this is not so, and so don't take undue stress over it. Yes, you must be determined to get good results. The determination should be strong and the motivation high, but exams should not become a burden for you. This is not the exam which will test your performance in life. So do not bother much about it.

Sometimes, don't you think we tend to make exams a huge burden? The reason behind this is 'comparison'. If we have friends and relatives who have children studying in the same class as your child, then there is a constant comparison? There is a feeling that our child should fare better than everyone else's child; even your own friend's children. And it is this constant comparison that creates pressure on your child. One feels that their child will earn a name amongst their family and friends. But is it really his name or your own prestige that you are worried about? Don't you feel that you are the one responsible for making your child a part of useless competition? Can't we associate him with a larger vision and a greater meaning of life? How will he cope with the competition to be the same as your neighbour's friend? Is this really what you want? Just give this a thought. Think, how in trying to compete with others, you have belittled your own child's life. Is it fair? When you talk to children, talk about big dreams, talk of greater heights that can be achieved, and you will see a change happening.

The Right Measure of Success

Friends, there is something that always bothers me. We always measure our success in comparison to others. Our entire energy is spent in useless competition. There are many points in life where competition is necessary, but for self-development, competition with others might not be a good motivator. However, competing with oneself, each day, should be the primary motivation. Concentrate on yourself, compete with yourself to do better, to do faster, to do more and to reach new heights and to make today better than the past. You will find that this spirit of competition will give you such joy and satisfaction that you yourself would not have imagined it. We remember the Russian athlete, Sergei Bubka, very fondly. This athlete broke his own record 35 times. He would test himself and would set himself a new challenge every time and scale new heights. You should also compete only with yourself, have faith in your own abilities, your preparation and then see that nothing can stop you from achieving success.

Dear friends, students also are of different types. Some people, irrespective of their exams, are always happy, while some just collapse under the burden of their examinations. Then there are some who keep hiding behind books in some corner of the house. However, in spite of all this, exams are still exams and are necessary to be passed successfully. I wish that you all pass with good scores. But sometimes you must have noticed that we seek reasons outside, when we are confused about ourselves. We do not have faith in ourselves and act as if we are giving some exam for the first time. If someone is watching TV and the pitch is loud, we get irritated. If our mother calls for food, we are irritated but at the same time if our friend calls up, we end up chatting for an hour. Don't you think that you have some confusion about yourself?

Friends, it is important for you to identify yourself. Just keep doing simple things; you do not need to go far. If you have a sister or your friend has a sister and who is appearing in a 10th or 12th standard exam, just observe them. You will see, be it 10th or 12th, the girls will definitely help their mothers in the household chores. Have you ever thought how do they manage to do such work and yet score well in exams? Nowadays, girls are far ahead of boys in their examination results. Do observe this around you.

This will make you realise that issues that bother you are not external; sometimes the reasons are purely internal. If you are in self-doubt, then confidence cannot help and you fall into a vicious cycle of blind faith. Some students are such that we call them Aarambhishura.

Dedication to Resolution Leads to Achievement

We need to realise that life is much bigger than just academic examinations. Everyday a new thought, a new desire, a new resolution arises, and then this resolution dies an early death and we are back to where we started from. I clearly believe that these ever changing desires are the 'whims' of people. You should not have fluctuating desires as that gives rise to a lack of resolve in one's life. People will make fun of you and hence, your desires should be stable. It is these stable desires, which will in turn become resolutions. And resolutions can never be futile. Resolutions are accompanied by goals. And when goals and action come together, resolutions are achieved. This is why I say *Desire* + *Stability* = *Resolution* and *Resolution* + *Action* = *Achievements*. I have complete faith that in your life too, achievements will be at your feet. And this will happen only when you stick to it with dedication.

Dedicate yourself to your commitment and be positive. Don't get bothered about defeating others. Think of making progress yourself instead of pulling someone else down. Test yourself everyday against your own limits, so that however big a challenge comes in life, you will not have any problem. And why should someone else take our exam? Make it a habit to examine yourself. Test yourself each day and see whether you have made any progress from where you were yesterday. See, if 'I have reached any farther than yesterday, have

I achieved more than what I achieved yesterday?' Each day, every moment, keep testing yourself. Then such tests will never bother you in life. Every exam will be an opportunity to test and regulate oneself and someone who can regulate himself, knows how to face challenges fearlessly. And so, who sets himself challenges of life, finds these classroom exams very small.

Sometimes, we far exceed our own expectations. Just try and remember the good work that you have done. You will be surprised at your own achievements. Last year, you were sick and yet you got good marks, or your uncle got married and one full week got wasted, however, you still managed to score very well. Earlier, you would sleep for six hours and then last year you decided to sleep for only five hours and you did it successfully. What advice can Modi give you? You become your own advisor and as Lord Buddha said, *"Appo Deepo Bhava"*. 'Be a light unto yourself.' Don't follow others.

It is my belief that one should recognise one's inner light, recognise one's potential. Those who set themselves a new limit each time are the ones who scale greater heights. Don't bother yourself with what the future will be. Also, leave the past. The present is what is important. A good batsman never thinks about his performance in the last match, or the last ball or for that matter what will be the outcome of the match. He only focuses on the particular ball at given point of time. He does not think of the next ball or of the match, or of the entire series. You should also fix your mind in the present. There is only one formula to win. Live in and connect with the present. Victory will be yours.

Realising One's Potential

My dear friends, do you think exams are meant to exhibit your capacity. If this is what you think then you are wrong. Whom do you have to show your capacity to? Whom do you need to demonstrate it to? You should understand that these exams are not to demonstrate your capacity, but to realise your own potential. If you make this basic mantra your calling, your confidence will get a new boost. Once you realise your potential and understand yourself, then you yourself will keep fostering your strengths; this strength will translate into a new potential and so don't take exams as a medium of exhibition, take them to be opportunities for you to shine. This is an opportunity to know oneself, to explore oneself and to be living with oneself. So live on, my friends.

My young friends, appear in your exams with self-confidence without getting nervous. Keep yourself away from meaning less thoughts like who have wished me luck and who haven't. Friends, rise above all this and do not get involved in such trivial things. Think of all this when your exams are over. If you have faith in yourself, then such things will not matter.

I know that some people have the tendency to become nervous. I believe that the reason for nervousness is the lack of faith in oneself. How do you achieve this faith in yourself? This can be done, if you gain mastery in your subject by working hard and doing multiple revisions. If you do so, you will never again have to face any nervousness.

Have Faith and be Confident about your Strengths

All the hard work that you have done in the past year, all those books that you have studied through the night, they will not go waste. It will be there somewhere in your mind. As soon as you sit at your examination desk, it will all start coming back to you. You should trust your knowledge and your information. Have the faith that all the hard work you have done will certainly bear fruit and also be confident about your strengths. You should have the faith that however difficult the exam, you will crack it successfully; however lengthy the exam is, 'I will successfully complete it.' You should be confident about the timing, be it a two-hour or a three-hour paper, that you will finish it before time. I still remember, maybe you have been told too, our teachers instructed us to attempt easy questions first and tackle the difficult ones later. Carry on your work as you have been guided.

Friends, I have received many suggestions and experiences on MyGov.in. I will pass them on to the Ministry for Education, but I would like to mention a few things here. Arnav Mohta writes from Mumbai, Maharashtra, that some people make these exams an issue of life and death. Vinita Tiwari writes from Varanasi that the news of children committing suicide on the declaration of the results frightens her. You too must be hearing such news, but I have got good response about it from another gentleman, Mr R Kamath, who has asked students not to get worried, but become warriors instead. We should really not sink in worries, but should be a warrior in the battlefield and march ahead with the belief that victory will be ours. Life is very long. There are ups and downs, but one should not perish with them. Sometimes, unwanted results are an indication to move forward. They give us the opportunity to find new strength.

I have also witnessed another thing, that as soon as they are out of the examination hall, they start estimating how they fared. Friends and family too ask the same question. How was today's paper? Please remember, whatever is finished is over, please forget about it. I would also request parents not to ask such questions. As soon as your child gets out of the examination hall, welcome them with a smile and say, 'Ok good, let us go and prepare for tomorrow'. If you discuss what was wrong or right in the paper, then tell me will it not impact your performance the other day? So why waste time and energy on this? After all the exams are over, whatever calculations you want to do you are free to do them. How many marks will be scored, that should not be your concern at the time of your exams. Gear yourself up for the next day's paper; forget that day's paper and you will see your burden lessening by 20-25 per cent.

Pariksha Utsava

I would like to ask my educators and academician friends, that can't we instead, celebrate a week-long exam festival (Pariksha Utsava), twice a year. It should have sessions on poetry, debate and cartoon competitions to reduce the "scare" of exams. There should be someone to lecture on the psychological aspects of exams so that this tension around them gets eliminated. If exams become a celebration, then students would not need to spend time the way they are doing today in hearing this. Students will themselves become confident. I also believe that while teaching the syllabus, a separate lecture should be conducted on topics pertaining to exams. It is important for students to discover themselves, and appear for exams fearlessly. A tense environment is not conducive.

Friends, I know that whatever I am telling you, you must have heard a lot more than that from your parents and teachers. I do not want to confuse you by talking more on this subject. I want to believe that all sons and daughters of this land who are going to give exams, will remain happy and joyful and will attempt their exams with a free mind.

I am talking to make you happy and to help you relax. You will get good results. You will be successful, make exams a celebration, give exams in a joyful mood, enjoy achievements each day, and change the entire atmosphere. Parents, teachers and schools—all should get together and experience what it is like to challenge the challenges, how wonderful it feels to convert each moment into an opportunity. And remember, you cannot please everyone in the world.

I had a penchant for writing poetry, I had written a poem in Gujarati, I don't remember it fully, but I had written something like, "if successful, then you are worth being envious of, if failed then you are nowhere." This is the way of the world. Be successful, not to defeat others, but to overcome your challenges; be successful for your own pleasure. Be successful for bringing pleasure to the lives of others living in this world.

I have this faith that you will succeed with happiness in your heart. You will have great success. And then, whether we could celebrate Holi or not, whether we could attend our uncle's marriage or not, whether we could attend our friend's birthday party or not, whether we could see the Cricket World Cup or not, all these things will eventually become immaterial, as for now your dimensions of happiness will be very different. My best wishes to you. The nation's future is as bright as your own future. India's future will be defined by India's youth, it will be defined by you. Be it our sons or our daughters, both have to work in tandem to take the country forward.

Be steadfast in your goals, firm in your resolve and success will follow you.

Come make the exam festival into a celebration. My best wishes to you!!!

For listening to the audio, please log on to http://www.narendramodi.in/mann-ki-baat or scan the given QR code.

CHAPTER 6: March 2015

Greetings to all my dear farmer brothers and sisters!

Today, I feel so fortunate to avail this opportunity to speak with my farmer brothers and sisters from different corners of the country. I am aware about the problems being faced by our farmers. When I speak to farmers, I speak to the village and its residents, and also to the farm labourers. I am also concerned about the mothers and sisters who work on farm fields. And in this context, probably this talk is going to be a different from all the other interactions I had through 'Mann Ki Baat' previously.

When I decided to speak about farmers in 'Mann Ki Baat', I never expected that farmers from far off villages across the country would be willing to ask numerous questions and would provide such information. I was taken aback to receive your numerous letters and questions in such large numbers. I am touched by the awareness of farmers, who have reached out in large numbers to express their views.

First of all, I would like to express my heartfelt greetings to you all. I have read your letters and understood the agony and the struggle in your lives. Despite bearing much misery my self, I cannot imagine what you have gone through in your lives.

You all have surprised me, but I take this 'Mann Ki Baat' as an opportunity for education and experience. My dear farmer brothers and sisters, I would like to assure you, that all your questions and queries from different aspects that you have brought to my notice, would be addressed by me and I will bring consciousness and sensitivity on those subjects in my government and not let my villages and my poor farmer brothers be forced to live in this pathetic condition. I am shocked, that our farmers not only face farming-related issues, but they also have to deal with issues like village mafias and gangs. I can understand the problems related to natural calamities, but they are also facing issues with small businessmen.

Some farmers have to drink contaminated water in their villages, while some have raised concerns on the lack of facilities like provisions of shelter for their cattle, and some other issues like lack of proper facility to dispose off dead animals. All this leads to spread of various diseases among villagers. I will not let farmers down and all the concerns raised by them will be addressed.

Empowerment of Farmers

Today through 'Mann Ki Baat', the governing bodies are getting a unique chance to understand numerous problems of farmers. We can attain our rights to govern the country only when we can understand and provide solution to all these small, but important issues. I feel so embarrassed when I read your letters and think about what we have done so far. I have no answer to this question. What have we done? My chief goal is empowering farmers. I will try my best to bring a change and would awaken the slumbering government to work in the most appropriate manner. This will be my primary focus and that is a promise from my side.

I am well aware about the great difficulties faced by you all last year due to the scarcity of rain. This year, due to unseasonal rains and hail-storms, all the states above Maharashtra, had to face a lot of difficulties. Farmers across the country had to face great difficulties. A poor farmer, who leads his life by slogging daily in the fields, has no other source of earning a living or an income. I am with you in this difficult time of your life. Our government is also taking stock of the situation minutely, of the various issues of the farmers and is in touch with different departments of the state. The ministers are also out in the field, visiting various states and collecting reviews and analysing the situation. I have also asked the state governments to work closely along with the Central government and strive to provide as much aid as possible to our farmer brothers and sisters in this difficult situation. I assure you, that the government will take proper steps and solve your problems promptly and help you in this difficult time. We will do whatever is possible to help you and do our best to fulfill our promises.

Farmers and their Issues

The villagers and farmers have raised various issues. Irrigation problem is one of the most important issues. Farmers are also angry because of the unavailability of roads, electricity and the increasing price of fertilisers. They are also unhappy about the fact that they are unable to educate their children. Mothers and sisters are angry with the drug abuse prevailing in villages. Some women have also addressed the issues of tobacco intake by their husbands. I can understand your pain. Farmers are not educated about the policies and plans of the government for their welfare. Some farmers feel that they only hear the strategies adopted by the government, but the benefits of such policies never really reach them. They have mentioned how they labour day and night to provide food to the entire nation, but they earn very little in return. When they go out to sell the crops and other farm products, there is no buyer, so, they are left with no other option, but to sell the products at lower prices. They are doomed in both the cases, whether they produce more or less. This means that farmers have brought to my notice their inner thoughts through their letters. I can assure all my farmer brothers and sisters that the state and central government will take all necessary steps actively from now on. I will inspire the government to speed up the actions and provide solutions to all your problems. I understand that you may be running out of patience. This is quite natural as you have waited for 60 long years. I will try to find a full-proof solution to this.

My farmer brothers, I have found one primary problem among your various questions that is the 'Acquisition of Land Bill', prevailing in almost all the states. I am shocked to hear these rumours spread across the country. It is good that you have raised such small issues and questions. I will try to bring the truth before you. You must be aware that the Acquisition of Land Bill was passed 120 years ago. Post-Independence, this law was in practise for 60-65 years. Today, activists, who call themselves as the supporters of farmers, also followed this law in the country, governed the country and the farmers got their share. Everybody believed that there should be a change in this law and I too believed in the change. We were in the opposition and we too believed in the change of law.

The New Law

In the year 2013, a new law was passed in haste. We too supported this law, extending our full support to the government. If a law benefits the farmers, who would not to support it, so we too supported the law. But after the initiation of the law, some grave concerns arose in our minds and we felt that in this way, we would be betraying the hopes of our farmers. On one side, when our government was formed, we saw that all states raised their voices to amend the law, or to improve the law; the law must be modified to plug the loopholes. On the other side, we found that no state was ready to implement the law, except the governments of Maharashtra and Haryana, which, under Congress rule, had implemented the law, proclaiming themselves to be the well-wishers of farmers. They brought an ordinance and decided to pay only half the decided amount as compensation to farmer. What kind of justice is this for farmers? After reviewing all these points, we felt that there should be some re-thinking. When things are done in haste, then some drawbacks remain. The intent might be good, but if there are drawbacks, then they should be rectified.

Now, I will speak of the most primary drawback, which you will all find quite astonishing. All those, who are self-proclaimed well-wishers of farmers, are not ready to give any answers to these questions. Are you all aware that there are 13 different laws in our country through which most of our country's land, like the Railways, national highways and minefields, is acquired. 13 areas have been excluded from the law, which meant that land could have been taken without the consent of the farmer. The farmers would receive the same compensation as they used to get under the previous law. We have modified this law and this, lacunae have been removed in the new law, so that farmers get full compensation. This is why we had brought an ordinance. If we didn't bring the enactment, lands of farmers would have been used in accordance with the previous law and they would not have received their compensation. When this law was passed, many in the government too raised their voice against it. Even those who were involved in the making of the law, got upset and said that this law is neither beneficial to the farmers, nor the village nor the country. This law can be useful, it was said, only to fill the treasury of the officers and for their enjoyment, to promote red-tapism. If this was the truth, then apt modifications should be done or not? Thus, we have tried to eliminate the drawbacks of the law and work on the direction of betterment of farmers. Firstly, we have included the 13 laws which were excluded under the Acquisition of Land Bill, so that farmers are provided with remuneration and all rights and they do not have to incur loss due to exclusion. I have heard the rumours being spread, that the Modi government is passing a law, which will provide less remuneration to the farmers and they will not receive the full compensation.

My dear farmer brothers and sisters, I cannot even think of committing this sin. In the year 2013, under the dispensation of previous government, the compensation which was decided has not been modified a bit. We have decided to provide four times the compensation than the one provided earlier. Not only this, we have also included the 13 areas which were excluded in the earlier law. We have also continued with the clause that in the case of acquisition of land for development of the city, the land owners will receive 20% of the developed land, so that they are benefited financially at all times. The youth of the family gets a job. We have also decided to provide employment to children of farmers. We have also added a new programme. The new addition is that the district authorities will have to make an announcement on who will be employed from the family, in what field they will be employed and what will be their work location. The government will have to provide written announcements for the same. We have fixed the government's responsibility by adding this feature. My dear farmer brother and sisters, we always want to use government land first and after that the barren land must be used. When there is no other option left, only then do we touch the farmlands. So, we have started a survey to locate all barren lands, and to place these under priority usage.

We have received complaints from our farmers that more than the required land for use is gobbled up. With the enactment of this new law, I can assure you that before using the land, a survey will be conducted, and only then will it be decided, so that more than the required land is not acquired. Sometimes, with the foresight that something may happen, there is lot of damage caused. In the name of Social Impact Assessment (SIA), if these judicial proceedings are carried on for several years, how can the farmer take the right decision in this situation? He cannot decide whether to grow crops in the field, as he is in a fix, since he will keep anticipating that the judgement may come any day. This will lead to two to four years of loss and things will be stuck due to red-tapism. Due to long and difficult judicial proceedings, a poor farmer is forced to beg before the officers to get his work done, – "Sir, please write this, please do not write this... this is going to happen, that is going to happen". I do not want my farmers to fall prey to these officers. I do not think this is the right thing to do. The procedure was complex and we are trying to make it simpler for farmers. My dear farmer brothers and sisters, the law was passed in the year 2014, but the states have not adopted the law yet. Farmers are still at the same position. The states have opposed this law. Please let me know whether I should listen to the states or not? Should I trust the states? How can a country run without trusting its own states? So, I believe we should trust our states and we should specially trust our central government. Firstly, I am willing to trust my states and secondly, the improvement we are trying to bring in the law by trying to eliminate the drawbacks and trying to better the conditions of the farmers. Even after this, if the states are not ready to support this movement, they are free to do so. This is why, I would like to request you all not to fall prey to these rumours. These rumours are absolutely 'against farmer' rumours. It is part of the conspiracy of keeping the farmers poor, like it in the past. This is a part of the conspiracy of not letting the country progress. We have to save ourselves from this conspiracy and save our country and our farmers as well.

Now, even farmers don't want that all members of their family should pursue the occupation of farming. They wish that at least one or two children should have jobs or be in other professions... So, the farmers' children too have to now move out and seek employment somewhere and arrangements need to be made for that as well. So we have decided that whatever is important for the welfare of the village and farmers and whatever is needed for the employment of the members of the farming community, all help should be provided. We are the ones who hold the belief, 'Jai Jawan Jai Kisan'. These two are important factors for the development of the nation. Jai Jawan is related to the security of the country. Jai Kisan is for the farmers. As far as the security of the nation is concerned, our soldiers are there, and similarly our farmers too never step back from their responsibilities. If some land is required for national security, we will have to ask the farmers for it. And I have complete faith that farmers will give us the land. So we have added the clause for taking land for such purposes like building canals and providing shelter to the poor. Tell me is this for the industrialists? Is this land being demanded for the ultra-rich? Try and understand the truth.

Yes, there is something I want to announce without a doubt. In the new ordinance too, any private industrialist, owner of a manufacturing unit, will have to follow the same set of rules that were laid out in the Land Acquisition Act of 2013. The rules for the corporates are the same as in 2013. Then why are these lies being spread. My farmer brothers and sisters, a misunderstanding is being created that you will not get your legal rights, and that you cannot approach the courts. This is entirely false. No government at the centre can take away your legal rights. The Constitution provided to us by Babasaheb Ambedkar ensures that you can approach any court in any part of the country. All we have done is to bring in some sort of a system to your doorsteps. We have created an authority. Now this authority will work at the district level and the issues of the farmers will be resolved at the district level itself by the authority. And if you are not satisfied with the solutions offered, then you can approach the courts as well. This is the arrangement we have made.

There is a misconception that the law related to returning the acquired land in five years has been scrapped. This is not true dear farmers; we have just added the timeline for the completion of projects. If the project is not completed in the specified time period, then whatever the farmers' wish has to be adhered to. So we have set a time-frame for government projects. What is the case scenario today, those lands which were acquired about 40 years ago, the government has not done anything on them. This cannot continue any longer. We have decided to set a time limit for governmental projects. Yes, there are projects which take time, maybe around 20 years. For example, if a 500 km long railway track is to be laid then it will take time. So we want it all written down, the time frame in which a project will be completed. So, what we are doing is fixing the liability of the government. We have fixed the government's responsibility.

Yes, the people sitting comfortably in their air-conditioned rooms have no idea about the ground realities of the villages. Whenever a dam is made or a reservoir is constructed, the rule is to acquire land till the point where there is a possibility of the water getting to the maximum level in a span of 100 years. So the water gets filled once in 100 years. For 99 years no water gets filled. Yet the land lies with the government. What is currently happening in the states is that land has been acquired, compensation paid and yet farmers are working on those lands. If the land gets flooded once in 100 years, that year the land can be taken. The law of 2013 denied the farmers the right to cultivate the land. All we want is that if the land does not get flooded then it should be available for farmers for cultivation. And hence that land should not be acquired from the farmer. This kind of flexibility is necessary. So the farmer benefits even after giving up the land and also get compensation in lieu of their land. This will doubly benefit the farmers. This kind of organization is both necessary and practical. And we are the ones who have thought about it.

Another misconception being spread is that, 'consent' is not necessary. I urge you, to protect yourself from such politically motivated propaganda. The law which was promulgated in 2013 has no provision for consent in schemes for which the government is acquiring land.

So people are being misled on this consent issue. The issue of consent did not exist previously, it does not exist now. And so my brothers and sisters, to say that it was beneficial for you before but it is not so now, this is an unfortunate attempt to mislead you. I assure you and insist that this consent clause is very much functional in case of private industries, corporate and individual enterprise.

Another thing I would like to share is that some people talk about the Public-Private Partnership (PPP) model. The PPP model means when someone else or some agency invests its money to complete government projects. The ownership and rules and regulations of the government will be framed on the working of the projects. The ownership of the land is with the government. The construction agency is different. The construction agency is different because the government does not have the requisite amount of money. The government wants that a road be constructed in the village, as well as hospitals and the poor children get education, for this monetary investment is required. The private investors construct roads but not for themselves. They do not take it with himself; they make it for the government. In a way they invest their money. This means in a government project someone else puts in the money which is called the PPP model. This is not only for villagers but would be used by other people too, and the ownership rests with the government and government means of all of you, of the 125 crore Indians and hence we have said there that there is no need for a consent. Hence it was necessary for me to dispel these myths around the PPP model.

Sometimes this issue of consent will increase red-tapism and nepotism. People think about their own benefits, but the government has to think about benefitting the whole nation at large. So, the consent clause gets eased in all these cases. For example, there is a village; a road has been constructed till that village, now a road has to be constructed till the next village which is 5 kms ahead. The road for the first village has been made, but land for the road to the other village lies with the previous village. So tell me will the villagers wilfully give land for road till the other village? Tell me will they give their consent? So what sins have the people of the other village committed? Should they not get the roads? Similarly, if I am making a canal, this village has got the water and we have to provide water supply to another village and the identified land is with the people of the previous village who already have water and they deny giving their consent for acquiring their land saying that they already have the water, and are not going to give consent for land acquisition for supplying water to another village. So tell me, should the people of the other village get water or not?

My brothers and sisters, this is a practical issue. So we are evolving a process which does not take long. This is for the farmers' rights, not for industries and industrialists. It is for the betterment of the villages, the villagers and for the benefit of their children.

There is another issue of concern. I have said this before as well. In every farmer's family, the farmer wants one son to do farming and the others to take up other means of employment. Such are the times today that different efforts need to be made to run the household. If we make a road and government establishes an Industrial Corridor next to it, which is not private. I reiterate that a corridor by the government, is not for the rich, or the industrialists, so if the government makes a Corridor on the left or right of a 50 or 100 km road, then all residents of the nearby villages—maybe 50, 100, 200 villages falling along it—will have an opportunity for employment, their kin will get employment.

Tell me dear brothers and sisters, do we want children of our villages to suffocate in the slums of Delhi and Mumbai. Should they not get an employment opportunity closer to their home, if a small industry comes up some 20-25 kms away from their village? So this corridor will be made by the government and will not be private. The government will make these Corridors and create employment opportunities for the villagers through this. This proposal is about government ownership, it is for the betterment of the villages, the farmers, and the future of the villagers; it is for the betterment of the poor people of the villages and to make electricity available to the villages. For these, there were some drawbacks in the last Land Acquisition Bill, which we have tried to resolve through the new Bill. Still I have maintained in the Parliament, that if anyone feels that there are still some short comings, we are ready to make further amendments. When we placed the Bill in the Parliament, certain leaders of the farming community gave us some suggestions and we added them. We still say that the land acquisition rules should be pro farmers and we are committed towards it. There are lot of lies being spread. I request you to not get swayed and don't make your decision based on these lies. The important issue is to how to make farmers strong and how to make our villages strong. The farmer should get the right price for his efforts; farmers should get a proper market, a proper storage for his produce. It is our effort to make right decisions for the betterment of the village and the farmers.

Dear brothers and sisters, it is our effort to see that the nation progresses and so do our farmers by increasing their yield. And so we have introduced the 'Soil Health Card'. If a person falls sick, a laboratory test is undertaken for them. Similarly a lab test can be undertaken for our motherland. So we are working not only towards protecting your land, but also trying to make it healthy.

And so, not land acquisition, but making the land healthy is our task. And so we have introduced the concept of the 'Soil Health Card'. Every farmer is going to benefit from it. Your undue expenses on fertilizers will be saved. Your yield will increase. We are working on issues like—proper pricing for your products, there should be proper granaries, proper rules and regulations and that you are saved from exploitation. I remember, when I was the Chief Minister of Gujarat, I worked a lot in this direction. The condition of farmers in Gujarat was very bad, we worked on issues relating to water and we saw a big change. Farmers made a huge contribution to the development of Gujarat, which was beyond all expectations. Entire villages would be deserted, but the change came about. We want this type of change in the entire country, which makes our farmers very happy.

The issue of the ordinance is making headlines every day and I chose to speak about it more. But my dear brothers and sisters, I will speak to you again and on other issues. But I want to assure you that through whatever you have written to me, I will shake the entire government and will make them see the reality about what is actually happening at the ground-level. I am happy that you have told me so many things, and I believe that you have told me all this because you trust me. I want to assure you that I will not shatter your faith.

I desire your love and blessings at all times. You are the elders of the nation and can never think wrong of others. You may rather suffer losses for other's benefits. This has been your tradition. It is important and my government's prime focus is to see that farmers do not suffer. Today, after hearing this 'Mann Ki Baat', many thoughts may have arisen in your mind. Please do write in to me at the Akashvani address. I will talk again. Based on your letters, I will try to rectify all the mistakes of my government. I will try to speed up the efforts and if somewhere injustice is being done, I will try and provide justice.

We are in the middle of the auspicious festival of Navratri. My Heartfelt greetings to you all!

For listening to the audio, please log on to http://www.narendramodi.in/mann-ki-baat or scan the given QR code.

CHAPTER 7: April 2015

My dear countrymen, namaskar!

I did not feel like doing Mann Ki Baat today. I am feeling heavy, burdened and a little distressed. There was news of hailstorm, unseasonal rains and damages to the farmer's crop when I talked to you all last month. Suddenly out of nowhere, strong winds blew in Bihar, causing the death of so many people and inflicting damages. And now, the earthquake has shaken the entire world on Saturday. It seems a trend of natural disasters has begun. Be it the Nepal earthquake or that in India, the earthquake took lives across various states of India. There has been loss of property because of the earthquake, however, the loss to Nepal is frightening.

Devastation caused by Earthquakes

I have seen the devastation caused by earthquake in Kutch (Gujarat) very closely on 26th January 2001. I can clearly imagine how devastating these disasters are and I can imagine what Nepal and the affected families there must be experiencing. But my dear brothers and sisters of Nepal, India is with you in this hour of grief. Work has begun to provide assistance to people facing crisis across several locations in India and Nepal. The first and foremost task is to rescue those people, who might still be alive under the debris and all efforts will be made to save them. A team of experts has been sent which is specifically trained for this task. Sniffer dogs have also been sent as they possess the ability to trace any individual alive under the debris. Our whole endeavour would be to save the maximum number of people. Post the rescue operation, there is a need to undertake relief work as well. Rehabilitation work will also continue for long. However, humanity has a power of its own. Nepal is dear to 125 crore people of India. Their grief is our grief. India will make sure to wipe away the tears of every Nepali, hold their hands and stand along with them in this hour of crisis.

Crisis in Yemen

Thousands of our Indian brothers and sisters were left stranded in Yemen, a few days ago. It was a very tough task to evacuate Indians alive, amidst a horrific situation, the tension of bombs, guns and firing; but we managed to do so. Not only this, we realized the power of humanity when our forces saved a week-old baby girl in Yemen. It brings a sense of satisfaction to me that such an act of saving the infant was possible.

India earned accolades from various countries for one thing and that was for saving citizens of nearly 48 countries of the world in Yemen. Be it the citizens of the US, UK, France, Russia, Germany, or Japan, we helped citizens of every country. This shows the spirit of serving people, irrespective of caste, creed and religion. And due to this, the world has experienced the old saying of India, *Seva Parmo Dharma,* meaning the greatest service to humanity is to serve others. Our Ministry of External Affairs, our Air Force and our Navy played a commendable role in rescuing people, and it will have indelible imprint over the world in the coming days.

This is what I believe in. And I am happy that all the people were evacuated safely without any damage or loss, and it should be noted that this is the culture of India.

Homage to Indian Soldiers in the Centenary Year of World War I

I am honoured to pay homage to Indian soldiers, during my recent visit to France, as I went to the memorial of the First World War there. The reason for visiting the place was that it is the centenary year of the First World War, as well as that of India's valour. Our soldiers who fought in foreign lands in the great war, have won the admiration of the world for dedication, loyalty, courage and sacrifice, as we Indians believe in *Seva Paramo Dharma*, meaning the greatest service to humanity is to serve others and this phrase has been lived up to by our country.

I am saying this because very few people would know that about 15 lakh Indian soldiers had put their life at stake during the First World War from 1914 to 1918. And the Indian soldiers did not die for India's cause. Neither did India want to capture any country, nor did it want to take away anyone's land. But the Indians had shown amazing strength. Very few people would know that about 74,000 of our soldiers sacrificed their life in the First World War. And this is also a matter of pride that about 9,200 soldiers, who lost their life, were bestowed with gallantry awards. Not only this, there were eleven such individuals who received the highest honour of Victoria Cross. About 4,700 Indians had sacrificed their life, especially during the World War in March 1915 in France, which has made a memorial as a mark of respect for their services. I would like to express my gratitude for the strength displayed by our ancestors.

If we see all these incidents, then we can rightly say to the world that our country thinks in the direction of world peace, happiness and welfare. The country keeps doing something in this direction and if needed puts its life at stake. India is among the highest contributors in the peacekeeping force of the United Nations. That is a matter of pride for us.

125th Birth Anniversary of Babasaheb

In the last few days, I got an opportunity to accomplish two important tasks. We are going to celebrate the 125th birth anniversary of respected Babasaheb Ambedkar. There has been a controversy regarding the land where his memorial was to be built for many years. Now the new government has completed this task and a grand memorial will be erected which will inspire us to work for Dalits. Similarly, there must be an International Centre in the name of Babasaheb Ambedkar in Delhi, so that the entire world knows this sage, his thoughts and his work. This was also a matter, which was pending for years. I completed it and laid the foundation stone of the memorial. I have pledged to finish the work in 20 months, a work which did not happen for 20 years. And at the same time, a thought came to my mind and we are working on it. Even today there are many families in our country that are forced to carry garbage on their head. Is it not a matter of disgrace for us that even today some families have to carry the burden of garbage on their head? With all earnestness, I said at a government forum that we had to get ourselves free from this blot in the year when we are commemorating Babasaheb Ambedkar's 125th birth anniversary. Now, the time has changed, we will not tolerate a situation in which the poor will have to take loads of garbage on their heads in our country. I believe that democracy runs through public participation. We can take the nation forward when we work together. For this, we need the support of the society, and the government must also shoulder its responsibility. I need cooperation of people as we have to do this work.

Upliftment of the Dalits

Babasaheb Ambedkar used to say 'Stay Educated' throughout life. Even today, education has not reached many Dalits—exploited, and deprived ones in the society, especially girls. We must also pledge on the occasion of the 125th birth anniversary of Babasaheb Ambedkar that there must be no sons or daughters of the poor who remain illiterate in our villages, cities and localities. The government must do its duty. And if it gets the support of the society, then we will definitely feel a sense of satisfaction.

Sportsman Spirit

I want to share a matter of happiness and share another matter of discomfort as well. I take pride in the fact that two daughters of India, Saina Nehwal and Sania Mirza, have made the country proud by becoming the world's no. 1 player in Badminton, and the world's top player in Tennis Doubles tournament, respectively. Congratulations to both and to all the other daughters of our country! I feel proud seeing the effort and strength of our own girls. We should always stand by our sportsmen whether they win or lose. The behaviour of our countrymen was not appreciable when the Cricket World Cup was on and we lost to Australia in the semi-finals. How can a game be played with no defeat? Victory and defeat are a part and parcel of life. If the players of our country have been beaten in a match, then we must encourage them in times of crisis. There must be an effort to create an environment to generate new confidence. I am sure that going forward we will learn from the defeats and will not lose control by indulging in aggressive behaviour. I really get disturbed and worried when some untoward incident happens all of a sudden, a mob behaves violently and creates fear in the minds of the peoples, disturbing the peace of the country. Accidents must not happen. Even the government must make full efforts to ensure that. But my dear countrymen tell me, by burning vehicles and being violent do the dead come back? Can't we depend on the law to take its due course by keeping our emotions in check?

Well, today my mind has been grief-stricken due to these incidents, especially due to natural disasters. But amidst this also, we will move forward with courage and confidence. Be it any individual of this country—the Dalit, the oppressed, the exploited, the tribal, the villager, the poor, the farmer, or the small businessman, we will move forward on the path of welfare for everyone. Examinations of students are over. Especially, the students of classes 10 and 12 who would have made a programme of celebrating the holidays. I wish all of you a very enjoyable and happy vacation! Use the opportunity to learn something new. And since you have worked hard the whole year, I wish that you also spend some time with your family with joy and happiness.

Best wishes to everyone.

Thank you!

For listening to the audio, please log on to http://www.narendramodi.in/mann-ki-baat or scan the given QR code.

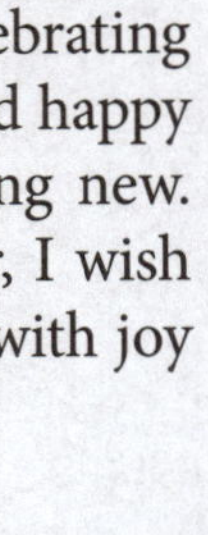

CHAPTER 8: May 2015

My dear countrymen,

Last time when I addressed 'Mann Ki Baat', I was extremely distracted and upset by the earthquake that had struck then. My mind did not allow me to speak much, but still I addressed 'Mann Ki Baat'. Today, when I am undertaking 'Mann Ki Baat', we are all surrounded by a severe hot weather, with all heat related problems and news pouring in across the country. I would request you all to take care of your health in this hot weather by following simple instructions, such as drinking ample water and covering yourself for protection from the heat. At the same time, I would also like to request you all to take care of the birds and animals in your neighbourhood and fulfill their requirements too. We should take this as an opportunity to give responsibility to our children to place a bowl of water for the birds in a suitable place where the water remains cool. By doing this, I can assure you that your children will imbibe good moral and cultural values. Moreover, in this extreme heat, this act will be a life saver for birds and animals too.

Choosing a Career Path—Transforming Dreams into Reality

The summer season is marked on the one hand by the extreme heat conditions, while on the other there is both happiness and sadness. After completing our exams, we are in a state of anxiety until the announcement of the results. Now, the CBSE and the other boards have declared their results and I would like to congratulate each and every student who has passed with flying colours. I came to know the significance of 'Mann Ki Baat' when many students, after obtaining their exam results, informed me that they listened carefully to my words on 'Mann Ki Baat' and followed them strictly during their exams. This proved to be quite fruitful and beneficial. Well friends, I am glad to know this through your letters. However, the true reason behind your success is not any 'Mann Ki Baat', but your hard work throughout the year and the consistent support from your entire family. Your school, your teachers and many others have a role to play in your success, and you have striven hard to attain this success, in order to meet everybody's expectations. 'Mann Ki Baat' is a kind of exam tip given before entering the examination hall. However, today I am pleased that 'Mann Ki Baat' has created a significant impact, and I am very happy about it.

While I speak about the happiness of some of our friends, who have passed with good scores, I would also like to make a mention of many of our friends who may have got low scores and some of them who were not successful. To all those who have passed, I would like to remind them that they are in that stage of their lives where they can steer their career in the right direction.

Now, you have the opportunity to decide the right path for your career according to your wishes and capabilities. Please also remember that your future will depend on the path that you choose. Generally, I have observed that most students have no idea about what they should study, why they need to study, or where they should study. They are also not aware of the aims of their lives. Many students mostly choose their career paths based on the opinions of their friends and families or based on the wishes of their parents. Our universe has expanded itself in all directions. There are no limits in the choice of subjects or opportunities. You must be careful and determined in choosing your career path, in accordance with your talent and capabilities. Why choose from the prevailing opportunities? Try your best, and strive to utilise the talents within you to gain new opportunities. At the same time, you should also think of how you can contribute to the betterment of your nation from what you have learned or what you become.

You will be surprised to know that, as compared to the number of museums built around the world, the number of museums in India is very small. It is very difficult to find the right staff members for these museums as it is not a conventionally popular field. I do not want to drag on with one topic, however, my only point is that our nation is in dire need of excellent teachers, soldiers, scientists, as well as artists and musicians. The field of sports is very broad, wherein other than players, various crucial human resources are also required for the success of any sporting activity. This proves that we are surrounded by a vast variety of opportunities on this planet, so we must all be determined to try. Your strengths, your capabilities, your dreams—all should be aligned to the dreams of our nation. This is your only chance to choose the right path.

To those who have not succeeded, I would like to tell them that success and failure is a part of life. Those who consider failure as an opportunity will always be on the path to success. Those who give up in life, due to failure, can never reach the heights of success. We can learn a lot from our failures. We should believe that our failures can provide us the opportunity to know ourselves better and understand our strengths, and by knowing our strengths and talents, we will be able to choose the right path in life.

I am reminded of our nation's ex-President, Dr APJ Abdul Kalam. In his book *My Journey—Transforming Dreams into Action*, he mentions an incident in his life. Dr Kalam says that he always aspired to become a pilot. However, when he tried to become a pilot, he failed and could not clear his exams. Now, you can see that this failure gave him a great opportunity in his life. He became a great scientist and also became the President of India. His contribution stands unparalleled in the field of nuclear energy in India. Therefore, friends, please do not crumble due to the burden of failure. Failure is a kind of opportunity. Do not let the failure go without learning a lesson from it. Try to search for the hope and opportunity that lies hidden in your failure. This is my humble request to all my young friends, and also to their family members—if your child fails, please do not create an atmosphere which can force him to lose all hope in his life. Sometimes, the child's failure is associated with the parents' dream which leads to various problems in future. This should not happen. Dealing with failures can provide us the strength to live our lives peacefully. I would once again like to congratulate all my young friends who have passed with flying colours. I would also like to convey my best wishes to my young friends who have failed, and I congratulate them for having received the opportunity of finding the right path in their lives. Please try and strive to move forward with hope and trust in your lives.

Meanwhile, many incidents have happened since my previous 'Mann Ki Baat'. Our government has completed one year. The entire nation analysed us quite minutely, and while some criticised us, many people gave us a distinction for our governance. In a democracy, I believe that it is very important to receive feedback from one's supporters as well as one's political opponents. We must try to understand our drawbacks and identify the areas in which we lag behind. It is also beneficial to understand our merits.

In my case, I am happy with all that has happened so far. My heart is always yearning to do something for the poor people in our country. I always think of novel ideas and welcome suggestions from others in order to help the poor. Last month, we launched three key policies to provide social security to the people of our society, that is Prime Minister's Suraksha Bima Yojna, Prime Minister's Jeevan Jyoti Bima Yojna, and Atal Pension Yojna. It has just been 20 days since the launch of these policies, and I can proudly say that due to your trust in our nation, our government and our programmes and policies, the common citizens of our country have joined hands with us in such huge numbers. I am extremely happy in sharing the fact that within a short span of 20 days, more than 8 crore and 52 lakh people have registered their names for these programmes. We have adopted important measures in the path towards social security and it will act as a boon for the people in future years.

For those who have not yet received this information, I would like to request them to acquire these benefits as soon as possible. No one could have imagined receiving Suraksha Bima Yojna by investing just one rupee per month or 12 rupees in a year. In order to get the benefits of Jeevan Jyoti Bima Yojna, you need to invest just Rs 330 in a year, which is less than a rupee per day. Therefore, by using these benefits, the poor will not be dependent on others for their living. The poor will become independent and self-confident. We are adopting different measures in this direction. I want to create an army of people, an army comprising poor people who will fight against poverty and defeat it. Our nation has been burdened with poverty for years now, and we will take appropriate steps to try and eliminate poverty from our nation. We are sure we will succeed.

Another important development is the introduction of a channel for farmers on television, and I am feeling positive about it. We have a number of channels on televisions in our country, such as cartoon channels, sports channels, news channels and entertainment channels. For me, the channel for farmers is very important as I can clearly see the future of farmers through this channel.

According to my view, this channel is like an open university for farmers and their farms. This is a channel where both students and teachers are farmers. These farmers can learn a lot of things through excellent experience and move from traditional farming towards modern farming. Only minimal areas are left for farming. The families of farmers are increasing in number, but the land area is reducing. Due to this problem, it is very critical to understand the ways to grow crops efficiently in such small areas. Now, we can get details about the weather forecast and plan accordingly. The channels for farmers will be focussing on these various issues. My farmer brothers and sisters, a system for monitoring farmers has been arranged in each of our districts. Please contact the respective district heads for availing this benefit.

Animal Husbandry

I would also like to speak to my fishermen brothers and sisters, and to all those who are involved with fishery. There are many things for them to learn from this channel. In India, animal husbandry has been a traditional segment in a villager's life, which provides a supportive role in farming. However, as compared to the number of animals and the amount of milk produced in various countries around the world, India is far behind. As compared to the numbers of animals, the commensurate amount of milk is not produced in our country. The process by which we can produce more milk per animal, the ways in which the animals can be taken care of and the types of food that should be provided to them, are some important factors to be considered. We take various measures based on our traditions, but we need to move forward by adopting scientific methods and technologies. By adopting these scientific methods, farmers as well as the animal husbandry sector can help us achieve financial strength. In this way, we can provide confidence and power to farmers and also animal keepers. We should get scientific guidance regarding the direction in which we should move forward and attain success in this area.

India and Yoga

My dear countrymen! Do you remember this date, 21st June? Generally, 21st June is remembered as the longest day of the year. But, recently this date has gained a new significance in the world. Last year, in September, I had raised a subject and proposed to celebrate 21st June as International Yoga Day while addressing the United

Nations Assembly. The whole world was astonished, and you will also be surprised to know that within a hundred days, we got support from 177 countries and this proposal was successfully passed. In the history of the United Nations, such a huge number of supporters from different countries was seen for the first time. This proposal was passed in a very short span of time, with the support of various countries around the world. This is a proud moment for every Indian.

So, now, this is our responsibility. Would we have ever thought that yoga can act as a connecting link between nations? *Vasudhaiva Kutumbakam* implies that our ancestors had imagined the same, where yoga would act as a catalyst in connecting the world. This news gives us utmost happiness and makes us proud. But to achieve its real significance, we need to project the real essence of yoga, and its real power, to the entire world. Yoga connects the heart and the mind, and acts as a medium for freedom from ailments and indulgences. I am realizing that yoga connects the body, mind and knowledge. Now, it is has been widely proven that yoga can also act as a medium for connecting the world.

Why are we not taking steps to become ambassadors for this venture? Why not move forward on this path of human development with the help of this vital knowledge of yoga? We must celebrate 21st June as Yoga Day, in every corner of India. Please call up your relatives and friends staying in different parts of the world and ask them to gather in groups and celebrate the day. If they have no knowledge of yoga, they should educate themselves with the help of books. Read and explain the importance of yoga in our lives. You can also read various letters on yoga. I strongly believe that by declaring yoga day, we have taken an important step in the development of the world. We have contributed to human development by removing stress from the lives of people, and by providing positive energy to those who have lost all hope in their lives. I want that what the world has accepted, what the world has respected, and what the world has given to India, should be a matter of pride. Three weeks are still left and you should make efforts to join and make others join.

One-Rank and One-Pension Scheme

I would especially like to speak to soldiers of the army, who are fighting for our country's safety, those who had joined the army and those who have sacrificed their lives for our country. Here I am not speaking to them as the Prime Minister, but from my inner self, inner truth and deep emotions that I have for my soldiers.

Questions about one-rank and one-pension (OROP) have neither been resolved nor answered for over forty years. There is no denial of the truth that the previous governments have spoken about this issue, but have never done something about it. I can assure you, and I have also promised my armymen, that my government will surely launch one-rank and one-pension. We know our responsibilities, and after the formation of our government, different departments have begun working on this issue. I used to consider this to be a simple issue, but it is far more complicated than I thought, and for forty years, the problems in this issue have been accumulating. In order to resolve this issue in a simpler way, I have asked the government officials to find solutions to this problem. It is not necessary to provide information to the media every single second. There is no need to have a running commentary on this issue. I would like to assure you, and I would like to repeat, that our government will launch one-rank and one-pension and provide solutions for all the related issues. Your life is very important to us, owing to the thought-process and ideals, with which we are moving forward.

I would like to connect with you and help you, not just as a part of any government programme, or any political campaign, but as a reflection of my patriotism. Once again, I would like to convey to all the soldiers of my country, that we are not one of those people, who, in the name of politics, played games with you for the past forty years. I am against this path, and I am not willing to take any step which would complicate the existing issues. I want you to trust me, even if people are against us and playing games in the name of politics. I would like to provide all assistance to my people who are sacrificing their lives for the country. These are my motives, and I believe that the words from my soul, which are nothing but the truth, will touch your heart as well. You have kept your patience intact for forty years. I need some time and opportunity to work. Once again, I would like to assure my countrymen that we will mutually work on this issue and find a solution for it.

Maintaining a Travelogue

You must have all visited different parts of the country during vacations. Some of you must be planning to visit places now. It is natural, as "Seeing is Believing". When we visit places, we may go to our relatives' place or go sight-seeing, we get to explore and understand the world. For a person, who has just seen a pond in his village, the experience of seeing an ocean cannot be expressed in words. He is unable to describe the size of the ocean in front of the villagers, as seeing is altogether a different experience. When on vacation, while you are travelling, with friends or family or planning to go, I do not know if you have the habit of writing a diary while travelling. I believe you must jot down your experiences, when you meet new people, and you should write down in words all that influenced you. When you see something, you should describe it in words. In other words, you must assimilate what you see or feel, within you. Travelling is a form of knowledge in itself. It is not possible for all of us to get a chance to climb the Himalayas, so one must read the adventure and travel stories, written by those who have got a chance to visit the Himalayas.

I am not saying that you should become a writer. We should travel, and strive to learn something new from our travels, understand our country, and know its varied diversity. We should not travel for the sake of travel. We can write about the peculiarities of a particular place, the food-habits of the people there, their clothing style, language, and culture, and also about their dreams, aspirations and problems. We are living in this vast nation. If we want to understand the entire nation, one life is not enough to do this. It is my earnest request to all of you, who are planning to visit or travel, to share your travelling experiences with me. I would be happy to read your stories. I would request you to mail me your photo and your experience with #*IncredibleIndia*, and I will share your impressive stories with others.

I would like to experience what you have experienced. I would to like see from far, what you have seen up-close during your travel. You can visit a sea shore and take a walk alone. Though I may be unable to do this, by reading your story, I would love to share your vivid experience with others.

On this note, let me remind you once again, please take care of yourself and do not fall sick. There are many ways to protect yourself from the summer heat, but please take care of the birds and animals around you too. I have articulated all that has come out of my heart. I will meet you all again, and will speak to you again. My heartfelt greetings to one and all.

Thank you all for your support.

For listening to the audio, please log on to http://www.narendramodi.in/mann-ki-baat or scan the given QR code.

CHAPTER 9: June 2015

Namaskar, my dear countrymen!

The last time in 'Mann Ki Baat', I had requested you to send me memorable pictures if you go out on a vacation anywhere in India, and if you do happen to find them, kindly post them under the 'Incredible India' hashtag. When I said that, I had never imagined that it would get such an immense response. Lakhs of people have posted photos on Twitter, Facebook and Instagram. I can say that, 'India is full of diversities', and I was able to witness so many magnificent scenes in those pictures; be it of architecture, art, nature, waterfalls, mountains, rivers or seas. The government of India had never thought that people could contribute to our tourism in such a massive way. I liked some pictures so much that I re-tweeted them. And as I understand, if someone had not posted the picture of Belum caves in Andhra Pradesh, many people would never have come to know that something like that exists in our country. Madhya Pradesh's Orchha Fort is another example of that. We assume Rajasthan to be a state with scarcity of water, but when someone sends a photo of the Menal waterfall, it is a matter of great surprise. Really, tremendous work has been done. We will promote and also continue doing such work and the entire world, our nation and the new generation, will watch it.

Worldwide Participation on the International Yoga Day

My beloved countrymen, though you have elected me as the Prime Minister of the country, at times, the human in me shuns all posts and prestige associated with it and submerges itself within it. I can say that 21st June, the International Yoga Day, affected me in the same manner. At that time, when I proposed the International Yoga Day, it was just an idea. But the scene that was witnessed on 21st June was such that wherever the sun dawned, wherever its rays reached, there was not a single landmass wherein, it was not welcomed by way of yoga. We can say with conviction that the sun never sets in the world of yoga practitioners. The way yoga was received and welcomed with open arms, around the world, I am certain that there is no Indian who is not proud of it. I too am delighted. And when the people of France chose River Seine and Eiffel Tower as places where they take pride in doing yoga, they gave an equal status to it as the River Seine and the Eiffel Tower. In New York, people did yoga at the Times Square. If we think about Sydney, Australia, then the picture of Opera House comes to our mind. The citizens of Australia gave equal respect to yoga by doing it in the Opera House. Whether it is North America, Silicon Valley or Milan's Duomo Cathedral, it is a matter of great pride for us. On 21st June when I saw UN Secretary General Ban Ki-Moon, doing yoga at the UN Headquarters, I was really delighted. Similarly, the UN Peacekeeping force did a spectacular display of yoga. In India, our soldiers too were doing yoga in Siachen on the white sheet of snow and on sea too, wherever our naval ships are posted, the yoga programme was being carried out by the Indian Navy. Delhi made it to the Guinness Book of

World Records. Rajpath turned into 'yogpath' that day. I am thankful to India and the rest of the world and can say that the International Yoga Day was not only in name. It seemed as if from every corner of the world, there was a new inquisitiveness, new joy, new hope and new connection.

Yoga as a Unifying Force

A few days back, when I tweeted a photo of a Vietnamese child doing yoga, it was such a sweet photo, that it got a lot of attention from the entire world. Everybody, be it men or women, old or young, village or city, developed or developing countries, everybody got connected with it. Yoga, in the true sense, became the core reason to connect the entire world. I do not know how the intellectual class, elites of the world would analyse this event. But I can feel and every Indian can experience, that the whole world is very curious to know more about India. Curiosity towards India has increased. The world wants to know about the values, the rituals and the heritage of India. It is our responsibility that without any artificiality we share our legacy and introduce ourselves to the world. We can only do this when we ourselves are proud of our traditions.

At times, we are so familiar with our values that we don't feel there is anything new in them, but we are ourselves unaware that our family values are considered to be a great thing across the world. Why don't we familiarise the outside world with our family values? The world would be very amazed, rather intrigued, to know about them. There are many things that our forefathers have given to us which are the best and the entire world also has a right on them. The success of the International Yoga Day has brought in a new responsibility along with it. It is our responsibility that we gift good/great/perfect yoga teachers to the world and see the entire tradition of yoga on one platform from the universe.

I request youngsters, especially IT professionals, to come together to create an online Yoga Activity programme. We should all get to know about every yoga organisations, yoga teachers and all the necessary information about yoga, from this online programme. One database must be prepared and I believe you can do it. One must start from somewhere and it would surely turn out to be a great power. I have seen and learnt from the perspective of recent occurrences that a government that works and a government that is action-oriented can bring in results if the targets are set. We should not forget that the only voice that could be heard one year ago was that 'nothing happens', 'nothing happens', 'nothing happens'.

Role of the Department of 'Ayush'

Can you imagine that there is a department under the government named *'Ayush'*? Nobody has paid attention towards this department. They only mention *'Ayush'* in some corner of the newspaper as being a small department, once in 2 to 5 years. But, it played a leading role on the International Yoga Day. It was this small department that organised this event across the world. This is an example that if there is an aim then even a small department can undertake a mammoth job.

Participation in MKB Initiatives

In the last few days, the world saw how we saved people from Yemen to Afghanistan. In a few hours, we reached

Nepal and helped people over there. When people wanted to open a bank account under the government's new scheme of *'Jan Dhan Yojana'*, we saw how the people working in banks helped them to do so and connected millions of Indians to the banks.

On 15th August last year, when I appealed from the Red Fort for toilets in schools, I had said that by the 15th of August next year, we have to complete this task. The work that could not be completed in the last 60 years was promised to be completed by the end of one year. The promise was really daring. Almost four and a half lakh toilets were to be built; but I can say this with satisfaction that though 15th August is still far away, the target of constructing toilets by people is nearing completion.

This means that the government, the people and the government workers, all have the urge to work for the country. If we pledge to work together in a selfless manner, 'Welfare for All, Happiness for All', then the government will also work efficiently. People who are a part of the government, will also work efficiently and the people of the nation will welcome them with open arms.

I have experienced this and this is the true strength that drives a nation forward.

Launch of Insurance Schemes

Last month, we had launched three insurance schemes. I had launched them from Kolkata and these schemes have received a commendable response in such a short span of time. There have been very few steps which have been taken from the perspective of social security, but though these three schemes we are taking a big leap. In such a short span of time, more than 10 crore people have become a part of these schemes, but we have to take it further. I have a thought which I want to put forth before you. Rakshabandhan falls in the month of August. Can't we start a massive movement before this festival and make every woman, be they our mother or sister, a part of this, thereby giving them benefit under this insurance programme. Be it a sister who is a domestic help in your home or your own sister; why can't we gift them a Rs 12 or Rs 330 scheme on Raksha Bandhan for their entire life. This can be an invaluable gift for a sister from her brother. Why can't we set the eve of Raksha Bandhan as a target? Why can't we, in numbers of 2 crores, 5 crores, 7 crores and 10 crores, try to reach out to our sisters so that they can reap the benefits of this scheme? Let's come together and try to work towards the fulfillment of this pledge.

On Monsoon and Rainwater Harvesting

Whenever I hold a 'Mann Ki Baat' session, many people send me suggestions. This time many people, like Yogesh Dandekar ji from Nagpur, Harshvardhan ji from Mysore, Praveen Nadkarni ji, and Divyanshu Gupta ji, have suggested that I say something about the monsoons in this session of 'Mann Ki Baat'. They have sent in some really good suggestions. Monsoon is a season of happiness. Each one of us, whatever our age, is definitely tempted to enjoy the first showers of monsoon. I am sure you too might be enjoying the rains with bhajiyas, pakoras, corn and a hot cup of tea. Just as the rays of the sun give us life, rainfall provides us life and sustenance. Every drop of water is precious. As responsible citizens and as members of the society, we will have to cultivate the habit of conserving every drop of water. It should be our pledge that water from the villages stays in the villages and water for the cities remains available to them. If the rain water does not flow away, it goes into the earth, the aquifers then get recharged and the year-long water woes get resolved. Rain water harvesting is not a new concept. It is being practiced over the centuries. Be it check dams, watershed development, small lakes or the small ponds in fields, we need to save precious water everywhere. I always tell people, that if you go to Porbander, the birth place of Mahatma Gandhi, you will be able to see a two hundred year old underground water tank which gets directly re-filled with rain water. You can still see it. If you ever go there, do visit the place. And you will find that even after two hundred years, it is still functional, brimming with water and the water does not even stagnate. Porbander is a coastal city, so potable water was collected through the rains for the entire year. Even in those days, a lot of care was taken. We too can do the same. This should, in fact, become a mass movement. Each and every village should have facilities for rain water harvesting.

Similarly, we find greenery so pleasing to our eyes. We all like green surroundings. Gardens and trees bring in an element of freshness in our lives. This monsoon season, there should be mass plant-sowing campaigns conducted by youth and the social organisations. I can take a leaf from my personal experience, which has been very successful, and offer you a suggestion. This is an intensely rural technology. Whenever you sow a plant, place an earthen pot near it. You just need to fill it once or twice in a month. You will see how fast the plant grows into a lush green tree. I have even been urging farmers to plant trees on the boundaries of their fields, instead of putting barricades. These will become your biggest asset in the long run.

It is true that rains, besides being enjoyable, bring in a lot of fun as well. It is also true that rains also bring in many diseases. Doctors have to then examine so many patients that they hardly get time to breathe. We all know that rains cause many water-borne diseases. Increased moisture in the environment leads to bacterial growth and so, keeping the environment clean becomes important. Cleanliness becomes even more important in monsoons. One is often asked to consume safe drinking water. Most people drink boiled water during this season. It has its own benefits. It is true that the more care we take, the healthier we would be. We need monsoons and we need water but we also need to stay healthy.

Dear countrymen, we have recently launched three schemes for the people in cities. We have around 500 small cities. Our policy is called 'Waste to Wealth'. We can earn from waste too. Garbage can be recycled to make fertilizers, bricks and even electricity. Contaminated water can be recycled to make it clean and to use it for irrigation of the fields. We have to take this movement forward.

In the Amrut scheme, we have launched a massive campaign and taken up initiatives to improve the quality of life in our cities. We should become a country which is able to match the living standards of the world. We should have smart cities, comparable to world standards. And yet at the same time, the poorest of the poor should have an accommodation of his/her own and that too, complete with water, electricity, sanitation and access to a school. In 2022 when India celebrates its 75 years of Independence, we wish that every Indian has a house of his/her own. Keeping all this in mind, we have launched three major schemes. I am optimistic that these schemes will bring about a qualitative difference in the lives of urban people.

I am myself connected to you via social media. I keep getting many new suggestions and new ideas and also good and bad information about our government.

And at times, a small comment from an individual in some remote village of India conveys something that just touches our hearts. You are aware that the government has launched the 'Beti Bachao Beti Padhao' programme. But you can't imagine the force that is lent to the programme when a village or a society adopts it. A few days back, a sarpanch in a small remote village of Haryana, Mr Sunil Jaglan ji, launched 'Selfie with Daughter' campaign. Such an environment was created that every father wished to click a selfie of himself with his daughter and post it on the social media.

New Schemes—Waste to Wealth, Amrut Scheme and Beti Bachao Beti Padhao

I liked this idea and that too for a special reason. In Haryana, the number of girls in comparison to boys is dismally low. Around another 100 districts in the country have a similar dismal situation of a skewed sex ratio. But it is the worst in Haryana. And these, if a sarpanch of a small non-descript village lends such meaning to the 'Beti Bachao Beti Padhao' programme, then I certainly get overwhelmed. It makes me happy and gives me a new hope and I do express my happiness. I request you all to take a selfie with your daughter and post it on *#SelfieWithDaughter*. And do not forget to post a tagline around the theme of 'Beti Bachao Beti Padhao' with it, whatever be the language—be it in Hindi, English or your mother tongue. And I promise to re-tweet the most inspirational tagline with you and your daughter's selfie. We can turn 'Beti Bachao Beti Padhao' into a mass movement. I urge you all to take forward the programme launched by Mr Sunil in Bibipur village of Haryana. I request you all to post on *#SelfieWithDaughter*. Let us all enjoy the rising honour and prestige of our daughters and see how joyful this entire experience of 'Beti Bachao Beti Padhao' becomes. Let us all rid ourselves of this bad name that we have for not respecting our daughters.

So my best wishes to you for the coming monsoon season. May all of you enjoy the rains. Make our country clean and green. And remember, the International Yoga Day was not a single day initiative. Continue practicing yoga, and then see what difference it makes to you and your life. And I say this from my experience. Please take this forward. Make yoga a part of your life. And on the initiative regarding Incredible India, do keep posting a picture of whichever part of the country you go to. The country and the world will awaken to our diversity. I feel that handicrafts have not received due attention. Do make it a point to post on social media the handicrafts of the local region you visit. There are so many things that people around you might be making, the poor as well as the skilled might be creating. Do keep posting their pictures regularly. We have to expand our reach to the world and make India known to the world. We have an easy medium at our disposal and so we will all do it.

My dear countrymen, that is all for today. I shall meet you again in the next edition of 'Mann Ki Baat'. Many people expect me to announce some huge schemes during this programme. Be sure, I am working day and night towards it. This is my time for some light conversation with you all. This gives me immense pleasure.

Thank you very much, Jai Hind!

For listening to the audio, please log on to http://www.narendramodi.in/mann-ki-baat or scan the given QR code.

CHAPTER 10: July 2015

My dear countrymen, namaskar!

This year the rains have started on a good note. This will definitely prove beneficial for our farmer brothers and sisters in the sowing of kharif crops. I am very pleased to share an extremely good news with all of you. We have always faced a scarcity of pulses and oilseeds in our country. Poor people require pulses and some amount of oil to prepare vegetables for their food. The good news for me is that there has been an increase of approximately 50% in the production of pulses and an increase of around 33% in the production of oilseeds. I would especially like to congratulate and compliment all my farmer brothers and sisters for this achievement.

Kargil Vijay Diwas

My dear countrymen, 26th July is marked as 'Kargil Vijay Diwas' in the history of our country. The connection that the farmers have with their land, is shared by our soldiers too, as they are connected to the land in the same degree. During the Kargil war, each one of our soldiers proved mightier than hundreds of soldiers of our enemies. I would like to salute all our brave soldiers who without caring for their lives, thwarted all attempts by our enemies. The Kargil war was not limited to just our borders, but each of our cities and villages contributed in this war. This war was fought by those mothers and sisters whose sons and brothers were fighting against the enemies at the border. This war was also fought by the daughters of our country, who were newly married with their henna was still fresh on their hands. Also, by the proud fathers, who saw themselves as soldiers, seeing their sons fighting for the country, and also by infants who had not even learnt to walk with the support of their father's fingers. It is because of these unmatched sacrifices that our country is proudly standing on its feet before the whole world. Hence, I would like to salute all valiant warriors on this occasion of Kargil Vijay Diwas.

The Website—MyGov.in

There is another reason why I consider 26th July quite important. It is because MyGov.in was launched a few months after our government was formed in 2014. Our pledge was to promote citizens participation in democracy and connect every citizen in the work of development. And after one year, I am pleased to share this today that nearly two crore people have visited the MyGov website. We have received comments from five and a half lakh people and I am extremely glad to mention that more than fifty thousand people took out time from their precious schedule to apply their mind and provide their suggestions on PMO applications as they considered this work important. Moreover, the suggestions we have received were quite significant. One of the suggestions sent from Mr Akhilesh Vajpayee from Kanpur is to provide a separate quota to the disabled for booking tickets on the IRCTC Website. It is quite unfair that our disabled citizens have to go through the same tiring procedure and buy tickets at the railway station. Though this is a very minor issue, The government had neither taken note of it nor thought about it previously. But on the suggestion of our brother Akhilesh Vajpayee, our government took this up seriously and implemented this facility in our system for our disabled brothers and sisters. We are receiving many positive suggestions on MyGov, it is also helping us in getting assistance in creating logos, tag-lines and formulating policies by the public. We are experiencing a fresh air in the administrative system. We are experiencing a new sense of consciousness. I am even receiving suggestions on MyGov as to what should be my speech on 15th of August!

We have received quite a few suggestions from Suchitra Raghavachari of Chennai in this regard. She has suggested that I should speak on topics like,—'Save our Daughters', 'Educate a Girl Child, Clean Ganga', and Swachh Bharat. With this, I got an idea and I am requesting all of you to send suggestions on what should be the topics for my 15th August speech. You can send your suggestions through MyGov, letters to AIR or write letters to the PM's office. I believe that this will be a great initiative for including people's suggestions while framing my speech for 15th August. I look forward to receiving your good suggestions.

Also, I would like to talk about an issue which is a matter of great concern. I neither want to sermonize nor am I trying to find an escape route from my responsibilities pertaining to the State Government, Central Government or units of local self-government.

Road Safety

Two days ago, a visual of an accident in Delhi caught my attention, wherein the victim on scooter was fighting for his life for ten minutes post the accident. He did not receive any help from passers-by. Otherwise also, I have noticed that I have been receiving suggestions to speak on road safety and make people aware of this issue. Be it Hoshakote Akshay from Bengaluru, Ameya Joshi from Pune or Prasanna Kakunje from Mudbidri, Karnataka—all these people have written to me, and there are many other names but I am not mentioning, who have raised their concerns. I agree that whatever you have put forth is valid.

My heart shivers when I look at the statistics of accidents. We are witnessing an accident every minute in our country. Due to these road accidents, we are witnessing one death every four minutes in our country. It is a matter of huge concern that out of these deaths, nearly one-third of the victims are of youth, being a part of the 15 to 25 years age group, and every death shakes the very foundation of an entire family. The government system will continue to work towards this, but I would like to request all parents to make their children aware of all Safety Rules pertaining to driving a two-wheeler or a four-wheeler—families should encourage discussion of road safety at home and create an atmosphere to promote road safety. We have seen the words "Papa, come home early" written at the back of auto-rickshaws, and after reading it we are so touched. And therefore, the government has taken a lot of new initiatives in this regard, be it the initiative of education on Road Safety, initiative related to road engineering or of enforcement of road safety laws and the discussion on emergency care to be provided after accidents. We are going to implement the Road Transport and Safety Bill for adopting these safety measures in our country. In the coming days, we are also planning to take many important measures for implementing the National Road Safety Policy and the Road Safety Action Plan.

Cashless Treatment for Accident Victims

We have undertaken another project called Cashless Treatment in Gurgaon, Jaipur and Vadodara, extending it to Mumbai, Ranchi, Rangaon and Mundiya national highways, and it will be further extended. The Cashless Treatment refers to the policy which ensures that for the first fifty hours post-accident—one need not worry whether one has money or not, or about who will pay the bills, leaving behind all these worries—one has to give primary importance to the road accident victim, so that he/she is treated and provided the best hospital facilities at the earliest. We have started a toll-free number 1033 for providing information about incidents across the country and for ambulance services, but all these services are for post-accidents. One must strive to avoid accidents in the first place, and it is also important for us to see this from the perspective that each and every soul, each and every life is precious.

Karma Yogis

Sometimes, I say that government employees are the Karma Yogis, or selfless workers. I recall a few incidents that occurred in the last few days which I liked and would like to share with you. Sometimes people get tired of their continuous jobs. In the initial few years the attitude is "okay, I get my salary so I will work". However, I came across an incident in the railway department a few days ago. A railway TTE, Vijay Biswal, from the Nagpur division who is gifted with painting skills, and who could have has chosen to showcase his skills in any field, continues to work with the railways and paints various scenes related to the railways alone. Through this, he gets an inner satisfaction from his job and also enjoys his hobby at the same time. Using his example, we can learn how to bring more joy into our own jobs. Vijay Biswal has shown us how we can connect our jobs with our hobbies, interests or skills. Who knows, Vijay Biswal's work may get recognised through his paintings across the nation in the near future.

Operation Malyuddh

I have come across a very inspiring initiative started by the entire team of government officials in Harda district, Madhya Pradesh. These officials, with their entire team, have started such a work which has touched me immensely and I really appreciate it—they have started 'Operation Malyuddh', and upon hearing this, you will feel that this project will go a long way. But the key focus of this operation is to give a new direction to Swachh Bharat Abhiyaan. These officials are working on operation 'Brother Number One', in which the brother has to gift one toilet to his sister on the occasion of Raksha Bandhan, so as to be 'Brother Number One'. They are influencing all brothers in the district to gift a toilet to their sisters, so that all mothers and sisters of the district avoid going to toilet in the open. This operation has given a new meaning to Raksha Bandhan and I would like to congratulate the entire government team of Harda district for this initiative.

I came across a news item a few days back and such small news really gives me immense pleasure and I would like to share it with you. There exists a small village called Keshla in Rajnandgaon, Chhattisgarh. The inhabitants of this village have tried in the last few months and led a campaign for building toilets in the village. Now, nobody from this village has to go to toilet out in the open. After completion of this campaign, the entire village celebrated this accomplishment just like a mega festival. These fine examples coming to me show how our society is bringing a change in human values and the human mind, and how the citizens of this country are taking the nation forward.

Act East Policy for the Northeast

Bhavesh Deka from Guwahati has written to me on the issues and problems related to the Northeast. I must say that the people of the Northeast are quite active. I really appreciate the fact that they write about a lot of issues. I would like to tell them with great pleasure that we have a separate ministry for the Northeastern region. When Atal Bihari Vajpayee was our Prime Minister, a Ministry called DONER 'Development of North-East Region' was formed. After our government was formed, the DONER Ministry took the important decision of not staying in Delhi alone and working from the centre for the Northeast. Instead, it was decided to send government officials and their team on a seven-day camp to the Northeastern states like Nagaland, Arunachal Pradesh, Tripura, Assam and Sikkim. These officials would visit the districts, villages and meet the local government officials and talk to people's representatives and citizens of those areas. They will listen to their problems and direct the government to take appropriate measures in solving those problems. This initiative will bring a fruitful result in the near future. The officials who will visit these states would realize the beauty of these states and will feel determined to work for their development and fix their problems. When they return with such a pledge, they can easily understand the problems of these states even when they reach Delhi. This is a great initiative to go to the East, and this act is called the 'Act East Policy'.

India's Mars Mission

My dear countrymen, we are extremely delighted and proud of the success of 'Mars Mission'. India's PSLV C-28 has launched five UK satellites, which are the heaviest satellites launched by India till date. Such news remains in the limelight for a few moments and disappears. Often, we do not remember these achievements for a long time. I am often worried by this thought that when we speak to the youth of our nation and ask about their dream job; only one out of 100 may express their interest in becoming a scientist. The youth are losing its interest in science, which is a matter of great concern.

Science and technology is a form of DNA for development. The youth of our country should dream about becoming scientists and develop interest in the fields of research and innovation. Their capabilities should be monitored and they must be led in the right direction to achieve success in this field. The Government of India's Ministry of Human Resource Development, has initiated a 'National Discovery Campaign'. It was inaugurated by India's former President, Dr A.P.J. Abdul Kalam. As a part of this campaign, the IITs, NITs, Central and State universities, being the mentors and guides, are going to educate and motivate aspiring students to choose the right path in their career. I always urge IAS officers of our government, who have reached great heights with their vast intellect and education, to visit nearby schools and colleges and share their knowledge for just two to four hours in a week. Their experience and intellect would certainly help the new generation to some extent.

Deendayal Upadhyaya Gram Jyoti Yojana

We have raised a very big issue regarding the supply of 24 hours electricity in the villages of our country. This work is difficult, but it must be done. We have inaugurated this scheme and in the coming years, the villages will get a supply of electricity for 24 hours. The students in the villages should not be affected by the shortage of electricity during their exams. There should be enough electricity for starting a small industry. Today, some villagers have to go to other villages for charging their mobile phones. Villages should be provided with all the facilities that are available in cities. For this purpose, we have launched the 'Deendayal Upadhyaya Gram Jyoti Programme'. I am aware that this country is quite vast and we have to reach the villages and far-off corners of the country. But it is for the development of the poor for which we have to work. We will achieve this goal and it is already in progress. We will certainly achieve this. Today, through 'Mann Ki Baat', I felt like expressing these myriad thoughts.

In a way, in our country, the months of August and September are the months for celebration of festivals. There are lots of festivals in these months. My greetings to all of you for the same. Please do send your suggestions for my speech on 15th August. Your opinions will really help me.

Thank you all very much!

For listening to the audio, please log on to http://www.narendramodi.in/mann-ki-baat or scan the given QR code.

CHAPTER 11: August 2015

My dear countrymen, greetings to all of you!

I have opportunity to be amongst you to share my 'Mann Ki Baat' once again.

Far south, people are engrossed in Onam festivities and yesterday the entire nation celebrated Raksha Bandhan. The Government of India has launched various schemes of social security for the common man. I am happy that in a very short span of time all these schemes have been accepted in large numbers.

Suraksha Bandhan

I had made a humble request to my countrymen on the occasion of Raksha Bandhan that we should give our sisters these insurance schemes as a gift. The preliminary information that I have, feels me that from its launch till the present, around 11 crore families have joined this scheme. And I have been told that almost half the beneficiaries are women—our mothers and daughters. I consider this as a positive sign. I offer my best wishes to all mothers and sisters on this blessed occasion of Raksha Bandhan.

Jan Dhan Yojana

Today when I talk to you, I want to mention that around a year back Jan Dhan Yojana was started on a large scale. A task that could not be achieved in the past 60 years, would it be possible to achieve it in such a short span of time? Many questions were being raised back then. But, I am happy to tell you that all units of the government and all banks have put in tremendous effort and as per my knowledge, till date, close to 18 crore people have opened their bank accounts, 17 crore 74 lakh to be precise. I saw the richness of the poor. They had to open zero balance accounts. But these poor people saved money and deposited a sum of 22,000 crores instead.

Bank Mitras

Banks are the mainstream of the economy and to help make this facility reach the homes of the poor, the programme of 'Bank Mitra' is being strengthened. Today, more than 1.25 lakh 'Bank Mitras' are working in the country. The youth have got employment this way. You will be pleased to know that in this one year, to connect the banking sector, the economy and the poor people, over 1 lakh 31 thousand Financial Literacy Camps have been organised. One just does not have to open an account and get stuck. Thousands of people under the Jan Dhan Yojana are now eligible to take an overdraft and they have availed it too. Now the poor have this faith, that they too can get money from the bank. I would again like to congratulate all those associated with this initiative and I would like to request our poor brethren, who have opened an account, to never severe this relationship. These are your banks and you should not leave them. I have brought them to you, and now it is your job to keep them going. All of our accounts should be kept active. I have the faith that you will definitely continue operating the bank accounts.

About the Violence in Gujarat

In the past few days, the events in Gujarat, the violence that occurred, has unsettled the entire country. It is natural that if something of this sort happens in the land of the Mahatma and Sardar Patel, the nation would be shocked and hurt. But in a very short span of time, my intelligent brothers and sisters in Gujarat brought the entire situation under control. They played an important role in preventing the situation from worsening further and once again Gujarat started its peaceful march. Peace, unity and brotherhood together form the right way forward. We have to walk together towards the path of development, which is the key to our problems.

The Sufi Experience

Sometime back, I had the opportunity to meet scholars of the Sufi tradition. I had the opportunity to hear them speak. And truly speaking of the experience and the manner in which they presented their views, sounded like music to my ears. The importance of Sufism could truly reflect the great teachings of Islam, as its message was of love, liberalism and peace. Their choice of words, their way of talking, the generosity of the Sufi tradition, its sublimity, its lyricism, I could experience it all. I felt very nice. I think it has become imperative to present Islam in its true form to the world. I am confident that the Sufi tradition, which is associated with love and generosity, will take this message far and wide and will thus benefit, not only humanity, but it will also benefit Islam. And I would like to tell all that whatever faith one follows, we should definitely experience Sufism once.

I am about to get another opportunity in the coming days and I consider myself fortunate to receive this invitation. Various Buddhist scholars from across the globe are coming together at Bodh Gaya and will discuss issues relating to humanity, at a global level. I have been extended an invitation to be a part of this event and I am glad to be invited for this. Pandit Nehru, the first Prime Minister of India, visited Bodh Gaya. And now, I will be going there with these scholars. This gives me immense happiness.

Voice of Farmers

My dear farmer brothers and sisters, today I would again like to especially share my 'Mann Ki Baat' with you. I have already mentioned this in the previous sessions of 'Mann Ki Baat' that every voice is important, but the voice of the farmer is extremely significant. You must have heard me speak in the Parliament, in public forums or on 'Mann Ki Baat' about it. I have always said that the government is open to all views and suggestions on the Land Acquisition Act, on which a debate is going on. I have reiterated again and again that I am open to any suggestion in the interest of the farmers. But today, I want to tell all my farmer brothers and sisters, that the request to reform the 'Land Acquisition Act' was raised by the states very emphatically. Everyone felt that if the welfare of the farmers is to be achieved, if the water has to reach the fields, if poles are to be erected to provide electricity, if roads have to be constructed in the village, if houses are to be made for the poor in the village, if employment opportunities are to be provided to the poor youth of rural areas then, we have to free the land from legal hassles and bureaucratic hurdles. Hence, this reformed proposal was introduced. But I saw how farmers were being misled and a fear psychosis created. My dear farmers, you should not be misled and definitely never be scared. And I do not wish to give anyone the opportunity to mislead you and scare you. For me, every single voice in the nation is important, but the most important one for me is the voice of the farmer. We had issued an Ordinance. Tomorrow, on 31st August, the deadline for this Ordinance ends. I have decided to let this Ordinance lapse. This means that the same situation will exist as it was prior to the formation of my government. But in the same Act, there was something which was incomplete. This was related to a list of 13 points which were to be completed within a year and so we brought the Ordinance, but due to these disputes the issue got stuck. The Ordinance is coming to an end, but those 13 points which were to benefit farmers, and are directly connected to the monetary issues of the farmers, will be made into a law, and will be implemented today itself, so that the farmers do not suffer any losses, especially in monetary terms. Hence, the task of implementing the 13 points, which was left incomplete in the earlier Act, is being accomplished today. I want to reassure my farmer brothers and sisters that, 'Jai Jawan Jai Kisan' is not a mere slogan, but our guiding mantra for the welfare of villages and the poor farmers. This is why, I declared on the 15th of August that it will not just be an agricultural Ministry, but Agriculture and Farmer Welfare Ministry will be created. We are steadily working on it. So my dear farmers, there is no need to be misled now and especially, there is no need for you to fear anything. Do not be scared even if someone tries to scare you.

50 Years of the 1965 War

I have to say something more. Two days back we completed 50 years of the 1965 war. And whenever we talk of the 1965 war, it is natural that we remember Lal Bahadur Shastri. It is also but natural that we remember his slogan, 'Jai Jawan Jai Kisan'. We can never forget the sacrifice of our Jawans, who sacrificed their lives to maintain the pride and honour of our Tricolour. I salute all those associated with the victory of the 1965 war and pay my tribute to the brave soldiers. May we continue to be inspired by such incidents of our history.

Scientists and their Phenomenal Work

Like I had the chance of meeting the Sufi scholars and I was pleased to listen to them, similarly I had another great experience as well. I had the opportunity to interact for hours with distinguished scientists of the country. I had the opportunity to hear them, and I was very happy to know that India is doing commendable research in the field of science. Our scientists are doing some excellent work. Now the challenge lies in taking these researches to the common man. How to convert these theories into machineries? How to connect the laboratory to the land? We have to take this forward as an opportunity. I got a lot of new information. Our scientists are doing phenomenal work. I can say that it was both inspiring and an educative experience for me. The way some of our young scientists were speaking, made me very happy. The young scientists were eager to explain their work, and their eyes were full of dreams. In the previous episode of 'Mann Ki Baat', I had said that our students should be drawn towards science. After this meeting I felt that there are numerous options and endless possibilities. I would like to reiterate once again that our young friends should take interest in science, and our educational institutions should also encourage students to take up science.

I receive many letters from our citizens. Mr Parimal Shah from Thane, talks about educational reforms on our portal, 'MyGov.in' and has written about Skill Development. Mr Prakash Tripathi from Chidambaram in Tamil Nadu emphasises the need for good teachers at the primary level and has emphasised on the need to bring in reforms in educational set ups.

I especially want to make a point for my young friends. I had asked from the Red Fort, on why should there be interviews for lower posts. And when the interview letter comes—the poor, widowed mother starts wondering whom to approach for a recommendation; who can help her child get the job; whose jack could be useful to get that job. I do not know what kinds of words are being used. Everyone wants to rush and this has seemingly increased corruption at lower levels. I had mentioned in my speech on 15th August, 2015 that this tradition of interviewing should at least end at some level. I am happy that in such a short span of time, it has just been 15 days and the government has been working at a very fast pace. Information is being disseminated and soon the decision will be enforced, and small jobs will be made free from any interviewing process. Now the poor will not have to run for recommendations and will in turn aid in countering exploitation and corruption.

Call for Action to Reduce Mortality Rates

These days, many guests from foreign countries have arrived in India. 24 countries from across the globe, discussed on the Indian soil, a 'Call to Action' to reduce Maternal Mortality and Infant Mortality rates. It was for the first time that this programme was organised in any other country outside America. And it is true that in our country, about 50,000 mothers and almost 13 lakh children die during delivery or immediately after, every year. This is a cause of worry and these figures are scary; although a lot of improvement has taken place. India is being appreciated at the international level for its efforts, but the statistics are not low. We became polio free and similarly, we became free from tetanus as a cause of maternal and child mortality as well. The world has accepted this, but we still have to work towards saving our mothers and infants.

Prevention of Dengue

Dear countrymen, there is news of dengue everywhere. It is true that dengue is dangerous, but prevention of dengue is easy. It is directly related to the Swachh Bharat Abhiyan, that I talk about. We watch the advertisement on TV, but do not pay attention. There are advertisements in the newspapers, but it escapes our attention. There are several ways of keeping the smallest thing in the household clean, by using pure water. Various Public Education Programmes are being conducted, but we do not pay attention. We feel, we live in very good houses, with proper arrangements, and are totally unaware that water gets collected at some location in our house, and this way we are inviting dengue. I would request you all to not make life so cheap. Life is very precious. A little carelessness about cleanliness and accumulated water can cause death, which I believe is not right. In the entire country about 514 centres have facilities for testing dengue cases absolutely free of cost. It is necessary to get ourselves tested on time to save precious lives. Cooperation from all of you is very important for this menace. And cleanliness should be given great importance. This is a time of festivals. Let's link them with cleanliness and continue working towards a clean India. You will thence see how a tradition becomes your habit.

Big Win for Tribals

My dear countrymen, I want to share a good news with you. As I had said we may not have had a chance to die for our country, but we can instead be fortunate to live for it. I congratulate two brothers from Nashik in Maharashtra, Dr Hitendra Mahajan and Dr Mahendra Mahajan, both with a keen desire to help our tribal population. These two brothers have made the nation proud. In America, a difficult cycle race of about 4800 kms, known as the Race Across America, is organised. This year, both these brothers have won this race. They have made us proud. But I was happier to know that they do all this for their campaign, 'Team India—Vision for Tribals'. See, everyone is doing their bit for taking the country forward. When you hear such things, the heart swells with pride.

Cycle Day

Sometimes we commit injustice to our youth, guided by a certain perception. The old generation feels that the new generation does not understand anything and I understand that this has been going on for ages. My experience regarding youth is different. Sometimes when we talk to youth, we learn so many things. I have met so many youngsters who have taken pledge of 'Sunday on Cycle'. Some tell me how they keep one day a week as the 'Cycle-Day', since it is good for their health.

It is good for both, the environment and one's health. Nowadays, many cities in our country are witnessing cycle use and there are many people promoting such usage. This is a good initiative, both for improving health and saving the environment. Today, when two youths from my country, made India proud in the US, I thought it worth mentioning.

Memorial for Babasaheb Ambedkar

Today, I especially want to congratulate the Maharashtra government because it has made me happy. The task for erecting a memorial for Babasaheb Ambedkar in the Indu Mill compounds had been stuck for long. The new government in Maharashtra completed this task and now a grand memorial will soon be erected, which will inspire us to work for the Dalits, the exploited and the marginalised sections of our society. But alongwith this, the house in UK, where BabaSaheb lived, 10 King Henry Road, has been purchased too. The globetrotting Indians on their trip to the UK, can visit the memorial being erected by the Maharashtra government. It will be inspirational to many. I congratulate the Maharashtra government on the accomplishment of both these tasks.

My dear brothers and sisters do share your views before the next 'Mann Ki Baat', for I believe that democracy runs through public participation. We can take the nation forward when we work together. I send my best wishes to you.

Thank you.

For listening to the audio, please log on to http://www.narendramodi.in/mann-ki-baat or scan the given QR code.

CHAPTER 12: September 2015

My dear countrymen, greetings to you all.

This is the twelfth episode of 'Mann Ki Baat', which means that we have completed one year. It was on 3rd October last year that I had the opportunity to conduct my first ever 'Mann Ki Baat'.

'Mann Ki Baat'—one year, many thoughts. I am not sure of what you have gained from 'Mann Ki Baat', but I can certainly say that I have gained a lot.

In a democracy, the power of the people is of great importance. This thought has been fundamental to my thinking and that is why I have immense faith in the power of the people. But with 'Mann Ki Baat', whatever I was taught, whatever I was explained, seems only the half-truth because the experiences I had have made me realise that the power of the people is immeasurable and it far exceeds that our thinking. Our ancestors would say that there is a divine element in each individual. My experience of 'Mann Ki Baat' has made me realise that the thinking of our ancestors was very authoritative and had great authenticity in it, as I have myself experienced it. I asked for a number of suggestions for 'Mann Ki Baat' and yet I could touch upon just 3-4 of them. But people continued to contribute actively in lakhs. This in itself is a great power. I do not feel that anyone got disheartened thinking that he wrote a letter to the PM or posted on MyGov.in, yet his suggestions were not accepted even once.

Contribution of Akashvani

Yes, these lakhs of letters did teach me something more and have made me aware of very minute problems associated with governance. I would like to congratulate Akashvani for treating these suggestions as expectations of the people and not mere bits of paper. It conducted programmes after that called in various departments and put across to them issues raised by the people. Akashvani even tried to get certain problems resolved. Various departments of the government analysed these letters and segregated them as related to policy matters, personal issues and some others as pointers to issue that the government was not even aware of. Many things arose from the grassroot level and reached the government. It is true that the basic principle of governance is that information should percolate upwards from the bottom and guidance should flow from the top to the bottom. Who would have thought that 'Mann Ki Baat' would become a source of information? But this has happened.

In the same way, 'Mann Ki Baat' became a platform to express the power of society. I had just casually mentioned about the selfie with daughter and what a movement it turned out to be. The whole world was amazed. Lakhs of people, perhaps from all countries of the world posted a selfie with their daughters. What dignity did it lend to our daughters? Anyone who clicked this selfie not only boosted his daughter's confidence, but also made a commitment to her. Whosoever saw it, realised that he will now have to give up the apathetic attitude towards daughters. This, in a way, was a kind of a silent revolution.

I had casually mentioned to my fellow citizens, keeping in mind the tourism industry of India, to send me good pictures of the destination they travel to, on the lines of Incredible India, so that I could also see them. People from every corner of India sent me pictures in lakhs. Neither the Government of India, nor the state tourism departments were aware of such heritage. All things were brought together on a platform without the government spending even a single penny. The people themselves took the task forward.

Khadi for Fashion

In October last year, I had my first 'Mann Ki Baat'. In that edition I had mentioned about Gandhi Jayanti. I told people that we were celebrating Gandhiji's birth anniversary on 2nd October. There was a time when there was Khadi for nation? Isn't it the need of the hour that there be Khadi for fashion? I requested the people to buy Khadi and to do their bit. Today, I can say with great satisfaction that in the past one year sales of Khadi have almost doubled. Now see, there was no government advertisement. Nor were lakhs and crores spent. A simple feeling and realisation by the people has brought this change.

Once I had mentioned in 'Mann Ki Baat' about the problems faced by poor families, like how their children cry because of the pollution affecting them when the smoke 'chullhas' are lit. Shouldn't they be getting gas cylinders? And I had requested the affluent to surrender their gas subsidy. Just think. Today I can say with great pride that 30 lakh families have given up their gas subsidy and these are not the rich people. I saw on TV, a retired teacher, a widow standing in a queue to give up her subsidy. Common people from the middle and lower middle classes have difficulty in giving up subsidy, still they did it. Isn't it a silent revolution? Isn't it a demonstration of the people's power?

The governments too will need to learn a lesson that there lies a powerful society which has tremendous capabilities, energy and the determination beyond the realms of their administration. There is more likelihood of the government being a catalytic agent of change if it is better connected to society. 'Mann Ki Baat' has turned my faith into belief and reverence and once again I would like to salute this humongous power of the people, through this platform. They took up every small cause and made it their own and tried to contribute to the welfare of the country. Can there be a bigger satisfaction than this?

Messages for MKB

This time I thought of conducting a new experiment through 'Mann Ki Baat'. I had requested people to call up telephonically and get their suggestions or queries recorded. I told them that I will take it up in 'Mann Ki Baat'. I am happy that we received more than 55,000 calls from across the country—be it Siachen, Kutch or Kamrup, be it Kashmir or Kanyakumari. There is no part of India from which I did not receive a phone call. This is a pleasant experience in itself. People of all age groups have sent messages. I listened to some message personally and I liked them. My team is working on the others. You must have spent just a minute or two but for me your phone calls are very important. The entire government will work on your suggestions.

But there was something which surprised me and made me equally happy. It is felt that there is negativity all around. But my experience was different. These 55,000 people expressed themselves in their own way. It was a frank interaction where they could say anything but I am surprised that all the things were in the shadow of 'Mann Ki Baat'. They were totally positive—suggestion oriented and constructive. Just see how citizens of the country are moving with a positive attitude; this is the nation's greatest wealth. There were serious complaints in about 1-2% phone calls. But more than 90% were energising and pleasant.

Another thing came to my mind for the specially-abled. And from amongst them, especially the kin of visually impaired, made quite a number of phone calls. The reason may be that they are not able to watch T.V, but they must definitely be listening to the radio. This made me realise how important radio is for the visually impaired people. I am seeing a new aspect as they put forth such good suggestions which are enough to make the governments more sensitive.

Pawan Acharya from Alwar, Rajasthan, has sent me a message. I believe that all of you should hear it and follow it. Please hear what he wants to say:

> *My name is Pawan Acharya and I belong to Alwar, Rajasthan. I want to give the message to Prime Minister, Mr Narendra Modi ji, to request all the people of India through his programme "Mann Ki Baat" to use as many earthen lamps (diyas) as they can this Diwali. This will not only help the environment, but will also provide employment to many potter families. Thank you.*

Pawan, I believe that this sentiment will definitely reach every corner of India. It is a good suggestion and the soil is priceless. So the earthen lamps will be valuable too. It is important from the environmental point of view and it is made in a poor man's home. Poor people earn their living this way. I request the citizens to follow Pawan's advice in the coming festivals. If we do so then the lamp may well be lit not only in our homes, but it will illuminate the house of the poor as well.

Gallantry of Armed Forces

My dear countrymen, on the day of Ganesh Chaturthi, I had the privilege of spending 2-3 hours with the *jawans* of the armed forces. The jawans from our Army, Navy and Air force who are guarding our land, waters and skies. We have completed 50 years of our war with Pakistan in 1965. To commemorate this event an exhibition named 'Shouryanjali' had been organised near India Gate. I saw it with immense curiosity. I went there for half an hour but when I came out it was more than 2.5 hours and I felt like seeing more. What was it that was not there? The entire history had been brought to life. From an aesthetic perspective it was excellent, from a historical perspective it was very educative and if we see it from the inspirational point of view, from the perspective to serve the motherland then there can be no greater inspiration than this. At that time there was not much photography or videography but still those proud moments of the war, those tales of valour and sacrifice of our great soldiers, which we had heard can all be experienced here through this exhibition.

Whether it is the battle of Haji Pir, Chaminda or Asal Uttar and the visuals of our victory near Haji Pir, we feel thrilled and immensely proud of our soldiers. I had the opportunity to meet the brave families, families of those who had sacrificed their lives and also those who had participated in the war and are in the twilight years of their lives. They too had come and when I was shaking hands, I was filled with great energy. It was very inspiring. If you want to create history, then it is necessary to understand the nuances of the past. History binds us to our roots. If we are detached from our history, then the possibilities of creating history comes to an end. This exhibition on valour and gallantry helps us to experience our past. It enlightens us about our history. And this is an opportunity to inspire people to sow seeds for creating a new history. This exhibition will be on display for a few days. I request you and your relatives living in Delhi and nearby areas to definitely visit it. And do not be in haste like me. I came back in 2-2.5 hours but you will need 3-4 hours, do see it.

Look at the power of democracy, a child has ordered the Prime Minister, although the child forgot to tell his name in a hurry. I do not have his name with me, but what he said is worth giving a thought, not only should the Prime Minister think about what he said but every Indian citizen should listen to what this child has to say:

> *Prime Minister, Modi ji, I want to tell you that, for the Swachhta Abhiyan (Cleanliness Drive) that you started, you should get dustbins installed in every street and every corner.*

This child is absolutely right. We should adopt cleanliness as a habit and should make provisions for cleanliness. I got great satisfaction from this child's message. On the 2nd of October, I declared this cleanliness drive and I think something like this has happened for the first time after Independence because even in the Parliament, cleanliness is being discussed for hours these days. Our government is criticised as well. I have to even listen to a lot of things; people say things like, "Modi ji used to talk big about cleanliness, but what has really happened?" I don't get offended by all this. I look at the positive side of it, which is that even the Parliament of the country is discussing the issue of cleanliness in India.

Look at the other side, on one hand the Parliament and, on the other hand, this child both are talking about cleanliness, can a country cannot be more fortunate than this. This ongoing movement of thoughts, the environment that's building against filth, there has been an awareness towards cleanliness. This will also compel the governments to work. The self-governing regional bodies, be it panchayats, municipal corporations, municipalities, municipal corporations of metropolitan cities, central government or state governments—everybody will have to work on this. We will have to take this movement forward despite its shortcomings and when we celebrate the 150th birthday of Mahatma Gandhi in 2019 in India, we should aspire to work in the direction of fulfilling his dream.

Do you know what Mahatma Gandhi used to say? He once said, "if I have to choose between freedom and cleanliness, I will choose cleanliness first and freedom later". For Gandhi ji, cleanliness was more important than freedom. Come let us all follow what Mahatma Gandhi said and take a few steps towards fulfilling his wish. Mr Gulshan Arora from Delhi has left a message on MyGov.in. He has written that he wants to know about the birth centenary of Deendayal ji.

My dear fellow citizens, the lives of great men will always inspire us. Is it not our responsibility to figure out the ideology of these great men? Everyone who lives and dies for our nation inspires us. In the coming days, we will get to remember a lot of these great men—The 25th of September, we shall remember Pandit Deendayal Upadhyaya, Mahatma Gandhi and Lal Bahadur Shastri on the 2nd of October, Jai Prakash Narayan ji on the 11th of October, Sardar Vallabh Bhai Patel on the 31st of October and there are innumerable names, but I have mentioned just a few because our country has an unending list of such gems.

You pick any date; you will certainly find a name of one or the other great personality from the kaleidoscope of history. We must all try to remember these great personalities in the coming days, take their message to every house and try to learn something from them.

I would like to request you for 2nd October specially. It's the birth anniversary of our beloved Mahatma Gandhi. I had told you last year as well, that you must have all kinds of fashionable clothing, all kinds of fabric, a lot of things, but you must also own Khadi. I am saying it again, that Khadi outlets have a sale from 2nd October onwards for one whole month. You must all avail yourselves of this discount. Along with Khadi, handloom must also be given equal importance.

Our weavers put in a lot of hard work. If 1.5 billion Indians buy a handloom product or Khadi for even Rupees 5, 10 or 50, that money will reach the poor weaver. It will reach the poor widow who weaves Khadi and this is why we must all spare some place for Khadi in our homes and on our bodies, this Diwali. I just have this small request, I do not insist that you only wear Khadi. But have a little collection of Khadi. This is my only request. Look, last year, we almost doubled the Khadi sale. A lot of the poor have been benefitted. Advertisements worth crores by the government, cannot achieve what has been achieved through your help. This is the power of the masses and this is why I request you to come forward and help once again.

Dear countrymen, my heart is filled with joy because of this one thing. I wish to share this joy with you as well. I visited Kolkata in May and the family members of Subhash Chandra Bose met me there. His nephew, Chandra Bose, had organised everything. I got the opportunity to spend quality time with Subhash Babu's family members. That day I decided to invite his great family to the Prime Minister's residence. Mr Chandra Bose and his family members were in the process of organising this and last week I received the confirmation that around 50 members of the Bose family are coming to the Prime Minister's residence for a meeting.

You can imagine how happy I must have been on hearing this news. Perhaps this is for the first time that Netaji's family members, must have been invited together to the Prime Minister's residence. More than that, I feel honoured that this opportunity for me in October will be a one of a kind opportunity for the Prime Minister's residence to offer its hospitality. More than 50 family members of Subhash Babu's family, who stay in different countries, are especially coming down to attend this meeting. It is going to be a joyous moment for me. I am very excited to welcome them and feel extremely happy.

I received a message from Bhargavi Kande and after listening to the way she speaks, I felt she is a leader or she is going to be a leader probably.

> *My name is Bhargavi Kande. I want to request the Prime Minister to make the young generation aware of voter's registration, this will increase the participation of the young generation in the times to come. In the future the young generation will provide its important contribution in selecting as well as running a government. Thank you.*

Bhargavi talked about registering the names in the voters' list and participation in the voting process. In a democracy, every voter determines the destiny of the country and this awareness is spreading gradually. The voting percentage is also increasing and for this I want to congratulate the Election Commission of India. Till a few years back, we saw that our election commission worked only as a regulator but it has changed a lot in the last few years. Today, our election commission does not work only as a regulator but has become a facilitator, voter-friendly and the voter is at the centre of all its policies and ideologies. It is a welcome change but we need more than what Election Commission can do. We must mobilise schools, colleges and societies—we must spread awareness always, not only during the time of elections. The voters' list must be updated; we must also keep a watch on it. This priceless right that I have, is it safe? Am I using it or not? We must all develop this habit. I hope that all the youngsters who have not been registered in the voters' list yet, get themselves registered and must vote too. I publically say during elections that one must cast his vote before one eats food. This is a holy act, everyone must do it.

I have returned from a visit to Kashi, day before yesterday. I met a lot of people and attended a lot of events. I met many people there, but these two kids I met there, had told me something that I want to share with you today. One of the boys, Kshitij, is a student of Class 7. He studies in the Kendriya Vidyalaya of Banaras Hindu University. He is a very smart kid with a surprising by high confidence level. I saw that at such a young age he was interested in research in the field of Physics. I thought he must be reading a lot books, must be surfing Internet, or watching new experiments. He was talking about things like, how to stop railway accidents, which technology to use, how to save money in producing energy, how to develop feelings in robots and what not. He was an amazing kid. Although I could not follow what he was saying, very closely, but I liked his confidence and his interest in so many things. I want that kids in our country should develop more and more interest in science. Kids should be very inquisitive, why? How? When? A kid should always ask these questions.

Similarly, I met a girl named Sonam Patel. She is 9 years old. She is the daughter of Sadavrat Patel, a resident of Sundarpur, Varanasi. Her family is very poor. I was surprised that the girl had memorised the Bhagvada Gita completely but the most interesting thing was that she kept reciting the shlokas along with their English interpretation and their definitions in English as well as Hindi. When I asked, her father told me that she started reciting these shlokas since she was only five years old. I asked where she learned it from. He said, "We do not have any idea." Then I asked if she only reads Gita, or does she read something else as well? Her father then told me that if she picks up mathematics once, she memorises everything by evening. If she picks up history, she knows everything by evening. He told me that the whole family is surprised at this amazing talent the girl has. I was really very impressed. Sometimes, kids become obsessed with celebrities; Sonam did not have any such obsessions. I felt this girl is God-gifted.

Meeting these kids was a very special experience that I had during my Kashi visit. So, I thought I must share it with you. We do a lot of things, other than what you see on the TV and read in newspapers. Sometimes, we enjoy doing these things as well. Similarly, I will always cherish the memories of this encounter with these kids.

I noticed that a few people bring a lot of work for me in 'Mann Ki Baat'. Look at what Sandeep from Haryana has to say:

> *Sir, I want you to do 'Mann ki Baat' as a weekly rather than a monthly programme because we get very inspired by your words.*

Sandeep ji, how much will you make me do? I have to struggle even to make it to the monthly programme; have to make adjustments to my time-table. Sometimes, our friends at Akashvani have to wait for an hour or so. I still respect your feelings. I am thankful to you for your suggestion. For now, we will stick to the one month programme only.

'Mann Ki Baat' in a way has completed a year. Do you know how much did Subhash Babu use the radio? He started his own programme from Germany and he would constantly update Indian citizens about the independence movement through radio. He started the

Azad Hind Radio, with a weekly news bulletin. English, The radio used to run in Hindi, Bengali, Marathi Punjabi, Pashto, and Urdu.

I have also completed a year since I started 'Mann Ki Baat.' My 'Mann Ki Baat' has in the true sense become your 'Mann Ki Baat.' I listen to you, I think for you, I look into your suggestions and that triggers a thought process in me which reaches you through Akashvani. I only speak, but the words are yours and this gives me immense satisfaction. We shall meet next month again for 'Mann Ki Baat'. Your suggestions should keep pouring in. The government benefits by your suggestions. It helps to initiate improvement. Your contribution is priceless for me.

Once again, many congratulations to all of you. Thank you!

For listening to the audio, please log on to http://www.narendramodi.in/mann-ki-baat or scan the given QR code.

CHAPTER 13: October 2015

Namaskar to all my fellow citizens!

Once again, I have the opportunity of connecting with you through 'Mann Ki Baat'. Today the fifth one-day cricket match is being played between India and South Africa in Mumbai. This series has been named the 'Gandhi-Mandela' series. It is at an interesting point with both teams having won two matches each. So the last game is significantly important. My best wishes to both the teams.

Spreading Awareness

Today, I would like to congratulate my friends at the Kannur Centre of Akashvani. I started this 'Mann Ki Baat' and people started connecting with it. One of them was Shraddha Thamban from Kerala, a grade class 12 student. The Kannur Centre invited her for a ceremony and a lot of feed back was received. It created an environment of belonging. The Kannur Centre appreciated Shraddha's awareness and rewarded her. The development at the Kannur Centre inspired me. I encourage all the Akashvani centres to pay attention and raise the level of awareness among the members and make them active in their region, so that our aim of governance with public participation gets a boost. My heartfelt greetings and congratulations to the team at Kannur station of Akashvani for their efforts.

Organ Donation

I would like to talk about Kerala again. Girl students from Saint Mary Upper Primary School from Chittoor in Kerala have sent me a letter. This letter is special in many ways. Firstly, these girls have created an image of mother India by thumb prints on a huge piece of cloth. They have sent me the image of mother India. Initially, I was surprised to see why they created a map of India using thumb prints. But when I read their letter, I realised how beautifully a symbolic message was given. It is not as if these girls have tried to just awaken the Prime Minister alone. They are trying to create awareness among the people in their region and their mission is organ donation. Organ donation is very important in this country. They are organising a public awareness campaign for organ donation. They have organised plays for creating an understanding about organ donation. Organ donation should become a habit as well as an instinct. They have asked me in their letter to appeal to people about organ donation in 'Mann Ki Baat'. The octogenarian Vasantrao Sudke Guru ji from Maharashtra has been running a movement for a long time. He says that organ donation should be celebrated as a festival. These days, I get a lot of messages on phone as well. Devesh from Delhi has also sent me a similar message:

> *I am very happy with the government's initiative on the organ donation and steps towards creating a policy on the same. The country really needs support in these things where people need to go out and help each other and the*

ambitious target of one per million organ donation is a very productive step taken by the government.

I feel that this topic is very important. The country needs more than 2.5 lakh kidneys, hearts and livers per year for the purpose of donation. However, in a country with 125 crore people, only 5000 transplants could take place. Each year, about one lakh eyes are in need of vision, and we are able to reach only 25,000 people who need it. It implies that we are able to provide eye transplant services to only one out of four needy persons. We should also know that if someone is killed in a road accident, then too the organs can be donated. There are some legal hassles involved. And efforts have been made to guide the states in this direction.

By reducing the paper work, some of the states have made a good effort in speeding up the process involved in organ donation. Today, I can say that Tamil Nadu ranks first in the field of organ donation. Many social organisations and NGOs are doing a commendable job in this direction. The National Organ and Tissue Transplant Organisation (NOTTO) has been established to encourage organ transplant. A 24x7 helpline facility is also available for the same. Its number is 1800 114 770. And there is a saying, *Tena Tyaktena Bhunjhita* (Enjoy through renunciation). The joy of sacrifice is beautifully described in this mantra. In the past few days, we saw on television that the wife of a poor hawker in Delhi received a transplant in Delhi's G.B. Pant Hospital. This liver was brought from Lucknow by making special arrangements. The transplant was successful. A life was saved. Organ donation is the biggest donation. Let us all realise the mantra of *Tena Tyaktena Bhunjhita* (Enjoy through renunciation).

India-Africa Summit

Dear countrymen, we recently celebrated the festival of Navratri and Vijayadashami. And after some days, we will celebrate Diwali too. We also enjoyed the festival of Eid and Ganesh Chaturthi. But amongst all these, another big festival is being organised which our countrymen should be proud of. In the National Capital of Delhi, an 'India–Africa Foreign Summit' is being organised from 26th to 29th October. For the first time, a programme of this scale is being organised on Indian soil. Leaders of 54 African countries and unions have been invited. This is the biggest conference of African countries, outside Africa. India–Africa ties are deep. The African nations have a population equal to that of India. If both are combined together, they become a third of the world population. And it is said that lakhs of years ago, it was all one landmass. Later, it got separated by the Indian Ocean, into two parts. There are a lot of similarities amongst us. The biodiversity of both the nations is similar. Our natural resources are similar. And almost 27 lakh Indians have settled in these nations since a long time. India shares a lot of economic, cultural and political ties with the African nations, and plays the largest role in training youth from African countries. More than 25,000 African youths have studied human resource development and capacity building in India. And many leaders from Africa have also studied here. So you can understand the depth of our relationship. And from that perspective, this Summit is very important. Generally, when there is a summit, the leaders of various countries meet. Similarly, in this summit, the leaders will be meeting. We are making efforts that the people should also meet.

And this time, the Government of India, especially the HRD Ministry, has done something really commendable. An essay competition was organised among all the CBSE-affiliated schools as well as a poetry competition to increase their participation. Almost 1,600 schools participated in the event. It included schools within and outside India. And thousands of children wrote on topics about strengthening the India-Africa ties. On the other hand, a mobile exhibition called "Memories of Mahatma", starting from his birth place, Porbandar, and travelling through the north, is about to reach Delhi on the 29th of October. Lakhs of school children enjoyed this exhibition. The villagers also had a glimpse. People realised the importance of the role of Mahatma Gandhi in developing ties between India and Africa and also the effect of his personality on these nations. Some excellent creations were received in this competition. One of the creations drew my attention and I want to share it with you. It reflects the talent, the broad vision and the depth of thoughts of students from small cities. Garima Gupta from Muzaffarnagar in UP writes beautifully, saying:

The river in Africa is Nile and the name of the sea is Red,
The continent is huge and the Indian diaspora happy
Like the Indus Valley is recognition of Indian civilisation
River Nile and Carthage are synonymous with African civilisation
Gandhi ji started his revolution in Africa
He wove a spell and won everybody's heart
Be it Johannesburg or Kingston, Zimbabwe or Chad
In each African nation, we can find our aloo chat
To write, a thousand lines can be written
But I want to mention that I love African jungles

The poem is very long, but I have read only a few lines to you. Though it is an India–Africa Summit, but how this too can become an opportunity to connect people is clearly evident here. I heartily congratulate Garima, the students and more than 1,600 schools who participated, and the HRD Ministry for this initiative.

Sansad Adarsh Gram Yojana

Last time on 15th August, I had proposed the Sansad Adarsh Gram Yojana. Since then, many parliamentarian friends have adopted it. They were deeply involved. Last month, a workshop was organised in Bhopal. All the pradhans, (village heads) collectors, parliamentarians villages who have adopted under Adarsh Gram, representatives of the Indian government and state governments, had an in-depth discussion on this programme. Many new and encouraging things came to our attention. I would like to bring to your attention a few things. Jharkhand, a huge state is primarily tribal. Unfortunately, whenever one talks of Jharkhand, what comes to mind is Maoism, violence, guns and a blood-soaked land. Many regions in the state have been ruined by these communist terrorists. But the MP from that region, a senior member who has also been our Deputy Speaker, Mr Karia Munda, has dedicated his life to the tribals. He chose Parsi Gram Panchayat from Khunti district to be adopted for Adarsh Gram. It is difficult for government officials to go to places ruled by Maoists. Even doctors cannot visit those places. He himself started travelling to this village, to instil faith and give a new lease of life to governmental organisations. He encouraged the officials to visit too and tried to change the existing mood of despondency and created the mood for achieving something. A successful effort has been made in the Parsi village to create awareness, along with infrastructure and organisational development. I would like to congratulate our Honourable parliamentarian, Karia Munda ji, for his effort.

I got similar information from Andhra too. The MP from Andhra, Mr Ashok Gajapati Raju, involved himself in this plan and chose Dwarapudi Gram Panchayat from the Vijaynagaram district for the same. Other arrangements are in progress, but he did something really innovative. He urged students to teach the elders of the village. The new generation in the village is fortunate to be educated, but the older generation is not literate. So he asked students of a higher age group to educate parents. So in the morning they are students, and by evening they become educators. Nearly 550 adults were taught by these children and made literate. Just see, no budget, no circular, no special arrangements, but by mere will power, a big change was brought in. This is amply demonstrated by the Dwarapudi Gram Panchayat.

Similarly, another respectable parliamentarian Mr CL Ruwala ji, is an MP from Mizoram, in our Northeast. He chose Khwalahilung village for Adarsh Gram and ran a special initiative. This village is famous for sugarcane production and Kurtayi jaggery. Ruwala ji started a Sugarcane Festival on 11th March. All people from the region came together for it. Senior members from social public life and retired government officials from the region also participated in it. They put up an exhibition on how to increase sugarcane production. They discussed how the village could be made the centre of economic activities and how it could market its produce. I congratulate Ruwala ji for his efforts to make this village not only an Adarsh Gram, but a self-dependent village too.

Clean India

My dear brothers and sisters, it is not possible that there be an episode of 'Mann Ki Baat' and we do not discuss cleanliness. Savita Rai from Mumbai has sent me a telephonic message:

> *Each year on Diwali, we clean our houses. This Diwali let us clean our environment along with our homes and maintain that cleanliness even after Diwali.*

She has drawn attention to this issue. I want to remind you, my dear countrymen, that last year the Indian media ran a special campaign and showed us all the places where crackers were lying and reminded us that it was not the right thing. This was an awareness campaign launched by the media. As a result of it, soon after Diwali, a cleanliness drive started all by itself. So what you are saying is true, that our concern before and after the festival should be the same. And we should express this concern on every public platform. And today, I especially congratulate all members of the Indian media fraternity.

Safaigiri Campaign

This 2nd October, on Gandhi ji's birth anniversary and also on the completion of one year of the 'Clean India Campaign', I had the fortune of participating in the 'Safaigiri Campaign' of the India Today Group. They gave away the Clean India Awards and I could see several initiatives being carried out. Different people were working as, 'One Life, One Mission'.

There are so many places in our country that have been kept so clean. All these things were brought to light and I offered my heartfelt appreciation to the India Today Group for their commendable efforts. Since the inception of the cleanliness drive, I have seen that from Andhra and Telangana, ETV and Eanadu have participated whole-heartedly and especially Mr Ramoji Rao, who is very aged, but beats any youth in his enthusiasm. He has made cleanliness his personal programme, his mission. He has been promoting the cleanliness programme through ETV for the past one year. Newspapers carry news about it and he has emphasised on positive news about cleanliness. He has been successful in bringing together around 51 lakh children from about 56,000 schools of Andhra and Telangana to this mission. Be it public places, stations, religious places, hospitals, parks or other places, he ran a cleanliness drive. All these news exhibit the power to realise the dream of a clean India.

ABP news has started a programme called 'Ye Bharat Desh Hai Mera'. In this program, they have shown how people are becoming aware of cleanliness and through this they are trying to awaken people about keeping their surroundings clean. NDTV has started a campaign called 'Banega Swachh India'. *Dainik Jagaran* has also encouraged this campaign, so has Zee TV and IndiaTV also started 'Mission Clean India'. Thousands of channels and newspapers in our country, I am unable to name them all due to time constraints, but they have all helped run this campaign. This is why, Savita Rai ji, the suggestion that you have given us, the whole nation has taken it upon itself to do this work and take it forward. The Governor of Meghalaya, Mr Shanmuganathan, wrote me a letter and talked about a village in Meghalaya, called Mawlynnong. He has written that for the last many years, this village has set out on a mission for cleanliness and more or less every generation is completely dedicated towards this cause. He has also mentioned that a few years ago they also got the award for the 'cleanest village' of Asia. The idea of a far-flung village situated in the north-eastern region in Meghalaya, which has been particular about cleanliness since years, makes me extremely happy. This has become the habit and the culture of the village. This is what reinforces our belief that our nation will be clean one day for sure. This will be possible because of the efforts of the people, and by the time we celebrate the 150th birth anniversary of Mahatma Gandhi, the 125 crore people of the country should be able to proudly proclaim that we have made India clean.

Recruitment Made Easy

My dear countrymen, I said this from the Red Fort on the 15th August that there are a few places where corruption is deep rooted. When a poor man goes for an ordinary job, he faces so many problems while trying to get a decent reference and has to go through a team of agents who take money from him in exchange for the position he is applying for. He loses money regardlen of whether he gets the job or not. We keep hearing things like this. This is when I had an idea. Why do we need to interview people for ordinary jobs? I have never heard of any psychologist in the world who can analyse a person completely in a 1-2 minute long interview. With this thought, I decided to end the tradition of interviews for small positions.

My dear young friends, I feel very proud to tell you all that the government has completed all the formalities and now there will be no interview for non-gazetted posts of Group 'D', Group 'C', and Group 'B' in the central government. This will come into effect from 1st January 2016. We will not interrupt the ongoing procedures now, but from 1st January 2016, this will be implemented. So, let me congratulate all my young friends for it.

Gold—The Financial Strength of Our Nation

We had declared an important scheme in the last budget. In our country, gold has become a part of our social life. Gold is considered the medium of financial security. Gold is considered to be the solution in difficult times. This has been an age-old tradition. I don't believe that anyone can reduce this love for gold that we have developed, but keeping gold as dead-money does not suit today's generation. Gold can become our financial strength. Citizens can start saving their assets in gold. Sovereign gold bonds will be more beneficial for bank customers. Hereafter, gold will be secure in your banks. Gold can become the financial property of the nation and every Indian must contribute to this. I am happy that the promise that we made of introducing important schemes, we will do so around Diwali and Dhanteras when people specially buy gold. We have introduced a 'Gold Monetisation Scheme'. Under this scheme, you can deposit your gold in a bank and the bank will give you interest, same as when you deposit your money and get interest from the bank.

Earlier, we used to keep our gold in lockers and paid for the lockers ourselves. Now, when you keep your gold in the bank, the bank will give you money as interest. Now, tell me my countrymen, can gold become a property or not?

Can gold be converted from dead money to a living strength or not? This is exactly what we have to do, and you must stand with me. Do not keep your gold in your homes. Avail dual benefits, its security and interest on the gold. You must avail this opportunity. Another thing is that in sovereign gold bonds you do not really get any physical gold in your hand. You get a sheet of paper and the value of that paper is equivalent to that of the amount of gold and the day you return that paper, you will get the amount that is equivalent to the value of gold on that particular day. Let us assume, you buy a gold bond worth Rs 1000 and five years later you go to return that bond, and at that time, the rate of gold is

Rs 2500; you will receive an amount of Rs 2500 in exchange of that bond. So, we are introducing this scheme now. Due to this scheme, all worries related with gold end and you will not have to buy gold now. You will not have to secure your gold now, or to take safety measures to keep it in a secure place. In the coming week, I will certainly put forward this scheme that guarantees security to the people of this country. I feel very glad to tell you that we are also introducing a gold coin with Ashok Chakra. It has been around 70 years since independence but we are still using foreign gold coins or gold bullion bars which are also used by the foreigners. Why should it not have the national emblem of our country? This is why we are introducing it in the market and it will be available for citizens in the coming week, before Dhanteras–5 gm and 10 gm of gold coins. Along with it a 20 gm gold coin bullion will also be available to people. I have full faith that this new scheme will usher a new change in the financial development of the country, and I will get your support in this.

Unity in Diversity

My dear countrymen, 31st of October is the birth anniversary of the Iron-Man of India, Sardar Vallabhbhai Patel.

Ek Bharat, Shreshtha Bharat.

A complete layout of India unfolds in front of us when we talk about Sardar Vallabhbhai Patel. This great man has contributed a lot in building the unity of India. He has proven his capabilities as the Iron Man of India. We will certainly pay tribute to Sardar Sahab, but along with that his dream of seeing India integrated, he made it possible geographically. Unity should be our medium. Unity in diversity is our country's pride. But this mantra of unity should be present in our thoughts, in our minds, behaviour and our expressions. India is full of diversities—many sects, communities, languages, castes, attires. It is this diversity that adds to its charm. If it was not for this diversity, we wouldn't have been so proud of our country. This is why diversity is the mantra of unity. Peace, social harmony, unity, these are essential elements of a society.

Since many years, 'Run for Unity' programmes have been organised in various parts of the country on the 31st of October, 'Ekta ki Daud'. I had a chance to run in one of these earlier. I have heard this year also this race is being planned at many places. People are excited to be a part of this race. In the true sense, 'Ekta ki Daud' is the true race for development. In other words, the guarantee for the race of development lies in the race of unity. Come, let us pay tribute to Sardar Sahab. Let us move forward with the mantra of unity.

Diwali Festivities

Dear brothers and sisters, you must all be busy in the preparations for Diwali, houses must be getting cleaned. You must be shopping for new things. The festival of Diwali is celebrated in various ways all over the country. I extend my good wishes to you on this sacred festival. We also get to hear of a few accidents around the time of Diwali. Fires break out due to firecrackers or lamps. Especially children suffer a lot because of fire crackers. I will advise and suggest all parents to be careful while enjoying Diwali. They should see to it that the children do not get hurt, or any untoward incident should not happen, and try to avoid unnecessary losses due to such accidents. I know you will be careful about this and of course, about keeping the environment clean.

Upcoming Trip to Britain

My dear countrymen, I have to leave for a trip to Britain the day after Diwali. I am very excited about my trip this time. There is a reason behind my excitement. A few weeks back, I went to Mumbai to inaugurate a magnificent memorial of Dr Babasaheb Bhimrao Ambedkar near his 'Chaitya Bhoomi'. Now, I am going to London to formally inaugurate the house where Babasaheb used to stay and which has now become the property of India. It is an inspiration for 125 crore of my countrymen, be they dalits, or underprivilegeds, victims, or any Indian who is leading a difficult life. This house inspires us to believe in the fact that if one has a strong will power, one can overcome the difficulties to tread on the path of success, one can get educated and this is the very place where Babasaheb Ambedkar used to meditate. The Indian government and the government of different Indian states award scholarships to promising students who go abroad to study and who belong to the dalit community, the tribal community or any other under privileged community. I believe that when these children go to Britain to study, this memorial of Babasaheb will become a pilgrimage for them, and will be a source of inspiration. Whatever you learn in life, you must use it later for the country and live for your country. Babasaheb gave this message and even lived it by himself. Let's work towards Babasaheb Ambedkar's mission.

I am very excited about my Britain trip this time. This issue has been lying entangled since many years, and now it has become the property of 125 crore of my countrymen and if the name of Babasaheb Ambedkar is attached, you all can imagine how happy it makes me.

I am going to get another opportunity in London, to unveil the statue of Lord Vishweshwara. Many years ago, what Lord Vishweshwara had done for democracy and empowerment of women can make for a very good subject of study. The unveiling of the statue of Lord Vishweshwara on the land of London is in itself a perfect example of the fact that the great men of India were very far-sighted. Now you see, when such incidents are connected, how excited we get.

My dear countrymen, you are connected with us through 'Mann Ki Baat'. I keep getting your suggestions, comments and queries through telephone and MyGov.in. Your letters are also discussed on Akashvani. Government officials are called in and discussions are held. Some people write down their grievances, there are efforts to solve their problems as well. We should learn more than one language in a country like India. I am fortunate enough to have learnt a few languages, but still there are so many languages that I could not learn. I am indebted to Akashvani because they broadcast this programme of 'Mann Ki Baat' by 8 P.M. in every state, in the regional languages. Even though a different voice is used, the thoughts are mine.

I will try to reach out to you in your language. We have formed a beautiful bond between us. Last time, I had completed a year in power. This time, we are entering a new year. Heartfelt congratulations to all my countrymen for Diwali and a prosperous new year ahead once again!

Jai Hind.

For listening to the audio, please log on to http://www.narendramodi.in/mann-ki-baat or scan the given QR code.

CHAPTER 14: November 2015

My dear countrymen, Namaste!

I believe you must have had a great time during your Diwali vacations amidst all the festivities. You must have had the opportunity to visit some other places. New trade and job transactions would have commenced with renewed vigour. On the other hand, Christmas preparations must have started too. Festivals have their own significance in social life. Sometimes festivities help to heal wounds and sometimes they are a source of renewed energy. But sometimes when a calamity strikes during festivities, it is very painful and it hurts even more. There is continuous news of natural calamities from various parts of the world. And sometimes the news is very bizarre, never seen or never heard of. We are now realising the effects of climate change very rapidly. In our country itself, we have experienced torrential rains, that too off season and for a very long duration. Tamil Nadu has suffered heavy losses and other states have suffered too. Many people lost their lives. My heart goes out to all those people in this hour of crisis. The state governments have braced themselves up for rescue and relief work. The Central Government too has joined them in their efforts. Right now, a team of Central Government officials is in Tamil Nadu. But I have full faith in Tamil Nadu's potential and know that post this crisis it will rise again, speedily move forward and will continue to play its role of taking the country forward.

Rising above Calamities

Now when there are talks of such crisis all around, we feel the need to bring in a lot of change. About 15 years back, natural calamity was a part of the Agricultural Ministry's realm because most of the calamities were limited to famine. But today, its form and format has changed. It has become important to work on our capacity building at every level. The government, civil society, citizens, and small organisations will all have to work for capacity building through scientific methods. After the Nepal earthquake, I talked to Pakistan's Prime Minister, Nawaz Sharif. I suggested that the SAARC nations should come together for a joint exercise on disaster preparedness. I am happy that a seminar/workshop on table talk exercises and best practices was organised in Delhi. This is a good beginning.

Good Farming Practices

Today, I received a phone call from Lakhwinder Singh from Jalandhar, Punjab:

> *I am Lakhwinder Singh from Jalandhar, Punjab. We do organic farming in our fields and also guide a lot of others on it. I have a question, "how to convince people that burning of farm remains or straw not only destroys the micro-organisms of the soil but also contributes to the pollution in Delhi, Punjab and Haryana.*

Lakhwinder Singh ji, I am happy to hear your message. I am happy that you are a farmer engaged in organic farming. And not just that, you also understand the problems of the farmers really well. Your concerns are right and this does not happen in Punjab and Haryana alone. It is a practice in the entire country and traditionally we follow this method of burning away the remains of the crops or straw. Initially, we were not aware of the damage. We did it because others did it too. Secondly, people are not aware of other available solutions. They have not been trained in it. And this practice kept on spreading and now it is contributing to global climate change. And now we are hearing more about it because it is affecting city life too. But the concern you have expressed is genuine. So the first solution is that our brothers and sisters engaged in agriculture need to be trained. They will need to face the fact that it is not true that burning the remains of crops helps save time and effort and prepares the field for the next crop. This is not the truth. The remains of the crop are themselves very valuable. They are organic fertiliser themselves. We are wasting them. Not only this, if they are chopped into small bits, they can act as food for cattle. Secondly, because of burning this, the top soil gets burnt.

My dear farmer brothers and sisters, just imagine if we have strong bones, a strong heart, a strong kidney, an overall healthy system, but our upper skin gets burnt, then what will happen? Even if the heart is strong, we will not be able to survive. So burning the stump of crops, not only burns them, but, it also burns the skin of our motherland. The top soil of our land is burnt and it pushes our fertile soil to death. Hence, some positive efforts need to be made. If these remains are once again buried inside the soil, then it will turn into fertilisers. If they are put in a pit and left with earth worms and water, good quality organic fertiliser can be made. So it can be used not only to feed animals, and save our land, but also to create good fertiliser. If this is added to the soil, it will be doubly beneficial.

Once I had the opportunity of talking to farmers involved in banana cultivation. And they shared a very good experience. Earlier as they cultivated banana, when the crop was over, the stumps of the tree would remain. To clear the stumps from the fields they had to spend Rs 5,000, 10,000 or 15,000 per hectare. And until people who would clear these stumps came with tractors, these stumps would remain standing. But some farmers chopped those stumps into 6-6, 8-8 inch pieces and buried them inside the soil. They realised that the banana stumps held so much water in them that no external water supply was needed for three months. Any plant or any crop sown over those stumps could flourish without water. The water in the stumps kept the crops alive. And now even their stumps are expensive. They are now a source of income. Earlier they had to spend money on clearing those stumps, and now those very stumps are a source of revenue. A small experiment can turn lucrative; our farmers are no less than scientists.

Organ Donation—A New Lease of Life

Dear countrymen, the entire world will remember the 3rd of December, as the 'International Day of Persons with Disabilities'. The last time in 'Mann Ki Baat', I talked about 'organ donation'. I talked about the National Organ and Tissue Transplant Organisation (NOTTO) helpline for 'organ donation'. I have been told that after that session, the number of phone calls has increased seven fold and the number of hits on the website increased 2.5 times. The 27th of November was celebrated as the 'Indian Organ Donation Day'. Many famous personalities including actress Raveena Tandon, became a part of it. 'Organ donation' can save many valuable lives. Organ donation can bring about immortality. When an organ moves from one body to another, it gets a new life, and the person receiving it gets a new lease of life. There can be no greater donation than this. I would like to inform those waiting for organs and those willing to donate, that a National Registry for organ transplantation has been launched on the 27th of November. MyGov.in organised a logo, donor card and slogan design competition for NOTTO and it surprised me to know that so many people participated and presented their ideas in such innovative ways and with such compassion. It is my faith that awareness in this field will increase and the needy will receive the best of help in the true sense. This help cannot be obtained till someone donates their organs.

Courage and Compassion in the Face of Adversity

Like I said earlier, 3rd December is being celebrated as the 'International Day of People with Disability'. People with physical and mental disabilities are capable of unparalleled courage and capability. Sometimes it hurts when they are laughed at. Sometimes someone expresses pity and sympathy. But if we change our outlook and our perspective towards them, these people can inspire us to live. They can inspire us to do a lot. We start crying even when a small misfortune befalls us. Looking at them we realise, our problem is so small; how do they survive? How do they live? How do they learn? And hence, all of them are a source of inspiration to us. Their will power, their struggle with life and their zeal to transform crisis into opportunity is worth a lot of praise.

Today, I want to talk about Javed Ahmed. He is 40-42 years old. In 1996, terrorists had shot Jawed Ahmed in Kashmir. He was a victim of terrorism but he survived. The bullet damaged his kidney and a part of his intestine was lost. He suffered serious spinal injury. He lost the ability to stand on his own feet, but Jawed Ahmed did not concede defeat. The grave injury caused by terrorist could not deter him. His zeal is commendable, but above all is the fact that an innocent man had to face such a predicament. His youth is in danger yet he harbours no grudge and no anger. He turned this crisis into compassion and dedicated his life to social work. The body does not support him, but for the past 20 years he has devoted himself to child education.

Creating an Inclusive Society for the Disabled

How to improve the infrastructure for the physically challenged?

How to develop systems for the disabled in government offices and public spaces?

Javed Ahmed is working on these issues. He turned the focus of his educational qualification to these areas. He was awarded a Master's Degree in social work and is now leading a silent revolution as a messiah of the disabled, working as an informed citizen. Is his life not enough to inspire people in every corner of India? I especially remember the life of Javed Ahmed, his dedication and devotion, especially on every 3rd December. I am just mentioning Javed's case because of lack of time, but such lights of inspiration are prevalent in every corner of the country. They are giving a new lease of life and illuminating the path for others. 3rd December is a day to remember all such people and get inspired by them.

Our country is very large. There are many things for which we are dependent on the government. Be it someone from middle class, lower middle class, dalit, exploited, victim or deprived, they have to continuously be in touch with the government or its various organisations. As citizens, we have surely had a bad experience with at least one government official in our lifetime. And that one experience shapes our perception of the government system for a lifetime. There is some truth to it. But at the same time, within this governmental system, there are lakhs of people who by their sense of duty, their dedication, do some amazing work which does not get recognised. Sometimes it happens so naturally, it is so organic, that one does not realise that some government employee has done it.

Operation ASHA: Bill and Melinda Gates Foundation

In our country, there is a network of ASHA workers. We have never discussed them in our country. I had not heard about them earlier, and I am sure, neither you. The success of the work of the entrepreneur couple, Bill and Melinda Gates, through their foundation, has become an inspiration. Last year, we honoured them with a joint Padma Vibhushan. They do a lot of social work in India. They are spending their entire retirement time and whatever they have earned on working for the poor. They are so full of praise for the ASHA workers with whom they work. They talk about their dedication and hard work and their zeal to learn about new things. They are full of such stories. In the past, the Odisha government especially facilitated an ASHA worker on Independence Day. She hails from a small village, Tenda Gaon in Balasore district, where most of the population is scheduled tribe. People are poor there and the area is malaria infested. The ASHA worker, Jamuna Mani

Singh, decided that she will not let anyone die of malaria. She would go to each household and would be the first one to reach if there was news of fever in any household. She would put to use the primary training she received and give treatment accordingly. She would reach out to every household to make them aware of the use of mosquito repellents and mosquito nets. The way we care for our children and their sound sleep, Jamuna Mani Singh would work with the same dedication for the entire village. She fought Malaria and prepared the entire village to fight against it. There might be so many "Jamuna Mani". There might be lakhs and lakhs of people around us. Let us show respect to such individuals. Such individuals lend power to our nation. They are partners to the joys and sorrows of others. I applaud all such ASHA workers through the story of Jamuna Mani.

A Call to the Youth to be a Social Teacher

My dear young friends, who are especially active on the internet and the social media, I want to inform you that I have kept 3 e-books on MyGov.in. These e-books are about inspiring stories of Swachh Bharat, the health sector and the Sansad Aadarsh Gram Yojana. I request you to see it. Don't just see it, show it to others too. Read it and you may find something to connect with it. Please do send it to MyGov.in. Such things do happen, though we may miss them, but they are the actual strength of our nation. Positive power is the biggest energy. You also share good episodes. Share these e-books, discuss these books and some enthusiastic young man can narrate these to the students of VIII, IX or X standard in nearby schools. So you can become a social teacher in the truest sense. I invite you to come and become a part of the nation-building process.

Energy Conservation

My dear countrymen, the entire world is worried about climate change. Climate change and global warming are being discussed in every nook and corner and now it has become an accepted standard for embarking on any new task. The earth's temperature should not rise anymore. This is everyone's concern and responsibility too. And to save us from rising temperatures, the first step is 'energy conservation'. 14th December is "National Energy Conservation Day". The government is running many schemes. There is a scheme to increase LED bulb usage. I had once mentioned that one can switch off the street lights on a full moon night and enjoy the moonlight for an hour. One should enjoy the moonlight. Some friend of mine had sent me a link and I had the opportunity to see it. I really wanted to share it with you. The actual credit goes to Zee News because the link was of Zee News itself.

There is a woman called Noor Jahan from Kanpur. While watching her on television, it seemed that she did not have much of a chance to receive education. But she is doing something which no one would have thought of. She is utilising solar energy to illuminate the houses of the poor. She is fighting darkness and bringing light to her own name. She has formed a *Samiti* (committee) of women who manufacture lanterns that run on solar energy. They rent the lantern for Rs 100 per month. People take the lanterns in the evening and return them in the morning to get them recharged. I have heard that people in large numbers, around 500 of them are using these lanterns. At a cost of Rs 3-4 per day, the entire house is illuminated. Noor Jehan works the entire day to recharge the lanterns in the solar energy plant. See what the big people of the world do climate change. Maybe Noor Jehan can act as an inspiration to many for the kind of work she is doing. In fact, 'Noor Jehan' means the light of the world. She is spreading light through her work. I congratulate her and Zee TV that they presented this effort from a remote corner of Kanpur, to the country and the world. Many congratulations to you.

The Prime Minister MUDRA Fund

I received a phone call from Mr Abhishek Kumar Pandey from Uttar Pradesh:

> *Namaste! I am Abhishek Kumar Pandey calling from Gorakhpur. I am working here as an entrepreneur. I want to congratulate the Prime Minister for starting a programme, MUDRA bank. I would like to know from the Prime Minister how this MUDRA bank can support entrepreneurs like us. What kind of cooperation can we expect?*

Thank you, Abhishek ji. You sent me a message from Gorakhpur. The Prime Minister's MUDRA fund is about funding the unfunded. Those who do not get funds may get funds. To put it plainly, the objective is 3E—Enterprises, Earning, Empowerment. MUDRA is meant to encourage enterprise; it is about creating earning opportunities. MUDRA will empower in the truest sense. It is meant to help the small scale enterprises. This initiative is yet to achieve the speed that I have aimed for. But the start has been good. Till now 66 lakh people have received 42,000 crore rupees through the Pradhan Mantri Mudra Yojana. It could be anyone a washerman, a barber, a newspaper vendor, milkman, just about anybody engaged in small enterprise. I am happy that out of 66 lakh recipients, 24 lakh are women. And most of the beneficiaries are from the SC, ST, OBC category who want to work hard and run their families independently. Abhishek has himself narrated his excitement. I too keep receiving various news. Someone just told me that there is one Shailesh Bhosle in Mumbai. He received a loan of 8.5 lakhs from the MUDRA scheme. He started the sewage dress and cleanliness business. I had said about my cleanliness campaign that it will create new entrepreneurs. And Shailesh Bhonsle proved it. He has purchased a tanker and I have been told that he has already repaid 2 lakh rupees in such a short span of time. This is our intention behind the MUDRA scheme. I have been told about Mamta Sharma from Bhopal. She received Rs 40,000 from the MUDRA Yojana. She is into the business of making purses. But earlier she would borrow money at high rates and barely manage her business. Now that she has a large sum of money in her hand, her work is going on smoothly. Earlier, the money that was lost in paying high interest and for other reasons could now be saved. She was able to save around Rs 1000 every month. The family's new enterprise started developing. I want this scheme to be further promoted. Our banks should become more sensitised and should help more and more people. Actually, it is these people who run the economy. People engaged in small enterprises give strength to the nation's economy. We want to strengthen these people. Whatever has happened is good, but more good needs to be done.

Ek Bharat, Shreshtha Bharat

My dear countrymen, on 31st October on the birth anniversary of Sardar Patel I had discussed about—"*Ek Bharat, Shreshtha Bharat*" (One India, Best India). Conducting such events creates continuous awareness in social life. "*Rashtram Jagryam Vyayam*" means, "internal vigilance is the prize of liberty". This tradition should be followed for national unity. I want to give "*Ek Bharat, Shreshtha Bharat*" the form of a specific scheme.

MyGov.in had invited suggestions for it. What should the structure of the programme be? What should be the logo? How to increase public participation? What should be its structure? I have been told that many suggestions have been received. But I am expecting more suggestions. I expect more specific schemes. I have been told that the participants will all receive a certificate. Many big prizes have been announced. You should also utilise your creative mind. How can we make this mantra of *Ek Bharat, Shreshtha Bharat* that connects each and every Indian? What should be the programme and what should be the plan. It should be grand and full of life. It should be simple and effective to be able to connect everyone. What should the government do? What should be done by the civil society? There can be many ideas. I have complete faith that your ideas will be really useful.

Physical Activity and Exercise

My dear brothers and sisters, winter is about to start. But it is also the season to enjoy eating and dressing. But I would request you to exercise. I request you to utilise this good season for some kind of physical activity and exercise. Create this type of mood in the family, make it a celebration, all should get together for an hour to do these exercises. See how an awakening starts. And see how your body helps you through the day. So make a good habit in this good season. My good wishes again to all my dear countrymen.

Jai Hind!

For listening to the audio, please log on to http://www.narendramodi.in/mann-ki-baat or scan the given QR code.

CHAPTER 15: December 2015

Fellow citizens, namaskar to all.

This will be the last edition of 'Mann Ki Baat' in 2015. The next edition of 'Mann Ki Baat' will be in 2016. We have just celebrated Christmas and preparations are now on to ring in the new year.

India is a land of diversities, and we celebrate a lot of festivals. One is not done with one festival, and in the meantime, another one comes along. In a way, one festival leaves us waiting for another. At times, it feels that India is one such country which has a 'festival driven economy'. It also becomes a source of economic activities for the poor sections of society.

Greetings from my end for a Merry Christmas to all of you and I also wish you all a Happy New Year. May 2016 usher in lots of joys in your lives. I hope that new zeal, new excitement and new pledges may take you to new heights. May the world be free of crises, be it from terrorism, from global warming or from natural calamities or man-made tragedies. There can be no greater happiness than that of humanity having a peaceful existence.

You are aware that I make full use of technology which provides me lots of information. I also keep a watchful eye on my portal, MyGov.

Cleanliness—A Social Cause

Mr Ganesh V Savleshwarkar has written to me from Pune saying that this is the tourist season, and a large number of foreign and domestic tourists travel across the country. People also travel to celebrate Christmas vacations. He says that while most of the facilities related to tourism are taken care of, but special emphasis should be laid on cleanliness at all places which are tourist destinations or famed tourist spots, religious destinations or stay overs. India's image will be enhanced in the world if our tourist destinations are clean. I appreciate the views of Ganesh ji and convey this message to the people of our country. We say "*Atithi devo bhava*" (Guest is Like God) and we strive to keep our homes neat and clean when a guest is due to arrive. In a similar manner, the onus is on us to keep our tourist destinations and pilgrim places neat and clean. I am very happy that a lot of new stories related to cleanliness keep appearing in the media. From day one, I have thanked our media friends since they have brought many such small and good success stories before the people. I came across a nice story in the newspaper and I would like to share it with all of you.

Dileep Singh Malviya is an elderly artisan from Bhojpura village in Sehore district of Madhya Pradesh. He is a mason by profession. He did something so extraordinary that the newspapers printed his story. And when it came to my notice, I wanted to share this story with you. Hailing from a small village, Dileep Singh Malviya, decided that if anyone could material for constructing toilets in the village, he will render his labour services free of cost. And hats off to him, so far he has constructed 100 toilets in Bhojpura village taking it as a sacred cause and providing his labour services without charging a rupee. My heartfelt congratulations to Dileep Singh Malviya, for his earnest efforts. Sometimes we hear disappointing news about our nation. But there are thousands of people like Dileep Singh who are doing something good for the nation on their own. This is the power of the nation. This is the hope of the nation and these are the things which carry the nation forward, so it is natural that we applaud Dileep Singh and his efforts in 'Mann Ki Baat'.

Due to the tireless efforts of many people, the nation is making rapid progress. One twenty five crore Indians are not only marching together but they are taking the country forward too. Better education, best talent and new opportunities of employment are being created. Be it providing insurance cover to citizens or providing them banking facilities, be it the 'Ease of Doing Business' in the world horizon or making facilities available for new businesses, we have done it all. People from normal backgrounds who could not step inside banks, can now avail loan facilities from the 'Mudra Yojana'.

The world's acceptance and fascination with yoga is a matter of pride for every Indian. When the world celebrated 'International Yoga Diwas' and got associated with it, we became proud of our country. Such emotions arise when we see the vastness of our nation. No one can forget the story of Krishna and Yashoda, where he opened his mouth and the mother was able to see the entire universe, and only then was his power realised. The yoga incident was a similar reminder.

Bringing Light to Lives

The echoes of the concept of cleanliness can be heard in every household. The participation of citizens is also increasing. Many villages have received an electric pole after so many years of independence. Those of us who live in cities are so accustomed to using electricity that we don't realise the extent of happiness and excitement that comes when darkness is removed from one's life. The power departments of the state and the Indian government were functional earlier as well but from the day the 1000 day target for providing electricity to every village has been set, we have been getting news every day that power supply is available in some or the other village, and the happiness of the inhabitants' knows no bounds. The media has not discussed this topic. But I am sure that the media will definitely reach such villages and will inform the nation about the happiness and excitement of the people there.

The biggest achievement of this task is that government officials involved in this task will have immense satisfaction that they have done something which will bring about such a big change in the lives of the people and the village itself. Be it the farmers, poor, young or women, should such things not reach them? Such news should reach them not to highlight any government's achievement, but to make them aware of their rights. They should not let go if it is their right. People should get information in order to avail their rights. We should all make such efforts that the right information, the good information and information which is useful to the common man reaches as many people as possible. This is also a kind of service. I too have tried to do this work from my end but I cannot do everything by myself. But if I am saying it, then I too should do something about it. Even a common man can download the Narendra Modi App and get connected to me. And I can share these small things with you through the app. It is a matter of happiness for me that people share all these things with me. You too can get connected with this initiative. We have to reach 125 crore Indians. How will I reach without your help? Come, let us collectively do such things of interest for the common man in their language and inspire them to avail of things which are their rights.

Start-up India, Stand-up India

My dear young friends, I made some preliminary observations about 'Start-up India, Stand-up India' in my speech on 15th August from the Red Fort. After that, every government departments started discussing it. Can India become a 'Start-up Capital'? Can our states work together for new start-ups for youth, and encourage innovations with start-ups, be it in the manufacturing sector, service sector or agriculture. Everything should be new, new ways and new thinking. After all, the world does not move ahead without innovation. "Start-up India, Stand-up India" brings in a huge opportunity for the young generation. My dear young friends, the government will launch the entire action plan for "Start-up India, Stand-up India" on 16th January. What will it be, how will it be and why will it be? You will be presented with a structure. In this program, all the IITs, IIMs, Central Universities, NITs, wherever there are young people, will be brought together via live connectivity.

There is an established thinking regarding start-ups that they are meant only for the digital world or for IT profession. This is not true at all; we need to modify it according to the needs of India. For example, when a poor person works somewhere as a labourer and there is a lot of physical effort involved, and if a young man innovates something which can reduce the physical effort and help the labourer, I will call it a start-up. I will ask the bank to help such an individual and I will tell him to move ahead with courage. You will get the market. Similarly, the thinking that intellectual wealth is limited to a few select cities is wrong. The Indian youth all over the country has talent, all they need is opportunity. This 'Start-up India, Stand-up India' should not be limited to a few cities alone. It should spread to every corner of India. And I will request the State Governments to take this forward. I will interact with you on 16th January and we will discuss this in detail. Your suggestions are always welcome.

National Youth Festival

Dear friends, 12th January is the birth anniversary of Swami Vivekananda. There are thousands like me who draw inspiration from him. Since 1995, 12th January, the birth anniversary of Vivekananda is celebrated as the National Youth Festival. This year it will be organised from 12th-16th January in the Raipur district of Chhattisgarh. This is a theme based event and I have received information that this time they have a very good theme which is 'Indian Youth on Skill Development and Harmony'. I have been told that 10,000 young people will gather from all over India. A mini-India will be created there. They will share dreams together. A feeling of determination will be experienced. Can you give me suggestions regarding this youth festival? I would request the youth to send me their suggestions directly on the 'Narendra Modi App'. I want to gain an insight into your thoughts. And to ensure that it gets reflected in the youth festival. I will give the government reasonable suggestions and information. So, dear friends, I will wait for your suggestions on the youth festival on the 'Narendra Modi App'.

Accessible India

Dilip Chauhan, from Ahmedabad, Gujarat, who is a visually challenged teacher celebrated 'Accessible

India Day' in his school. He called me to express his feelings:

> *Sir, we celebrated 'Accessible India Campaign' in my school. I am a visually challenged teacher and I addressed 2,000 children on the issue of disability and how we can spread awareness and help differently-abled people. The students' response was fantastic, we enjoyed in the school and students were inspired and motivated to help the disabled people in the society. I think it was a great initiative by you.*

Dilip ji, thank you very much. Since you are also working in this field, you understand everything and you must have faced a lot of difficulties as well. At times, when we meet someone in society with a different ability, a lot of things come to our mind. We express our perception of him based on our thinking. There are people who lose a limb or a body part in an accident. Some people are born with some defects. And for these people, different words are used and a lot of thought goes into the usage of these words. All the time people feel that this kind of identification does not sound nice and respectable. At some point, we heard handicapped, then it was disabled and somewhere it is specially-abled. So many words have been used. It is true that words have their own significance. This year when the Government of India started the 'Sugamya India' programme, I was supposed to attend it but could not make it because of the severe floods in Chennai and other areas of Tamil Nadu. However, since I had to attend that programme, some thoughts kept coming in my mind. At the time, I thought that we call or know these people as handicapped because they lack in some ways in terms of their body structure or because their organs do not function properly. However, when we interact with them, we realise that we only see the deficits while. God has bestowed them with some different power which we cannot see. It is only when we see them in action that we realise their talent. We think, "Oh great! Look how he/she works". It is only upon looking at them with our eyes that we feel that they are handicapped, but·experiences tell us that they have some extra power. So I thought, why not use the word 'divyang' instead of 'viklang' in our country. They are those people who have one or more such organs which have divinity, where divine power flows, which we normal bodied people do not have. I like this term. My dear countrymen, can we make it a habit to use the word 'divyang' and make it popular. I hope that you will take this forward.

Sugamya Bharat

That day we started the 'Sugamya Bharat' campaign. Under this campaign, we will improve both the physical and virtual infrastructure, and make it accessible for the 'divyang' people. Be it schools, hospitals, government offices, bus depots, railway stations, amenities like ramps, accessible parking, accessible lifts, braille, will be made available. To make things Sugamya—we need innovation, we need technology, we need systems and we also need empathy from people. We have taken the initiative. We are receiving public participation too. You can also join in the manner you deem fit.

Schemes and Subsidies—Reaching Beneficiaries

My dear countrymen, government schemes will continue to exist and run but it is necessary that these schemes always remain operational. The schemes should be operational till the last individual has benefitted from them. They should not exist only in government files. After all, these schemes are meant for the common man, the poor people. In the past few days, the government has made an effort to ensure that the benefits of schemes reach out to the rightful owners. In our country, we give subsidy for gas cylinders. Crores of rupees were spent on it, but we did not know whether it reached the right people or not, and whether this subsidy reached people on time or not? The government has made some changes in the scheme. The government undertook the largest 'Direct Benefit Transfer Scheme' to provide subsidy directly in the bank accounts of the beneficiaries with the help of 'Jan Dhan Account' or the 'Aadhar Card'. I am happy to share with all of you the fact that this scheme has earned a place in the Guinness Book of World Records as the largest 'Direct Benefit Transfer Scheme' which has been implemented successfully. This scheme is known as '*Pahal*' and this experiment has been very successful. Till November end, around 15 crore LPG customers have become its beneficiaries. Government money is being directly transferred to the accounts of 15 crore beneficiaries. No middlemen, no need for recommendations, nor is there any possibility of corruption. On the one hand was the Aadhar Card Scheme, and on the other was the Jan Dhan Account. Thirdly, the state and the Government of India have compiled the lists of beneficiaries. That was connected to their account and Aadhar. This work is still in progress. Nowadays, even the MNREGA scheme which provides employment opportunities in villages is being connected to it. There were earlier lots of complaints about this scheme. In many places, the wages of the labourers are now being directly transferred into their accounts. There were complaints about student scholarships too. The amount for this too is being transferred into their accounts. This has been started and will be gradually taken forward. Till now, around 40,000 crore rupees has directly reached the beneficiaries through various schemes. According to my rough estimate, around 35-40 schemes are now under 'Direct Benefit Transfer.'

Our Constitution—The Fountainhead of our Rights and Duties

My dear countrymen, 26th of January is a golden moment in the life of Indian democracy. This is a beautiful coincidence that the 125th birth anniversary of Babasaheb Ambedkar, who is the maker of the Indian Constitution, will be celebrated this year. We organised a two day special discussion on the Constitution and it was a very good experience. All the parties and all the members deliberated on the sanctity of the Constitution, its importance, to understand the true interpretation of the Constitution. It was an excellent discussion. We should take this forward. Can Republic Day be an opportunity to connect the masses with the system, and the system with the masses? Our Constitution grants us several rights and there have been many discussions on it, as should be, as it is important. But the Constitution lays equal emphasis on duty also. However, it is seen that duties are hardly discussed. At the most, whenever there are elections, we see advertisements all around us, they write on the walls, and hoardings are put up to remind us that to vote is our sacred duty. There is a lot of talk about duties during elections but why not discuss our duties in life in general too. This year, when we are celebrating the 125th birth anniversary of Babasaheb Ambedkar, can we make 26th January a medium to organise debates, poetry, slogan competitions regarding duties in our schools, colleges, villages, cities and various organisations and societies. If 125 crore Indians take dutiful steps, one after the other, they can make history. But at least lets start with discussions. I have an idea: send an essay or poem about duty to me, before 26th January, in Hindi or English or your mother tongue language. I want to know your views. You can send them on my portal, 'MyGov'. I would like to know what the young generation thinks about its duties.

Cleanliness—A Voluntary Initiative

I want to make a small suggestion. On 26th January, we celebrate Republic Day. So, can we citizens, school and college students, take up the initiative of cleaning the statues of the great men that are installed in our city, and also clean the premises. We can undertake the best of cleanliness and the best of decoration on the occasion of 26th January. And I am not saying this on government lines. We become so emotional about getting the statues of great personalities erected, but become equally complacent when it comes to maintaining them. As a society, as a nation, can we make it a natural tendency to respect the statues of our great people? On this 26th January, let us make an effort that we will respect such great personalities, and keep their statues and surrounding premises clean. But this should be willingly done by citizens.

Dear countrymen, greetings to you for a Happy New Year 2016.

Thank you very much!

For listening to the audio, please log on to http://www.narendramodi.in/mann-ki-baat or scan the given QR code.

CHAPTER 16: January 2016

My beloved citizens, this is the first 'Mann Ki Baat' of 2016. 'Mann Ki Baat' has tied me with all of you in such a manner that if I see anything, or any thought comes to my mind, I feel like sharing it with all of you. I went to Rajghat yesterday to pay tribute to our beloved *Bapu*. This programme, to respect all the brave martyrs, is conducted every year. It is a great honour to be able to observe, a two minute silence exactly at 11 A.M. as a mark of respect for our brave martyrs. But there are many among us who would not have done this. Don't you think that such an attitude should be inculcated; we should consider it as our national responsibility. I know that this will not happen through a single 'Mann Ki Baat'. But if the entire nation observes silence on every 30 January at 11 A.M., you can imagine the energy that one single moment will generate. And these are the talks which provide motivation to live for the good of the country. You can imagine the strength this action will have within itself. And the correct message, as given by our Shastras:

> *We all should walk together, talk together, our hearts should be one.*

This is the true strength of a nation and these occasions give life essence to this strength.

The Khadi Revolution

My beloved citizens, a few days back, I was reading the ideas of Sardar Patel. I considered a few messages and I found his one particular message to be very interesting. In terms of Khadi, Sardar Patel has stated that:

> *The Freedom of India is in Khadi, the civilization of India is in Khadi. In India, we consider non-violence as our supreme religion that non-violence is in Khadi and the farmers of India, for whom you all show such spirit, their welfare is also in Khadi.*

Sardar Saheb had the habit of being straightforward in easy vernacular and he has explained the importance of Khadi very effectively. Yesterday on 30 January which is the day of Bapu's martyrdom. By means of a letter, I have tried to reach out to as many countrymen as possible on Khadi and Gramodyog. *Bapu* was an revered abider of technology, so I also made use of technology and tried to reach out to millions of our brothers and sisters. Khadi has now become a symbol, acquiring a different identity. It is also becoming the centre of attraction for the younger generation, especially for those who have a preference for holistic healthcare and organic products. For these people, it has become an excellent choice. In terms of fashion also, Khadi has made its own niche and I salute those connected with Khadi for trying to bring a new uniqueness in it. The market has its own importance in an economy. It has become important for Khadi to make a niche in the market. I asked people that when they have so many different kinds of fabrics then they should also have at least one in Khadi. People are slowly coming round to the idea that though they cannot become complete Khadi users, but since they already have ten other types of fabrics, one more can also be considered. Also, owing to my ideas, there is a positive approach emerging in the government. Many years ago, there was a very high usage of Khadi in the government. But slowly, in the name of technology, the usage of Khadi took a downward plunge and our poor people, who are connected to Khadi, lost their jobs. Khadi has the potential to provide employment to crores of people. A few days ago, many governmental institutions like the Railway Ministry, the Police department, Indian Navy, the Postal department of Uttarakhand, have taken good initiatives to increase the usage of Khadi and I have been told that as a result of these initiatives, the requirement generated will need an extra 18 lakh man hours from the people working in the Khadi industry. 18 lakh man hours-this will be a great leap in itself. Our revered *Bapu* was also conscious and appreciative about the upgradation of technology and that's why our looms upgraded and have been reached to where they are now. These days using the loom with the help of solar energy, linking solar energy to the loom has been a very successful experiment. Because of this, manual labour has reduced, productivity has increased and a qualitative transformation has been achieved. Especially for the solar loom. People regularly send me a lot of letters. Geeta Devi and Komal Devi from Dausa, Rajasthan and Sadhna Devi from Nawada district, Bihar have revealed in their letters, that there is a radical transformation in their lives because of the solar loom. Their sales have doubled and the market attraction towards their thread has also increased. All these talks help in enhancing motivation. And 30th January, when we remember revered *Bapu*, I will repeat this again that among all of the clothes we use there should be at least one made of Khadi, so that we appreciate Khadi.

Republic Day Celebrations

My beloved countrymen, the festival of 26 January was celebrated with much happiness and exaltation by all of us. Despite the concern of actions by of terrorists, all countrymen displayed gallantry and courage and celebrated the festival of democracy with fanfare and commotion. But a few people did things in a different manner and I would like to throw some light on these events, especially the exceptional experiment under taken by the states of Haryana and Gujarat. This year, to hoist and pay respects to our National Flag at the government school of every village, these states invited the most learned girl of that village. Haryana and Gujarat gave importance to the daughter. They tried to give an exemplary message of 'Save Daughter—Teach Daughter'. I admire and congratulate both the States for their imaginative thinking and I also congratulate the daughters who got the opportunity to hoist and pay respect to our National Flag. In Haryana, families, in which a girl was born in the last one year, were extended special invitations and were seated in the first row like a V.I.P. It was such an honourable moment in itself and I am so delighted that I started 'Save Daughter—Teach Daughter' campaign from Haryana because the sex ratio in Haryana was very unstable. The number of female child birth as compared to 1000 male child births was very less. It was a time of great worry, as the societal balance was in jeopardy. And when I chose Haryana, my delegates advised me against this by saying that the ambience was negative there. But I did my work and today I commend the people of Haryana with all my heart as they accepted this idea as their own and the number of female child births is rising at a great pace.

I truly appreciate the change in societal living that has been experienced in Haryana.

Protecting Our Statues

The last time in 'Mann Ki Baat', we discussed two ideas. Firstly, as citizens shouldn't we clean the statues of great people. When it comes to the installation of such statues we grow emotional but soon afterwards we become apathetic. Secondly, we discussed how we should emphasise our responsibility regarding the festival of democracy, how we should discuss responsibility. Many discussions have taken place regarding freedom and they will take place in future too, but discussions should also take place regarding responsibilities. I am delighted that at many places across the country, people have stepped forward, societal institutions have stepped forward, educational institutions have stepped forward, some holy people have also stepped forward and all of them have cleaned statues and their surroundings. It's a good beginning and this is not just a cleanliness campaign but also a campaign for respect. I am not mentioning everyone but the news that I have received has been very satisfactory. Some people don't provide news because they are shy. I request all such people to upload the photo of the statues cleansed by them, on my government portal, so that people from all around the world see them and feel proud of them. In a similar manner, on 26 January, I asked for people's opinion of on 'Responsibility and Freedom' and I am delighted that thousands of people have participated in that.

The Prime Minister Crop Insurance Scheme

My beloved fellow-citizens, I require your help in accomplishing one little work and I am sure you will help me. In our country, a lot is said and discussed in the name of the farmers. Nevertheless, I don't want to get entangled in these disputes. But one of the biggest crises that a farmer faces is natural calamity, which destroys all the hard work done by him. His year is ruined. Only one way comes to mind so that farmers can be ensured safety and that is Crop Insurance plan. In 2016, the Indian Government has given a very big gift to the farmers –'Prime Minister Crop Insurance Scheme'. But this plan is not for praising, applauding, a congratulating the Prime Minister. For so many years Crop Insurance has been under discussion but not more than 20-25 per cent farmers have been able to gain from it. Farmers in general have not been able to get attach to it. Can we take the resolution to cover at least 50 percent of the nation's farmers under Crop Insurance? Here, I need your help. If the farmer binds himself with crop insurance, it provides him with a big help in the time of crises. This time the 'Prime Minister Crop Insurance Plan' has been accepted on a large scale by the people because it's broad, it's easy, the technology input has been great and not only that, it has even promised help if nothing happens even after 15 days of the crop harvest. How to speed up the process of receiving money from insurance without delay, using technology, all these things have been taken into consideration. And the best thing is that the crop insurance premium's interest has been lowered to such an extent that nobody, probably, even thought of it. According to the new Insurance programme, the maximum premium for the farmers of the Kharif crop will be 2 percent and for the Rabi crop will be 1.5 percent. Now tell me if any of my farmer brother does not get this, won't it be a loss? You may not be a farmer, but you are still listening to my thoughts. Will you transmit my words/ thoughts to the farmers? And here is why I want you to advertise this as this time I have brought a scheme even for you. I want that my, Prime Minister's Crop Insurance Scheme, thought/talk should reach the people. And it is correct that you listen to my 'Mann Ki Baat' on the T.V. or radio. But what if you want to hear it later? Now I am here to give you a new gift, so that you can listen to my 'Mann Ki Baat' even on your mobile phone and that too, whenever you want. All you have to do is give a missed call from your mobile phone. The mobile phone number selected for this is 8190881908, i.e., Eight one nine zero eight eight one nine zero eight. You can give a missed call and after that you can listen to 'Mann Ki Baat' anytime. For the time being, it is available only in Hindi, but quite soon, 'Mann Ki Baat' will also be available to you in your own mother tongue/language. For this, the process is already underway.

The Start-up Programme

My beloved youngsters, you have done something amazing. When the 'start-up' programme was held on 16 January, I felt a new wave of energy, enthusiasm, hope and happiness. Lakhs of people registered to come to that programme. Even though most of you could not come because of paucity of space, as the programme was held at the Science Hall, you have all still participated for the full event online. It rarely happens that lakhs of people/youth stay connected to any one programme for hours. But this happened. And I was seeing what hope 'start-up' has. But there is one thing, a common man thinks that 'start-up' means I.T. related talks and is a very sophisticated industry. But after this event, that misconception is gone. I.T. related start-ups are just a very small part of it. Life is very large, necessities are immeasurable. 'Start-up' also brings limitless opportunities.

A few days back, I had gone to Sikkim-which is now an organic State and there I had invited agriculture ministers and scientists from all over the country. I had the opportunity to meet two young people there, both Indian Institute of Management graduates—Anurag Agarwal and Siddhi Karnani. They went for the 'start-up' and I met them in Sikkim. They both work in the Northeast in the field of agriculture, and grow herbal and organic products. They do global marketing for these products. Now that is something.

The last time I told people connected with my 'start-up', that they should send their experiences on the 'Narendra Modi App'. Many have sent, but I will be happy if more such experiences come in, however, the ones that have come in are really inspiring. There is this young man, Vishwas Dwivedi who has an online kitchen start-up and provides tiffin service to the middle class people, who come for their bread-and-butter. There is one Mr Dinesh Pathak. He has made up his mind to work on providing food to farmers, especially for the cattle, animal food. If the animals of our country get good food, only then will we get good milk. Only then will the youth of the country become strong. Manoj Gilda, Mr Nikhil, have started an Agri-Storage start-up, which is developing a Bulk Storage System with a Scientific Fruit Storage System for the farmer's produce. This means that a lot of new ideas have come. Do send me more. I feel good and I will have to talk about 'start-up' in 'Mann ki Baat' again and again. Just like I talk about cleanliness every time, I will talk about 'Start-up' also because your struggle is my strength.

Cleanliness

My beloved citizens/countrymen, 'cleanliness' is now being connected with 'beauty'. For years we have shown disapproval of pollution but pollution didn't go. Now people have stopped talking about pollution and have started talking about cleanliness and somewhere or the other, some work is being done on cleanliness. But now people are getting one step ahead. They have linked cleanliness with beauty. This is most evident at railway stations and it is seen that in a number of railway stations across the country, local people, local artists, students are decorating the city railway stations. Keeping the local art in consideration, walls are being painted, sign boards are being made in a better way by using an artistic outlook. Such things are being incorporated there to make people aware. I have been told that at Hazaribagh railway station, tribal women have decorated the full station with local vase and Kohabar. More than 300 volunteers from Thane District have decorated King Circle station, Matunga, Borivali, Khar. News is also coming in from Sawai Madhopur, Kota, Rajasthan. It looks like our railway stations have become the identity of our culture/tradition. Now people will not have to peep outside the coach windows for tea and snacks carts, but look at the walls to see the local specialties/delicacies just sitting in the train. This was not an initiation by the railways or by Narendra Modi. This was by the locals. Look at how the locals do it. I am looking at some of the photos received but my heart wants to see more. Can you, who have done undertaken some cleanliness drives along with beautification at railway stations or anywhere else, send me some photos. Do send them. I will see them, others will also see them and be inspried. What has happened at railway stations, can also happen at bus stations, also in hospitals, in schools, around temples, in parks and gardens as well. So much can happen. Everyone, who have thought of this and who have started it and who have taken it ahead, should be congratulated. But yes, you need to send me more photos. I also want to see what you have done.

International Fleet Review

My fellow citizen/countrymen, it is a matter of pride that in the first week of February, from 4th to 8th, India shall be a major host for a major event. The whole world will come here as our guest and our Navy is making full preparations for this event. Submarines and Navy ships from many countries around the world will gather at the Visakhapatnam Seaport in Andhra Pradesh. The International Fleet Review will take place at an Indian sea port. This is a competition between the world's armed forces versus the Indian armed forces. It is a big opportunity. You will get information on television and media in the coming few days because this is a very big event and everyone is supporting it. It is important for a country like India because Indian history at sea has always been glorious. The ocean is called *Udra* or *Saga*r in Sanskrit, it means endless/infinite. Borders may divide us, land may separate us, but the ocean joins us. We can join each other with the ocean. We can join with anyone. Our ancestors, centuries ago, showed us that power, when they undertook explorations at sea, carried on world trade via sea. Be it Chhatrapati Shivaji or the Chola dynasty, they made a big name when it came to sea power. There are a number of states with traditions connected to the sea that are still alive and are celebrated in the form of festivals. When the world will be a guest the India Navy will show its power. For everyone to see this is a very good opportunity. I will also be honoured to be present on this special occasion.

South Asian Games, 2016

SAARC (South Asian Association for Regional Cooperation) countries are as it is at the games festival at the eastern end of India in Guwahati. Thousands of players from the SAARC countries are coming to Guwahati. The excitement of the games; the grand celebration of the new generation of the SAARC countries is to happen in Guwahati, Assam. This is also a good opportunity to have new ties with the SAARC countries.

My beloved countrymen, I have told you earlier that whatever comes in my mind, whatever I feel, I share it with you. We will be beginning with the 10th and 12th standards' board examinations soon. The last time on 'Mann Ki Baat' I had talked to students about exams. This time I want to know about the success that the students have achieved and their tension free exam days, what was the atmosphere in the family, what was the role of teachers, what were your own efforts, what did the seniors tell you to do? These must be good experiences. What we can do this time is that you send me your experiences on the Narendra Modi App and I will request the media to broadcast all the good experiences in the coming months of February and March, so that students countrywide can know them, watch it on T.V. and they also know the secrets of taking tension free exams and I am sure that my friends from the media, will definitely help in this work. But they will only do this, if all of you send in your inputs.

Promise me, you will send them in.

Thank you very much friends. We will meet once again on 'Mann Ki Baat' next month.

Thank you.

Jai Hind.

For listening to the audio, please log on to http://www.narendramodi.in/mann-ki-baat or scan the given QR code.

CHAPTER 17: February 2016

Fellow citizens, Namaskar!

You might be listening to 'Mann Ki Baat' on the radio, but you would be occupied with your children's exams which begin tomorrow. For Class 10th and 12th, the exams start from March 1. I too want to join this journey of yours. I am as much concerned about the exams of your children as you are. If we change our attitude towards exams, probably we will be relieved of anxiety.

In the last edition of 'Mann Ki Baat', I had requested you to share your experiences and suggestions on the Narendra Modi App. I am glad that thousands of people have shared their views with me. These include teachers, successful students, parents and social thinkers. Two things have touched me especially. First, all those who have written to me, have stuck to the subject. Second, thousands of people shared their views. It is a reflection of how important the issue is. We have restricted exams to school premises, students and parents. A large number of views shared on my App show that student-related issues should be discussed continuously across the country.

In this edition of 'Mann Ki Baat', I want to discuss something with students, parents and teachers. I will share whatever I have heard, read and have been told. I will also share my thoughts and I feel that 25-30 minutes discussion will be very useful for the students appearing in the exams.

Sachin Tendulkar's Success Mantra

My dear student friends, before I say something why not open this edition of 'Mann Ki Baat' with the batting maestro, Sachin Tendulkar. Let's find out what made him successful. His experience will certainly help you. I want you to listen to the message sent by the pride of Indian youth and Bharat Ratna Shri Sachin Tendulkar:

> *Namaskar! This is Sachin Tendulkar. I know exams are going to start in a few days, some of you may be tense. I have a message for you. Your parents, teachers, family members and friends will expect many things from you. Everybody will ask about your preparations and expected marks. I just want to say that you set targets for yourself and do not buckle under any pressure. Work hard and set a realistic and achievable target for yourself. When I used to play cricket, there were innumerable expectations from me also. Over the past 24 years, many difficult moments came. Some nice moments were there as well. Public expectation was always there and it increased with the passage of time. I found a way to deal with it. I decided to set my own targets and to achieve them. If I set my own targets and achieve them, then I am doing something good for the country. I have always tried to achieve those targets. My focus was on the ball and targets were achieved automatically. Please keep your thoughts positive which will definitely yield positive results. Hence, be positive and by God's grace you can always expect best results. My best wishes for your exams. Write your exams in a tension-free manner and come out with flying colours. Good luck!*

Friends, see what advice Sachin Tendulkar has for you. Never get bogged down under the pressure of expectations. You have to build your own future. Set targets for yourself with a free heart, free thinking and free capability. I am sure that Sachin's advice will help you a lot. And it is true; why waste our time in competing with others? Why not compete with ourselves? Why not try to break our own earlier records? You will see that nobody will be able to stop you from going forward. You will not expect any praise from anyone when you will break your own record. You will be satisfied internally.

Friends, do not consider exams as a number game. Life should be linked with great purposes. We should pursue our dreams and stay focused. Exams only tell us, whether we are treading the right path or not and is it with the right pace or not. Therefore, if dreams are big, this exam will become enjoyable. Every exam is a step towards achieving that great purpose. Every success will become a key to achieving that great purpose. Therefore, do not limit yourself to what will happen in this year's exam. Work with a much bigger purpose. Even if you fall short a little, you will not feel disappointed. You will get more courage to achieve that purpose.

People have shared their views on my App. One Mr Shrey Gupta has emphasised that a healthy mind resides in a healthy body. Students should take care of their health also along with their studies. So that you can write exams while you are in good health. On this last day, I will not ask you to exercise or run for three or five kilometers. But your routine, especially during exams, is important. During all 365 days, our routine should be according to our dreams and commitments. I agree with what Shri Prabhakar Reddy has said. He has suggested that students should sleep on time and should do their revisions after getting up early. Students should reach the examination centre before time, with their admit cards and other essential things. Shri Prabhakar Reddy has said this and I may not have said this, because I am a little unconcerned about sleep. My friends also keep telling me that I sleep very less. I will try to do something about it. But I definitely agree with this. Stipulated time to sleep and a sound sleep are as important as your other day-to-day activities. And this is possible. I am fortunate that I sleep less, but have a very sound sleep. And it is also enough for me. But I have one request. Some people have a habit of talking on the phone for a long time before sleeping and those thoughts occupy their mind, so how will they really sleep? When I ask you to sleep, I am not asking you to sleep only for exams. To perform well in exams, I am asking you to sleep, tension-free. I am not asking you to keep sleeping. It shouldn't happen that when you score less and your mother asks you the reason, you say that Modi ji was the one who asked me to sleep and so I slept. I really hope you will not do that!

Discipline is the Foundation of Success

In life, discipline is a big reason for success. It provides a strong foundation. Unorganised and indisciplined people, who complete their day's work in the evening, think that they have done the job, but so much of energy is wasted and much tension lingers on every moment. In case of our body also, even if one part of it is paining, the whole body feels uncomfortable. Not only that, our routine also gets disturbed. And that is why, we should not consider any thing as small. You should never compromise on your decisions. Decide and try to do it.

Friends, I have seen two types of students who appear in exams. One type is where students concentrate on their strengths and learning. The second type is of students who doubt their abilities and worry too much about their question paper. You would have seen these two types of people. Concern about the question paper, has a negative impact on one's results too. The one, who is confident about whatever he has learnt, is able to handle anything that comes up.

Viswanathan Anand's Words of Wisdom

Someone who can say this better than me is chess champion Shri Viswanathan Anand. He will share his experiences and tell you how to checkmate in exams:

> *Hello, this is Viswanathan Anand. First of all, let me start off by wishing you all the best for your exams. I will now talk a little bit about how I went to my exams and my experiences for that. I found that exams are very much like problems you face later in life. You need to be well rested, get a good night's sleep, you need to be on a full stomach, you should definitely not be hungry and the most important thing is to stay calm. It is very similar to a game of chess. When you play, you don't know, which pawn will appear, just like in a class you don't know, which question will appear in an exam. So if you stay calm and you are well nourished and have slept well, then you will find that your brain recalls the right answer at the right moment. So stay calm. It is very important not to put too much pressure on yourself; don't keep your expectations too high. Just see it as a challenge—do I remember what I was taught during the year, can I solve these problems. At the last minute, just go over the most important things, and the topics you feel that you don't remember very well. You may also recall some incidents with the teacher or the students; while you are writing an exam and this will help you recall a lot of subject matter. If you revise the questions you find difficult, you will find that they are fresh in your head and when you are writing the exam, you will be able to deal with them much better. So stay calm, get a good night's sleep, don't be over-confident but don't be pessimistic either. I have always found that the exams go much better than you fear. So stay confident and all the very best to you!*

Viswanathan Aṇand has said a very important thing and you would also have seen him playing international matches in good health. He plays with so much concentration and stays focussed. We used to hear about Arjuna, how he used to concentrate on the bird's eye. Similarly, Viswanathan Anand's eyes are fixed on his target when he plays and that is the expression of his inner peace. It is difficult to say whether we will get inner peace just by someone's words. But we should strive for that, smilingly. Even during the exams, if we smile and laugh, we will start experiencing the inner peace. You can't have inner peace when you are not talking to friends and walking alone, trying to read so many books at the last moment. Laugh with your friends. Share jokes. You will feel a peaceful environment around you, automatically.

Peaceful Mind Leads to Successful Exams

I want to share a small thing with you. Just imagine, you are standing near a pond and have a nice view of the water, but suddenly, if someone throws a stone in it! Now, the nice view which you were enjoying will not be there anymore. If water is still, no matter how deep the things are, they look clear. But, if the water is not still, then nothing is visible inside. There is a lot inside you, like the labour done by you, the whole year. But if your mind is not at peace, then you can't find that treasure. If you have a peaceful mind, then you will be able to use your treasure of knowledge and the exams will become very easy.

I want to tell you something about myself. When I go to attend some lecture or in the government also, there are subjects on which I need to concentrate. When I try to understand by concentrating more, then I feel an inner pressure. Then I realise that I need to relax a bit. So I developed a technique of deep breathing and so I take three to five deep breaths. It takes me around 30, 40 or 50 seconds, but then my mind becomes calm and ready to understand the matter. This is my experience and it may work for you too.

Shri Rajat Aggarwl has written a good thing on my App. He said, we should relax with friends and family for at least half an hour every day. This is a very important thing said by Shri Rajat. Most of the times, when we come back from the exam, we start calculating about right and wrong answers. And if parents are educated and more so, if they are teachers, then they ask the exact questions. They calculate whether you will score 40, 80 or 90 marks. Your mind is still entangled in the exam that is already over. You also share with your friends, the answers in the question paper and we get entangled only in that. Friends, please do not do this. Once an exam is over, it's over. Chat with your family on other subjects, remember old memories. Try to remember the scenes of a location you had visited with your parents. Spend half an hour on this. What Shri Rajat has said is absolutely correct.

Friends, what can I tell you about peace? Today, before you take your exams, one such person has sent you his message; someone, who is himself a teacher. He teaches us the values of life. By interpreting the *Ramcharitmanas* in the present context, he teaches us values. He is revered as Morari *Bapu*, He has given some important tips for you. He is a teacher and a thinker as well, therefore his words have a combination of both:

> *I am Morari Bapu speaking. My advice to all students is that at the time of examination you unburden your mind and with a clear, calm and concentrated mind take the exam. And then accept whatever situation comes. My view is that by accepting the situation as it is, we can be more happy and peaceful. Take the exam with a light and calm mind, you will get sure success, you will not feel guilty if you fail*

and not feel arrogant if you succeed. I end with a couplet 'It is not necessary for everybody to have success in this world, learn to live with failures'. I thank our honourable Prime Minister's programme 'Mann Ki Baat'. I wish all of you the best.

I am grateful to our revered Morari *Bapu* for his inspiring message. Friends, I want to talk about one issue. In their responses, people have invariably mentioned about yoga. It is a matter of satisfaction for me that when I meet people from different countries, a mention of yoga always comes up, may be briefly. I feel proud that there is so much curiosity about yoga. So many people have, Shri Atanu Mandal, Shri Kunal Gupta, Shri Shashank Kumar, Shri KG Anand, Shri Abhijeet Kulkarni, and other innumerable people have referred to yoga and meditation on my mobile App. I do not say that you start practicing yoga from tomorrow. That will be injustice to you; however, those who practice it should not stop doing it just because of exams. However, it is true that, be it one's student life or the latter part of one's life, yoga is an important key for the development of one's conscience. And it is a key which is most accessible and simple. You should definitely think about it. If you search around yourself and find a yoga teacher, they can definitely suggest a few things which you can practice for a few minutes and which will benefit you during exams. See if you can. I have great faith in it.

Let's not Rush

My young friends, you are in great hurry to enter the examination hall. You want to take your seat quickly. Why do you do this in a hurry? Why should you not manage your time in such a manner that even if you are stuck in traffic, you will still reach on time for the exam. Otherwise, the hurry adds to the tension. You should read the instructions for the question paper very carefully. Sometimes we think it is a waste of time, but it is not the case. Let it take 2 minutes, 3 minutes, 4 minutes, but read the instructions very carefully. You will clearly know what is to be done and it will ensure that you do everything properly and you will not have to regret later. I have observed that sometimes one comes to know only during the exam that there is a new pattern, but if you read instructions carefully, you will be able to cope with it. So please read the instructions very carefully.

Mr Yash Nagar has written on my App that when he saw the paper for the first time, it appeared very difficult. However, after the second look, it appeared easy to him. Questions were the same as those which he knew, only they were asked differently. It is very essential to understand the question. Sometimes when we do not understand the question properly, they appear difficult to us. I emphasise this view of Yash Nagar. Read the questions several times and try to match your knowledge with them. You will see that the question will appear easy, even before you attempt it.

Professor CNR Rao's Message of Patience

It is a matter of great happiness to me today that Bharat Ratna and renowned scientist Professor CNR Rao has stressed on 'patience'. He has given a brief, yet a very effective message, to all students. Let us listen to the message of Sri Rao:

> *This is CNR Rao from Bangalore. I fully realise that examinations cause anxiety. That too, competitive examinations. Do not worry, do your best. That's what I tell all my young friends. At the same time remember, that*

there are many opportunities in this country. Decide what you want to do in life and don't give it up. You will succeed. Do not forget that you are a child of the universe. You have a right to be here like the trees and the mountains. All you need is doggedness, dedication and tenacity. With these qualities, you will succeed in all examinations and all other endeavours. I wish you luck in everything you want to do. God Bless!

See how amazing is the way of expression of a scientist? For which I take half an hour, he took only three minutes to communicate. This is the strength of science and a scientific mind. I am very thankful to Mr Rao for inspiring the children of the country. What he has highlighted are the qualities of dedication, determination, diligence. Remain steadfast friends, if you do not give up, fear will run away. For achieving good things, a bright future awaits you.

Seeds of Success

In my App, Ruchika Dabas has sent a message, sharing her exam experience. She said that in her family, there is a conscious effort to create a positive environment during examinations. Similar efforts were made in her neighbouring families too. And this was emphasised by Mr Sachin Tendulkar also, that a positive approach and a positive frame of mind, gives rise to positive energy.

Sometimes many things happen, which inspire us. And please don't think that they help only students. In every phase of life, good examples, give us strength, inspiration and show us the way out of troubles. We have all read about Thomas Alva Edison, the inventor of electric bulb. Have you ever thought how many years he devoted to achieve this feat? How many times he faced failures, how much time was wasted, how much money was spent, how frustrated he must have felt due to repeated failures? But today, the electric bulb is illuminating our lives. That is why it is said that 'seeds of success are inherent within failures'.

Who doesn't know Srinivasa Ramanujan—one of the greatest mathematical minds of the modern world? You will know that he did not have any formal training in mathematics and still made great contributions towards the fields of mathematical analogies and number theory. His was a life filled with pain and sorrow, and he still made a great contribution to the world.

JK Rowling is a brilliant example of the fact that anybody can achieve success anytime. The 'Harry Potter series' is now popular all over the world, but it was not the case in the beginning. Imagine how many difficulties she had to face, and how many failures. Rowling herself has said that in the times of crisis she used to focus her entire energy on the job which was most meaningful to her.

Nowadays, exams are not merely for students, but they are a test of the whole family, teachers and schools as well. However, without the support system of parents and teachers, it is difficult for a student to cope with such pressure alone. If students, parents, teachers and even seniors work as a team and proceed in a planned manner, examinations become easier.

Mr Keshav Vaishnav has written on my App, he has complained that parents must never pressurise their children to attain more marks. They should merely encourage them to prepare well and should be concerned about keeping them relaxed.

Vijay Jindal writes that our own expectations must never be imposed on children. Children must be encouraged as much as possible and they must be helped to maintain their confidence. Please do not pressurise children. Do not stop him from talking to his friends;

do create a lighter, positive environment and you will see your children grow in confidence. This confidence will be visible to you as well.

Innovative Changes

Friends, I want to tell it to our young friends—our lives have significantly changed from the previous generations. We are witnessing every moment, a new innovation, new technology and a new face of science. The best part is we are not merely dazzled by all this and rather want to move ahead in tandem with the pace of science.

I am highlighting this point because it is the National Science Day today. Every year we celebrate it as the national festival of science. On 28 February 1928, Sir CV Raman had announced his famous discovery, 'the Raman Effect', for which he won the Nobel Prize. Therefore, the country celebrates 28 February as the National Science Day. Curiosity is the mother of science. Every mind should have a scientific temperament and the quest for science. Each generation will have to lay emphasis on innovation. And innovation is not possible without science and technology. On National Science Day, let us resolve to make science and technology an essential part of our lives. This year, the theme on the National Science Day is, 'Make in India—Science and Technology Driven Innovations'. I bow to Sir CV Raman and appeal to all of you to inculcate scientific temper.

Friends, sometimes success comes very late and when the person is successful, his views about the world also change. You may have been busy preparing for exams and some news events might not have registered in your minds. I still want to repeat a story which you must have heard recently, that a great discovery has been made in the field of science. Scientists of the world worked relentlessly, several generations of them contributed, including our own scientists who discovered the gravitational waves. It is a very far reaching achievement in the field of science. The discovery not only proves the theory of Albert Einstein, but is also a quantum leap for physics. This is indeed a great achievement for entire mankind and also a matter of great pride for us, since many Indians were involved in this discovery. I want to extend my heartiest congratulations to all these scientists. In the future too, our scientists will work towards consolidating such gains and in all the other international scientific endeavours. We have recently taken an important decision to set up LIGO—Laser Interferometer Gravitational Wave Observatory in India. There are only two such laboratories in the world and India will be the third country. The process will gather momentum with the involvement of India. Despite its meagre resources, India will definitely be an active partner in the endeavour of great importance for mankind. I once again congratulate all the scientists.

Mann Ki Baat in Regional Languages

Fellow citizens, I want you to note down a number. From tomorrow, if you give a missed call to this number, you can listen to my 'Mann Ki Baat' in your regional language. The number is 8190881908. I repeat 8190881908.

Friends, your exams are going to start; I too have to appear in an examination tomorrow before 125 crore countrymen. Don't you remember! Tomorrow is 29 February, the Budget Day. Still, you must have noticed by my voice, how calm and confident I am. Let my exam get over tomorrow and yours begin day after.

Wish me success and let all of us come out with flying colours, so that our country succeeds. Friends, my best wishes to all of you. Move ahead without the tension of failure or success. Do not give up. Thank you.

For listening to the audio, please log on to http://www.narendramodi.in/mann-ki-baat or scan the given QR code.

CHAPTER 18: March 2016

My dear fellow citizens,

Let me begin by wishing 'Namaskar' to all of you. Today, Christians are celebrating Easter the world over. I extend my warmest greetings to one and all on this occasion of Easter.

Some of my young friends must be busy with their examinations and some of them must have now gotten free. For those of you who still have exams, it must be a testing time with the exams on one hand and the T20 Cricket World Cup on the other. I am sure you are eagerly waiting for the match between India and Australia this evening.

I congratulate team India for their twin successes against Pakistan and Bangladesh. We are seeing a fine momentum building up in this T20 Cricket World Cup. Today, I convey my best wishes to India and Australia for a big match in the evening.

Ushering Revolutionary Changes in Sports

With the young comprising 65% of our population, there should be no reason why we should be away from the world of sports. This will not do. We need to usher in revolutionary changes in sports. We can see that happening in India, like cricket, there's now increasing interest in football, hockey, tennis and kabaddi as well.

It is really a wonderful feeling to inform you all that India will be hosting the FIFA Under-17 World Cup next year. Twenty-four teams from all over the world are coming to play in our country. The Indian Football team won the gold medal at the Asian Games in 1951 and 1962, and secured fourth position in the 1956 Olympics. Unfortunately, over the decades, we have slipped from there to the lowest rank. Today, our ranking in FIFA is so low that I feel hesitant to even mention it.

On the other hand, I have been noticing that an interest in football, among the Indian youth, has been on the rise—be it for the English Premier League, the Spanish League or the Indian Super League matches. Young Indians take time out to get the latest information on these matches and watch them on television. What I mean to say is, given this increasing popular interest in football and the opportunity of hosting the FIFA Under-17 World Cup, shall we just play the role of a host and fulfil our responsibility? Or shall we use the opportunity to our advantage to promote sports?

We should create an atmosphere of football all around, through out the year, in schools, colleges, indeed, all over India. Our youth, the children in our schools, should be sweating by just playing football. If that happens, we shall have real fun playing the host. So, all of us should endeavour to ensure football reaches every village, boulevard and alley. Till the commencement of the FIFA Under-17 World Cup in 2017, we should infuse a spirit of enthusiasm in the youth. One advantage of playing the host for this event is that a whole lot of infrastructure will get created with the addition of sports facilities. But I personally shall be content when we are able to link every youth of our country with this game.

Friends, I would like to hear your views on how best to use the 2017 FIFA Under-17 World Cup to our advantage. How should this event be? What kind of programmes should we organise the whole year to facilitate the event gain impetus? How should it be publicised? What improvements do we need to bring in? How can we augment interest of our youth in sports through the 2017 FIFA Under-17 World Cup?

How can we initiate an element of competitiveness in governments, educational institutes and social organisations to associate with the game?

We can see all this happening in relation to cricket; but we should now endeavour to bring these elements in relation to other sports as well. The FIFA event offers us a unique opportunity to do so. Can you send me your suggestions on how best to use this opportunity? I view the FIFA event as a great opportunity to establish India as a global brand; an opportunity to let the world know of India's youth power—not in terms of winning or losing a match. In the run-up to and preparation for the 2017 FIFA event, we can harness and display our varied strengths; while doing so, we can do image-branding for India as well.

I look forward to your suggestions on the 2017 FIFA Under-17 World Cup, which you can send me through the Narendra Modi App. Do let me know what should be the logo and the slogans. How should we propagate this event throughout India? What should the songs be like? What should be in the souvenirs? Ponder on it friends. I would like every youth to become an ambassador for the 2017 FIFA Under-17 World Cup. You should vigorously participate in this event. It's a golden chance to build India's image.

Role of Travel in Shaping Our Lives

My dear students, you must have thought of travelling to places during holidays. Very few go abroad; most people visit places within their own States for a week or so. Some people also go outside their States. Last time too, I had requested all of you to upload photographs of the places you visit. And I have noticed that the kind of work which our Department of Tourism, Department of Culture, State Governments and the Government of India cannot do has been accomplished by millions and millions of Indian tourists. Photos of such magnificent places were uploaded that it was truly a delight to view them.

We have to take this task forward. Do it this time as well. But this time, along with a photo, please write and send a few lines about the place you visit, thus displaying your creative prowess. One gets to learn a lot by visiting new places. Things we cannot learn in a classroom, within our family, from our friends, can be learnt by travelling. We experience something fresh with each new place we visit—we learn about people, their languages, foods and lifestyles. Someone has rightly said, "A traveller without observation is a bird without wings". "If you have a desire to truly view, you should also develop an insight." India is full of diversities. Once you set out to see the country, for the rest of your life you will keep seeing new things and still never get enough of it. I have been fortunate that I had a lot of opportunities to travel. I travelled a lot when I was neither the Chief Minister nor the Prime Minster, and was only a youngster like you. There is hardly a district in India which I have not visited.

Travel plays a very strong role in shaping our lives. Now-a-days India's youth is being driven by a spirit of adventure and curiosity. Unlike before, they do not want to go to the places they have already visited or tread the oft beaten track. They want to do something new, see something new. I see this as a good sign. Our youth should be bold. They should be brave. They should have the courage to set foot on places where no one has been before.

In this context, I would like to specially congratulate Coal India. Western Coalfields Limited at Savaner near Nagpur, where there are coal mines, has developed an Eco-friendly Mine-Tourism Circuit. Generally we do not think of coal mines as places worth visiting. Pictures of mines make us wonder what it must be like out there. We even have a saying, "Coal blackens your hands", and hence people tend to stay away from coal mines. But Western Coalfields Limited has made these same coal mines a destination for tourism. Though this is only the beginning, but nearly 10,000 people have already visited this Eco-friendly Mine-Tourism site at Savaner near Nagpur. This in itself gives us an opportunity to see something new.

I hope that when you set out on a journey during the coming holidays you can contribute something to cleanliness too. Now there is greater awareness about cleanliness and people are making an effort to keep tourism destinations litter-free. Both tourists and local residents of these places are contributing to it. Maybe it is not being done in a very scientific way, but it is being done. Can you too, being a tourist, lay stress on cleanliness at tourist destinations? I am confident that our youth will definitely help me in this task.

Tourism is a sector that provides maximum employment. Even the poorest person gets a chance to earn from tourism. When tourists visit a place, even the not-so-well-off among them spend money, and rich tourists are bound to spend more. There are many employment opportunities created by tourism.

Compared to other nations, India lags far behind in tourism. But if we, 125 crore Indians, decide to give importance to tourism sector, we can certainly attract the world, draw tourists in large numbers to our side and thereby, can provide new employment avenues to several million young Indians. Be it the government, institutions, society, citizens—we all have to come together to make this happen. Come, let's make an endeavour in this direction.

Enhancing One's Personality in Holidays

My dear young friends, I do not like the holidays being just frittered away. You too should think along these lines. Will you let your holidays during the most important years of your life slip away just like that? I will give you something to ponder upon. Can you resolve to add one skill, one special attribute to your personality, during your holidays? If you do not know how to swim, can you resolve to learn swimming during the holidays? If you do not know how to cycle, can you resolve to learn cycling during the holidays? Or you could tell yourself, "I type with just two fingers on the keyboard, so shouldn't I learn the proper way of typing?" There are so many skills to develop our personality. Why not learn them? Why not overcome some of our shortcomings? Why not add to our strengths? Do give it a thought.

It is not like you need lots of classes, a great trainer, hefty fees or a big budget for this. You can find something around you. Let's say you decide to make the 'best' out of 'waste'. Just look for some waste material and start creating something from it. You will enjoy it. By the time evening falls, you will marvel at what you have created from that rubbish. Suppose you are fond of painting and you do not know how to paint, just start painting and gradually you will get better at it. You must spend your holidays on building your personality by developing some new talent, acquiring some new skill. There can be countless areas where you could do so; it is not as if these are confined only to the ones that I am spelling out for you. This will help you in carving out your own identity and raising your self-confidence tremendously. Just try it for yourself. When you return to school or college and tell your classmates about what you learned during the holidays, and when your friends find that they have not learned anything new, they will realise that they wasted their time. They will have a high regard for you and say, "You are a very determined man, my friend, you have accomplished something concrete." This may perhaps emerge to be a big thing among friends. I am confident that you will surely do it and, yes, do share with me what you have learned.

Suggestions received on MyGov.in

This time a lot of suggestions have come for 'Mann Ki Baat' on www.mygov.in. Here is one such:

> *My name is Abhi Chaturvedi. Namaste dear Prime Minister, you had said during the last summer holidays that even birds feel the summer heat so we should fill a bowl with water and place it in the balcony or the terrace so that birds can come to have water. I did this and enjoyed it and in this way I made friends with a lot of birds. I request you to repeat this task in Mann Ki Baat. Thank You.*

My dear fellow citizens, I would like to express my gratitude to this little boy, Abhi. He called me up and reminded me of what I had said. Frankly, I had forgotten about it. And I did not have it in my mind that I would say something on this topic, but Abhi has reminded me that last year I had asked you to put an earthen bowl filled with water for the birds.

Friends, I want to thank this boy, Abhi Chaturvedi. He has reminded me of a good deed by calling me up. Last summer I had remembered it and asked you to put water in earthen bowls for the birds during summers. Abhi has told me that he has been doing this for a whole year and many birds have now become his friends. The great Hindi poetess Mahadevi Verma used to love birds. She wrote this in one of her poems, "We shall not let you fly far way, we shall fill the courtyard with grains and fill the tank with sweet and cool water..." Come, let us also do what Mahadevi ji used to do. I greet Abhi and thank him for reminding me of this very important thing.

Shilpa Kukke from Mysore has raised a very humane issue. She says milkmen, newspaper vendors, postmen come close to our homes. Sometimes utensil hawkers and cloth sellers too pass by our homes. Have we ever offered them water to drink during the summer days? Shilpa, I am very grateful to you that you have articulated something so sensitive in so simple a manner. It is a small gesture but when the postman comes and we offer him water, he will feel good. Of course, it is a part of our nature in India. But I am glad, Shilpa, that you have observed these things.

Kisan Suvidha App

My dear farmer brothers and sisters, you must have repeatedly heard the term—Digital India. Some people feel that Digital India is meant for the world of the youth in our cities. No, it's not so. You will be happy to learn that a 'Kisan Suvidha App' has been launched to cater to your interests. If you download this 'Kisan Suvidha App' on your mobile phone, you will receive a lot of agriculture and weather related information. On this App there are many topics, such as what is the state of the market, what is the position of the wholesale market, which crops are doing well these days, which are the appropriate pesticides. Not just this. There is a button on the App which will connect you directly with agricultural scientists and link you with the experts. If you pose a question to them, they will reply to it; they will explain things to you. I hope that my farmer brothers and sisters will download the 'Kisan Suvidha App' on their mobile phones. Why don't you have a look at this gift for you and give it a try to see if something in it is of use to you? If you feel it lacks in anything, you can complain to me also.

Campaign for Water Conservation

My dear farmer brothers and sisters, summer, a holiday for others, is the time for you to sweat it out even more. A farmer waits for the rains and before that, he pours in his life and soul to ready his field so that not even a single drop of rain water goes waste. For farmers, the season just before the onset of farming is of utmost importance. We will have to give a thought to what will happen if there's no water. Can we not utilise this time to visit ponds, check routes through which water flows into these ponds and spot the places where garbage or something else blocks the water from flowing, because of which reservoirs get depleted. Cannot we remove the blockage and clean the inlets so that more water collects? If we manage to save and collect more water during the first rainfall and fill up our ponds, rivers and streams, then even if rains fail later, our losses will be reduced. But this can be possible only when we conserve each and every drop of water.

You must have noticed that this time it has been decided to construct five lakh ponds and farm water reservoirs. Under MNREGA also stress has been laid on creating assets for water conservation. Every village should save water. Think how can we save every drop of water during the coming rains; how do we begin an exercise to ensure that every drop of water in the village stays within the village? You should devise a plan and get connected with Government schemes so that we can start a people's movement which will help us understand the importance of water. Then everyone can join the campaign for water conservation. There must be many such villages in the country, many progressive farmers and many conscientious citizens who have already done this kind of work. But we still need to do much more in this direction.

Kisan Mela—Improvement in Agricultural Sector through Scientific Methods

My dear farmer brothers and sisters, a few days ago the Government of India had organised a very big Kisan Mela-'Farmers' Fair'. There I saw the modern technology now available for use of farmers and how much change has come into the agriculture sector. But we have to ensure that this technology reaches the fields. Now even the farmers have started saying that the use of fertilisers should be curtailed. I welcome this. Excessive use of fertilisers has made our Mother Earth unwell. We are the children of our soil, so how can we watch our Mother Earth suffering? Addition of spices and condiments to our food adds to the taste, but if we add too much of even the best of the spices and condiments to it, would one want to eat it at all? The same food would taste so bad, isn't it? The same is true of fertilisers as well.

Even the best fertilizers, if used beyond a limit, become the cause of ruination. A balance in everything should be maintained. This will reduce your expenses and you will end up saving money. Our stand is clear: "Less Cost, More Output. Invest Less and Reap More". We should move forward with this 'mantra' and improve our agriculture sector by using scientific methods. I hope we will do, with full concentration, whatever is necessary for water conservation. We have a couple of months till the onset of monsoon. Do remember, the more we save water, the more the farmers will benefit and more lives will be saved.

Beating Diabetes

My dear fellow citizens, the World Health Day falls on 7th April. This year the theme of the World Health Day is 'Beat Diabetes'. I call upon all of you to defeat Diabetes which plays host to so many diseases. Once it enters yours body, a whole lot of unwelcome guests in the form of illnesses follow it. It is said that in 2014 India had about six and a half crore Diabetics. Diabetes was found to be the cause of death in three per cent of all deaths. Diabetes is of two types - Type 1 and Type 2. Type 1 is hereditary; if the parents have it, so shall their child. Type 2 is due to your habits, age and obesity. The world is worried about Diabetes and so it has been chosen as the theme for World Health Day on 7th April.

We all know that our lifestyle is the biggest cause for Diabetes. Physical labour is getting reduced. There is not a trace of sweat; there is just no walking around. Even if we play games, we play them online; very little happens offline. Can we not, drawing inspiration from this year's World Health Day and its theme, do something to defeat Diabetes in our personal lives? If you are interested in

Yoga, then do Yoga. Or else, the least you can do is to go for a walk or a run. My country will be healthy if every citizen of my country is healthy. Sometimes we are reluctant to get our medical check-up done. When the condition worsens then only does it come to our notice that Diabetes is to be blamed for it. What do you lose in getting a check-up done? Please get this much done at least. Everything is available and a check-up can be done easily. Please do be concerned about this.

Free India from Tuberculosis

On March 24th, the world observed Tuberculosis Day. When I was a child we would be scared by the very mention of the word TB. It would seem death was inevitable for anybody suffering from this dreaded disease. But now we are not scared of it because everybody knows it is curable and can be easily cured. Paradoxically, when TB was linked to death we used to be afraid of it; but now that it is curable, we have become almost careless about it. Compared to the world, we still have a large number of TB patients. If we want to free ourselves and our country from TB, then we need correct treatment, as well as complete treatment. If we leave the treatment mid-way, it can create new complications. Tuberculosis is one disease that even the neighbours can spot. "Oh look! You have a persistent cough and fever and you have lost weight. Go get it checked. You must have got TB." This shows TB is one illness that can be detected fast.

My dear fellow citizens, a lot of work is being done in this direction. There are more than 13,500 Microscopy Centres, more than four lakh DOTS providers, various advanced laboratories. And all these services are free. Please go and get a check-up done. This disease can be got rid of. All one needs is the correct treatment and the treatment must continue till the illness has completely disappeared. I would like to appeal to you all, whether it is TB or Diabetes, we have to conquer these. We have to eradicate these diseases from India. But this cannot happen with just the efforts of the government or by doctors or medicines till you do not do something about it. So I call upon all of you today to defeat Diabetes and free ourselves from Tuberculosis.

125th Birth Anniversary of Baba Saheb Bhimrao Ambedkar

My dear fellow citizens, a number of important occasions are coming up in April, especially on the 14th of April—the birth anniversary of Baba Saheb Bhimrao Ambedkar. His 125th birth anniversary was celebrated all over the country. The five pilgrimage spots associated with him—Mhow, his birthplace; London, where he was educated; Nagpur, where he had his 'Deeksha'; 26, Alipur Road, Delhi, where his soul left him for its heavenly abode; and the cremation ground in Mumbai where his last rites were performed. We are making a constant effort to develop these five pilgrimage spots. I am fortunate to get a chance to visit Mhow, the birthplace of our revered Baba Saheb Ambedkar, on 14th April this year. Baba Saheb has given us a lot to help shape us into ideal citizens. We can best pay our homage to him by following the path set by him and by becoming good citizens.

In a few days from now, the new year of Vikram Samvat will begin. It is celebrated in different States in different forms. Some call it Nav Samvatsar, some call it Gudi Padva, some Varsh Pratipada, some Ugadi, but it holds importance in nearly all the States of India. My greetings to everybody, on this auspicious New Year.

As you know and I had said it last time too, you can now listen to my Mann Ki Baat in about 20 languages whenever you wish to. You can choose your own convenient time to listen to it. You can listen to it on your own mobile handset. All you have to do is to give a missed call. I am happy to state that although it has been barely a month since this service was launched, 35 lakh people have availed themselves of it. You too can note down the number. 81908-81908. I repeat—81908-81908. Give a missed call on this number whenever it is convenient for you. Even if you wish to listen to any previous episode of 'Mann Ki Baat', you can listen to it in the language of your choice. I will be happy to remain connected with you.

My dear fellow citizens my heartiest best wishes to you all. Many, many thanks!

*For listening to the audio, please log on to **http://www.narendramodi.in/mann-ki-baat** or scan the given QR code.*

CHAPTER 19: April 2016

My dear fellow citizens, Namaskar!

It's summer. Everybody makes plans for their summer holidays. Since this is the season of mangoes, we crave for the flavour of this fruit. Sometimes we feel that a nap in the afternoon would be nice. But this year the sweltering heat has played spoilsport for each one of us.

Initiatives for Water Conservation

It is quite natural for people to feel concerned about the unrelenting heat. On top of it, due to a continuous drought over the past couple of years, the usual water storage facilities have been adversely affected. Sometimes due to encroachment, sometimes due to silting, the inflow of water into reservoirs and other water bodies gets blocked. As a result, the reservoirs store much less water than their capacity. Worse, because of this cycle which has been going on for years, the capacity of these reservoirs itself is gradually reduced. To cope with the drought and to provide relief from the water crisis, governments are making efforts. But that's not all. I have noticed that citizens are doing commendable work to help deal with the situation. Awareness is now seen in many villages. Only those who have faced shortage of water know the real value of water. Hence, in such places they are very sensitive towards water and are equally active in doing something to deal with its shortage.

I was recently told that in Ahmednagar district of Maharashtra, the Hiware Bazar Gram Panchayat and its villagers have addressed the problem of water shortage by treating it as a major and delicate issue. One can find many villages where there is a desire to store water. At Hiware Bazar, the farmers tackled the issue by changing the cropping pattern. They have decided to give up the cultivation of those crops that require a lot of water, like sugarcane and banana. It sounds very simple, but in reality it is not so. What a big collective decision this must have been? If one tells the owners of the factories that consume a lot of water about the consequences of their consumption and requests them to shut down their units, one can well imagine what the response would be. But see the sensibility of these farmer brothers. When they realised that the cultivation of sugarcane should be given up because it consumed a lot of water, they went ahead and did it. Instead of sugarcane, they have now taken to fruits and vegetables that require much less water. Farmers in this village have taken so many initiatives such as using sprinklers, drip irrigation techniques, water harvesting and water recharging, that today their village is strong enough to cope with the water crisis that they face. I might be talking of a small place like Hiware Bazar, but there must be many other such villages. I extend my hearty felicitations to such villagers for their fine work.

I was told that in Dewas district of Madhya Pradesh, the Gorwa Gram Panchayat took up the drive to create farm ponds. They have already created 27 farm ponds. Due to this, there has been an increase in the ground water level. Whenever water was required for crops, farmers had access to it. This panchayat has given a rough estimate that their agricultural production has increased by 20 per cent. Not only has water been saved, the quality of water has also vastly improved with the water level increasing. World over it is said that potable water can contribute as a factor for GDP growth. It certainly contributes to better health.

When the government used railways to transport water to Latur, it became news for the world. There is no doubt that the swift manner in which Indian Railways has acted is praiseworthy. But villagers who have taken various initiatives to save water also deserve equal amount of praise. Indeed, I would say they deserve greater praise. There are several such schemes and programmes that are run by citizens but these don't get our attention. The good work done by the government sometimes does come to our notice. If we look around us, we will see that people are making an effort to combat the menace of drought by trying to find solutions that are new and innovative.

It is human nature that no matter how many perils people face, when they hear any good news from any corner, they feel as if the entire crisis is over. Thus, ever since the day it became public knowledge that rainfall this year is expected to be between 106% and 110%, it seems as if tidings of peace and happiness have come. There is still some time left before the monsoon arrives, but the news of good rains has already brought joy. At the same time we must remember that a good monsoon offers both, an opportunity and a challenge. Can we start a drive to save water in every village from now on itself? Farmers need fertile soil in their fields to grow crops. This time why can't we take the soil from the bottom of our ponds for our fields? If we were to do this, the quality of the soil in our fields would improve and the capacity of ponds to store water would increase. Can we fill empty cement and fertiliser bags with pebbles and sand and use them to stop water from flowing out through breaches? If we were to stop water from draining out for five days, for seven days, it would seep into the ground and the water level would come up. There would be sufficient water in our water-wells. Thus, we should strive to retain as much water as possible. The water of a village will be preserved there if we collectively work for it in a determined manner. Therefore, notwithstanding the current water scarcity and drought situation, we have an opportunity, during the coming one and a half months, to prepare to harvest rainwater.

I have said earlier that people who visit Porbandar, the birthplace of Mahatma Gandhi, can also see there the underground tanks constructed about 200 years ago, that were built to save rain water. Water collected in these tanks remained pure.

Cleaning the Ganga

Mr Kumar Krishna has asked on MyGov whether "the cleaning of Ganga will be possible while we are alive". His concern is quite natural because it has been nearly 30 years since work began in this direction. Many governments came, plans were made to clean the Ganga, and a lot of expenditure was incurred without showing results. For this reason there must be crores of Indians like Kumar Krishna who have the same question in their hearts. For those who are religiously inclined, Ganga is the path to salvation for them. I too accept this importance of Ganga. But more than that, Ganga is the giver of life. We get our daily bread from Ganga, we get our earnings from Ganga, and we get a new source of energy from Ganga to lead our lives. The flow of Ganga adds momentum to the economic pace of the country. Bhagirath did bring down the river Ganga for us, but to save it, we need crores of Bhagiraths. The project to clean Ganga cannot be successful without a mass participation by the people. So we will all have to become agents of change to achieve cleanliness. We shall have to continuously keep on repeating this thing. There are many efforts being made by the government. We are seeking the full cooperation of all the states through which Ganga flows. We are also trying to get voluntary organisations to join us in this effort. We have taken several steps for surface cleaning and to stop industrial pollution. Every day, effluents and garbage, in a large quantity, flow into Ganga through drains. At Varanasi, Allahabad, Kanpur, Patna – trash skimmers have been deployed which clean the river while floating on it. All local bodies have been given this facility and they have been urged to carry on with this work continuously and clean all the garbage from the river. I have been told a few days ago that in places where this work is being carried out properly nearly 3 to 11 tonnes of garbage are being taken out of the river every day. So it would be right to say that pollutants in such a large quantity are being stopped from getting into the river. In the coming days, we have plans to deploy such trash skimmers at other places also and the benefits of it will be felt by the people living on the banks of Ganga and Yamuna.

To monitor and control industrial pollution, an action plan has been prepared with the pulp and paper, distillery and sugar industries, and it has also been implemented to some extent. I feel it will yield good results. I am very happy that in Uttarakhand and Uttar Pradesh, which had discharge from distilleries, there has been a change for the better. Officers have told me that they have been successful in securing zero liquid discharge. The discharge from the pulp and paper industry or the liquor industry is almost coming to an end. All these things are a sign that we are moving in the right direction and awareness has also increased. I have seen that not just on the banks of Ganga, even in the far off South if one meets a person, he is sure to ask, " Sir, will Ganga be cleaned?" This faith and hope of the common people is going to ensure success in the cleaning of Ganga. People are even giving donations for this. Thus, this effort is being made quite meticulously.

Panchayati Raj Divas

My dear fellow citizens, today is the 24th of April. This is observed as Panchayati Raj Day in India. On this day, the Panchayati Raj system was implemented in our country. Panchayati Raj system has gradually spread to the entire country and is functioning successfully as an important unit of our democratic system of governance.

We celebrated 14th April as the 125th birth anniversary of Babasaheb Ambedkar and today we celebrate 24th April as Panchayati Raj Day. This was such a fortunate coincidence. From the birth anniversary of the great man who gave us the Constitution of India, to 24th April, the Panchayati Raj Day was introduced in our country to empower our villages, which are the strongest link of our Constitution. It inspired linking these two dates. For this reason, the Government of India, along with the cooperation of the State Governments, has launched a campaign – "From Gram Uday to Bharat Uday" – From the Rise of Villages to the Ascent of India, over a 10-day period between 14th April and 24th April.

It was my good fortune that on 14th April, the birth anniversary of Babasaheb Ambedkar, I had the opportunity to visit his birthplace Mhow and pay my respects at that sacred place. And today, on 24th April,

I am going to Jharkhand, where mostly my tribal brothers and sisters live. In Jharkhand I am going to celebrate Panchayati Raj Divas. At 3 in the afternoon I shall be talking to all panchayats of the country. This campaign has worked in a major way to generate awareness. How can democratic institutions at the village level, in every corner of India, be strengthened? How can villages become self-reliant? How can villages plan programmes for their own development? There should be due importance laid on physical and social infrastructure. There should be no school dropouts in villages and the campaign to educate the girl child (*Beti Bachao, Beti Padhao Abhiyan*) should be successfully carried out. The birth of the girl child should be celebrated in a big way. There should be some plans to do that. In some villages people organised food donation on this occasion. It happens very rarely that so many different programmes go on at the same time in so many villages of India. I congratulate all the State Governments and the village heads. They have gone about these programmes in a very novel way for the welfare of villages, for the development of villages and for the strengthening of democracy. The awareness that has come about in villages guarantees a new progress for India. The foundation for the progress of India lives in the rise of its villages; so if we keep laying stress on the progress of the villages, we shall continue to get the desired results.

Improving the Quality of Education

Sharmila Dharpure from Mumbai has expressed her concern to me through her phone call saying:

> *Mr Prime Minister Namaskar. I am Sharmila Dharpure speaking from Mumbai. I have a question for you about the*

school and college education. For the last so many years, a strong need for reforms has been felt in the education sector. Either the requisite numbers of schools and colleges are not there or quality in education is lacking. It has been often found that children complete their schooling but they still don't have knowledge about the most basic things and so they lag behind in this competitive world. What are your views? How do you wish to bring about reforms?

Sharmilaji, your concern is quite genuine. Today in every home, the first thing that parents dream of, is to give their children a good education. A house and a car, all come in late into the picture. And for a country like India, this common people's sentiment is a very big force. To educate their children and to educate them well, this concern for a good education for their children should increase further and a greater awareness should come about among people. I believe that when there is awareness in the family, it impacts the school and has an impact on teachers as well. The child is also aware of the purpose for which he or she goes to school. So I would appeal to all guardians and parents to give not just enough time and attention to their children, but also to everything that's happening in their school. And if something strikes your attention, please visit their school and discuss it with the teachers yourself. Vigilance can be of help to reduce many shortcomings in the education system. People's participation will go a long way in achieving this.

Every government in our country has laid stress on education and all of them have made efforts for it in their own ways. It is true that for a long time our focus was on setting up educational institutions, expanding the system of education, building schools, building colleges, recruiting teachers and ensuring maximum attendance of children. So priority has, in a way been given to the spread of education. This was necessary. But today more than expanding education what is necessary is the improvement of the quality of education. We have already done a lot towards expanding education. Now we will have to focus on quality of education. We will have to shift our priority from literacy campaigns to good education. Till now we have concentrated on the outlay for education. The time has come to focus on the outcome of it. Till now the stress has been on how many are attending school. From now onward, more than schooling, we will have to lay stress on learning. Till now we have heard the echo of the mantra of Enrolment! Enrolment! Enrolment! But now we will have to turn our attention to providing good and worthy education to children who have made it to schools. You must have seen the budget of the present government. An effort is being made to provide quality education. But it is true we still have a long way to go. If we, 125 crore Indians, resolve, we can cover that distance. Sharmila ji has rightly said that we do need to bring reforms for quality education.

You must have noticed in the Budget that we have decided to do something unconventional. In the Budget, we have made 10 government universities and 10 private universities free from government control and have asked them to accept the challenge of flourishing on their own. We have asked them to come up with what they would like to do to become the best universities. We have done this with the intention of giving them a free hand. Indian universities can also compete with world class universities, and they should. Along with the importance being given to education, it is necessary to give equal importance to skill as well. Likewise, technology plays a very big role in education. Long distance education and technology will make the task of education simpler. I believe that the results of this move are going to be seen in the near future.

Infusing New Life in the Youth Organisations

For quite a while people have been asking me questions on this one topic. Some have written on my web portal, MyGov.in, and others have written to me on the Narendra Modi App. These questions have mostly been written to me by the youth of our nation.

Mr Prime Minister Namaskar, I am Mona Karnwal from Bijnore. For youth today, along with studies, sports are also of great importance. They should have a feeling of team spirit and the qualities of a good leader for their overall holistic development. I state this from my own experience because I have served in the Bharat Scouts and Guides and this had a very good impact on my life. I want you to motivate the youth as much as you can, and I want the government to also promote NCC, NSS and the Bharat Scouts and Guides as much as possible.

You people have been writing and sending me so many suggestions that one day I felt that I must, first of all, talk to such people. It was due to the pressure created by you, and by following your suggestions, that I recently called for a meeting with the chiefs of NCC, NSS, Bharat Scouts and Guides, Red Cross and the Nehru Yuva Kendra. I asked them if they have ever had a meeting before, and they said that since independence, this was the first time that they were attending a meeting like this. So first, I would like to felicitate my young friends who put such intense pressure on me, the result of which was that I held this meeting. I felt glad that I met them. I felt the need for greater coordination. They are doing a lot in their own way, but if work is done collectively and in an organised manner, then these various organisations of ours can bring about huge results. They are spread so wide, and are reaching out to so many families. They were filled with enthusiasm and they had the resolve to do something for the matter.

It's true that I myself have been a cadet in the NCC and so I know first-hand how one acquires a fresh perspective through such organisations. Children draw inspiration and develop a national perspective. I did get the benefit of that in my childhood myself. I believe that we should infuse a new life, a new force into these organisations. This time I put some issues before them. I asked them whether, for this season, all these organisations and our youth can make an effort for water conservation. We could collectively try and stop open defecation in so many blocks and so many districts. What kind of programmes can we make to unite our country? Can we have a common youth song for all these organisations? We spoke on and discussed such varied issues.

Today, I appeal to you all as well. Please suggest good ideas for these youth organisations. Do we need to add anything new in their functioning and their programmes? If you write to me on my Narendra Modi App, I will send your suggestions to the right place. After this meeting, I have a strong feeling that they are going to gain a new momentum. Now even you will wish to join one of them.

Subsidy on Gas Cylinders given up by One Crore Families

My dear fellow citizens, I now wish to talk about something that will compel all of us to think. I view it also as something that is going to shake us all. You must have seen for yourself that the political situation in our country is such that in the previous elections, political parties made promises of giving each household 9 to

12 gas cylinders. And each political party felt that if they had to politically approach the middle class then the gas cylinder was a major issue. On the other hand, economists have applied constant pressure to reduce the subsidy on gas cylinders. For this reason, many committees would sit and receive many proposals and suggestions on the issue of lessening the gas subsidy. Crores of rupees would be spent on these committees. But the matter would remain unresolved. This has been everybody's experience. No one ever thought beyond this.

Today, my dear fellow citizens, I have utmost pleasure in placing before you all, my own account on this. I have chosen the third way out and that is the path of placing trust and confidence in the people and the masses. At times we political leaders should trust our people more than we trust ourselves. We should have implicit faith in the people. I had once told you that if you can bear the expense of 1500-2000 rupees per year, then why don't you give up your subsidy on gas? This could be of use to innumerable poor households. I had just randomly mentioned this, but today I can say with confidence that I am indeed very proud of you all. One crore families have voluntarily given up their subsidy on gas cylinders. These one crore are not wealthy families. Among them are retired teachers, retired clerks, farmers and small shopkeepers. These are middle class and lower middle class families which have given up their subsidy. Now look at the other, rather unique, side of it. They could have given up their subsidy through the App on their mobile, going online or by giving a missed call over the telephone. There were many options. But it has been estimated that more than 80% of these one crore families chose to go to the distributor, stand in a queue and give in writing that they wish to surrender their subsidy.

My dear fellow citizens, this is not a small matter. If the government gives even a small concession on tax or exemption from tax, then for a whole week one hears praises for that government, being splashed around on TV channels and in newspapers. Here, these one crore families have given up their subsidy. In our country subsidy has turned into some kind of a right that people expect and it is exemplary to know that people have chosen to give up such a right for the betterment of so many others.

I would like to salute those one crore families. I humbly bow to them because they have compelled political leaders to think of coming up with something new. This has also forced the economists of the country to think differently. Even global economic experts, who used to live in a world of their own calculations, would find this phenomenon to be beyond the limits of their traditional wisdom. At some point of time they will also have to think of this novel experience that has defied conventional thinking. Imagine the quantum of the achievements of one crore families giving up their subsidy on gas cylinders and in return, one crore poor families getting gas cylinders with that money which is saved from the subsidy given up by one crore families. Externally, it appears just as a small incident, but, its extraordinary lesson is that if you place faith in the people, it leads to most the striking achievements.

I would like to specially appeal to the entire political class to place implicit faith in the people. It will fetch such terrific results that one can never have ever imagined. We should move in this direction. I have always felt this way, as when I felt as to why Class 3 and Class 4 employees should be made to go through interviews. We should trust the person who has given the exams and submitted the marks.

Sometimes I feel that we should publicly announce that today on this railway route there will be no ticket checker. Let's see what happens when we place such faith in the people of India. We can undertake several such experiments. Once we place faith and trust in the people of India, we can get incomparable results. Anyway, these are just some personal thoughts. We cannot turn these into government rules, but we can certainly create such an atmosphere. This atmosphere has not been created by any political leader but by one crore families of India.

Transforming India

A person called Ravi wrote to me – "Good News Everyday", he wrote, "please ask your officials to post about one good incident every day. Each newspaper and news channel has bad news for its every 'breaking news'. Is there nothing good happening around in this country, populated by 125 crore people? Please change this situation."

Ravi ji has expressed his anger, but I think he is not venting his anger on me, but on the prevailing conditions in the country. You may remember that the former President of India, the late Dr APJ Abdul Kalam, used to always say and used to continuously repeat:

"Please print only positive news on the front page of the newspaper".

Some days back, a newspaper had written a letter to me saying that they had decided that on Mondays they would not give any negative news, but only positive, happy news. These days I have noticed that some T.V. channels have begun setting aside some time for positive news as well.

Thus it is right to say that there is an atmosphere of positive news all around, and everybody feels that people should get the right news and good news. It is true that even if the most highly placed men and women narrate the best possible things in the best possible words and in the best possible manner, good news has a better impact than that. Good news becomes the greatest reason and inspiration to do something good.

It is true that the more we give prominence to good things, the less space there will be for bad things. If we light a lamp, the darkness is sure to be dispelled. You must all be aware that the government has started a website, 'Transforming India'. On this you get news of positive happenings, not just of the government, but also of the people around. This is a portal where even you can send news of any good thing that has happened to you and contribute to the site.

Raviji, you have given a good suggestion, but please don't get annoyed with me. We should all strive together to do something positive, talk about something positive, to spread something positive.

Kumbh Mela

There is one great speciality of our country—the *Kumbh Mela*. The *Kumbh Mela* can become the centre of tourist attraction as well. Very few know that since ages, crores and crores of people have gathered on the river-banks for this festival. The peaceful atmosphere at the *Kumbh Mela* gives moments of tranquillity to the soul. These festivals, from the point of view of organisation, event management and people's participation, set new and high standards. I have been noticing for the last two days that many people have uploaded pictures of the *Simhastha Kumbh Mela*. I would like the Tourism Ministry of the

Government of India and the state government to hold a photo competition on this occasion. People should be encouraged to take the finest photographs and upload them. What an atmosphere that would create! People will also come to know of the myriads of different activities going on in every corner of the *Kumbh Mela*. This can surely be done.

It's true that I met the Chief Minister of Madhya Pradesh recently and he told me that they have laid special emphasis on cleanliness. It is not that the cleanliness remains confined to that place. People should carry back the message of cleanliness with them. I believe that even if the *Kumbh Mela* is a religious and spiritual occasion, we can turn it into a social occasion. We can turn it into an occasion of imbibing good values. It can become a reason to carry good resolutions and good habits to all the villages. We should use each *Kumbh Mela* to make people aware of how we can increase our value for water, our faith in water; how we can spread the message of water conservation. We should do this.

My dear fellow citizens, I will surely meet you all once in the evening on this important occasion of Panchayati Raj Divas today. My sincere gratitude to all of you. As always, the unshakeable bond between your inner thoughts and mine, gives me immense pleasure.

Many thanks!

For listening to the audio, please log on to http://www.narendramodi.in/mann-ki-baat or scan the given QR code.

CHAPTER 20: May 2016

My dear countrymen, Namaskar!

Once again I have got an opportunity to talk to you about matters close to my heart, through 'Mann Ki Baat'. For me, 'Mann Ki Baat' is not a matter of ritual; I myself am very eager to talk to you. And I am really happy that I am able to connect with all of you in every corner of India through this programme—'Mann Ki Baat'. I am grateful to All India Radio that they have also been successfully broadcasting 'Mann Ki Baat' in regional languages at 8 P.M. I am also very happy that the people, who listen to me, later communicate their feelings to me through letters, telephone calls, the website MyGov. in and also through the Narendra Modi App. A lot of what you say is of great help to me in the functioning of the government. How active should the government be in terms of public service? How much priority should be given to public welfare activities? In terms of these matters, this dialogue, this link that I have with you all, is of great use. I hope that you will now be even more actively and be enthusiastically involved in ensuring that our democracy should function with people's participation.

The summer heat is increasing day by day. We were hoping for some respite, instead we are experiencing a continual rise in temperature. And, in the midst of this, came the information that the monsoon will perhaps be delayed by a week, which has added to the worry. Almost the entire country is reeling under the scorching impact of a severe heat wave. The mercury continues to soar. Be it animals, birds or humans, everyone is suffering. These problems have been getting increasingly worse due to environmental degradation. The forest cover has kept receding due to indiscriminate felling of trees. In a way, the human race itself has paved the way for self-annihilation by destroying the environment.

Saving the Environment through People's Participation

It is the World Environment Day on 5th of June. On this day, discussions expressing concern on the issue are held all over the world for saving the environment. This time, on the occasion of World Environment Day, the United Nations has given the theme 'Zero Tolerance for Illegal Wildlife Trade'. This topic will, of course, be discussed, but we also must talk about saving our flora and fauna, conserving water, and on how to expand our forest cover. You must have seen in the last few days, how forest fires have raged in the lap of the Himalayas in Uttarakhand, Himachal Pradesh and Jammu and Kashmir. The main cause of these forest fires was dry leaf littering combined with carelessness, which led to the massive inferno. And so, it becomes the bounden duty of each one of us, to save forests and save water.

Recently, I conversed at length with the Chief Ministers of eleven states, reeling under severe drought—Uttar Pradesh, Rajasthan, Gujarat, Maharashtra, Madhya Pradesh, Chhattisgarh, Jharkhand, Karnataka, Andhra Pradesh, Telangana and Odisha.

As per the conventional government precedent, I could have had a combined meeting with all the drought affected states, but I chose not to do so. I had a one-on-one meeting with each state, devoting about two to two–and-a-half hours with each one. I carefully heard what each state had to say. Usually such talks do not go beyond discussion on how much money was granted by the Central Government state-wise, and how much money was actually spent by each state. Thus, it came as a surprise even to the officers of the Central Government that some states have indeed made some very commendable efforts related to water, to environment, to tackling drought, caring for animals as well as affected human beings. Based on inputs from all corners of the country, irrespective of the ruling party there, we found that we had to give a thought to finding not only permanent solutions but also devising practical ways and means to deal with this long-standing problem. In a way, It was a kind of a learning experience for me too. And I have told the *Niti Aayog* that they should work on how to incorporate the best practices across all states.

Save the Water Campaign

Some states, especially Gujarat and Andhra Pradesh, have made full use of technology. I would also like that in future, through the *Niti Aayog*, the exceptionally successful efforts of these states should be applied to other states well. People's participation is a strong base for solving such problems. And for this, I believe that if there is a confluence of perfect planning, use of appropriate technology, and time-bound action, then we can achieve optimum results in drought management, for water conservation, to save every single drop of water. My belief is that water is a gift from God. When we go to a temple, we are given an offering of Prasad and even if a small bit of that spills, we feel bad. We not only pick it up, but also pray five times for God's forgiveness. Water is also an offering from God. Even if a drop of water is wasted, then we should feel remorse and pain. And so water storage, water conservation and proper water irrigation are all of equal importance. And so there is an urgent need for implementing the maxim 'Per Drop More Crop' through 'micro-irrigation' and cultivating crops that require minimal water intake. At present, it is indeed good news that in many states, even sugarcane farmers are using micro irrigation techniques, some are using drip irrigation techniques and some are using sprinklers. When I discussed with the eleven states, I noticed that even for cultivating paddy for production of rice, some of them had employed drip irrigation successfully and got higher yields, thereby also reducing the requirement for water, as well as for labour. I also found that there were many states which had taken on very big targets, especially, Maharashtra, Andhra Pradesh and Gujarat - these three states have done massive work in the field of drip irrigation. And they are striving hard to bring every year 2 to 3 lakh hectares of additional land under micro- irrigation. If this campaign gets underway in all the states, then not only will it benefit cultivation, but more water will also be conserved. Our farmer brothers in Telangana, through 'Mission Bhagirathi' have made a commendable effort to optimally use the waters of Godavari and Krishna rivers. In Andhra Pradesh, 'Neeru Pragati Mission' has been using technology for ground water recharging. People are devoting hard work and contributing financially as well to the mass movement that has been started in Maharashtra; I feel that the 'Jal Yukt Shivir' is one such people's movement which is really going to be of great help in saving Maharashtra from water crisis in the future.

Chhattisgarh has started the 'Lok-Suraj, Jal-Suraj' campaign. Madhya Pradesh has started the 'Balram Talaab Yojana' and dug nearly 22,000 ponds, which is no small figure and work is also being carried out there on the 'Kapil Dhara Koop Yojana'. In Uttar Pradesh there is 'Mukhya Mantri Jal Bachao Abhiyaan'. In Karnataka water conservation efforts are in the form of 'Kalyani Yojana', under which they are trying to revive wells once again. In Rajasthan and Gujarat there are many ancient *baudi* - deep tanks or masonry wells with steps going down to the water. These states are making a very big effort to revive these as 'water temples'. Rajasthan has started the Chief Minister's Jal Swawalamban Abhiyan - Water Self Sufficiency Campaign. Jharkhand, although being a predominantly forest area, still has some parts which face water problem. They have launched a very big campaign for building 'Check Dams'. They have started an exercise to check and stop the flow of water. Some states have started a campaign and made a number of small dams at distances of 10 to 20 kilometres in the rivers themselves to check the flow of water.

This is a wonderful experience. I urge the people of India that during the period of June, July, August and in September this year, we should resolve that we shall not let a single drop of water be wasted. We should decide this right now for places where we can conserve water and where we can check the flow of water. The Almighty blesses us with water according to our needs, nature fulfils our needs. But if we become careless when water is abundant then during the lean water season we land into trouble due to water scarcity, how can this be allowed? And the issue of water is not just for farmers. This concerns everybody—the villages, the poor, the labourers, farmers, the urban people populace, the country folks, the rich and the poor. And for this reason, now that the rainy season is approaching, saving water should be our priority. And when we celebrate Diwali this year, then we should also revel in how much water did we manage to save and how much water we stopped from flowing out. You will see for yourselves that our joy will increase manifold. Water has this power, no matter how tired one is, just a bit of water splashed on the face makes one feel so refreshed. No matter how tired we are, when we see a large lake or an ocean, how magnificent that sight is. Such a priceless treasure it is, bestowed upon us by the Almighty! Just connect to it with your heart. Conserve it! We should harvest water. We should also store water. We should also modernise water irrigation. This I say as an earnest appeal. We should not let this season go waste. The coming four months should be transformed into a 'Save the Water Campaign', to save every drop of water. And this is not just for governments, not just for politicians, it is a task that has to be carried out by the people at large. Recently the media reported about the water crisis in great detail. I hope that the media will show the way ahead to people on how to save water, start a campaign, and also share the responsibility to free us all from this crisis forever; I invite them as well.

Moving Towards a Cashless Society

My dear Countrymen, we have to build a modern India. We have to make a transparent India. We have to make many services uniformly available across the entire country, from one corner to another. So we will have to change some of our old habits as well. Today I want to touch upon one topic in which if you can be of great help to me, then we can together achieve progress in that direction. We all know and we were taught about it in school that there was a time when there were no coins, no currency notes; there was a barter system. If you wanted vegetables you could give wheat in return. If you wanted salt, you could give vegetables in exchange. Business was carried out only through the barter system. Then gradually came currency - coins came, notes came. But now times have changed. The whole world is moving towards a cashless society. Through the facility of electronic technology, we can get money and also give money; we can buy things and pay our bills too. And with this there is no question of our wallets being stolen from our pocket. We need not worry about keeping an account; the account will be maintained automatically. In the beginning it may appear to be a bit difficult, but once we get used to it, then this arrangement will seem very easy for us. And this possibility is there because under the 'Pradhan Mantri Jan Dhan Yojana', that we have started recently, nearly all families in the country have had their bank accounts opened. On the other hand, they have also got their Aadhar numbers. And the mobile phone has reached the hands of almost every Indian. So, Jan Dhan, Aadhar and Mobile—Jam—J. A. M.—by synchronising these three, we can move ahead towards a cashless society. You must have seen that along with the Jan Dhan account people have been given a RuPay card. In the coming days, this card is going to be useful as both—a credit and a debit card. And now-a-days a very small instrument has come which is called the 'point of sale'—P. O. S.—'Pos'. With the help of that, be it your Aadhar number or your RuPay card, if you have to pay money to someone, you can do it through that. There is no need to take out money from your pocket and count it; there is no need to carry around any cash with you. One of the initiatives in this regard that has been taken by the Government of India is about how to make payments through 'Pos', how to receive money. The second endeavour we have started is 'Bank on Mobile'. The 'Universal Payment Interface' banking transaction – UPI, will change the way things work. It will become very easy to carry out money transactions through your mobile phone. And I'm happy to tell you that the NPCI and banks are working together to launch this platform through a mobile app. If this happens, perhaps you may not even need to carry a RuPay card with you.

Across the country, nearly 1.25 lakh young people have been recruited as banking correspondents. In a way we have worked towards providing the bank at your door step. Post offices have also been geared up for banking services. If we learn and adapt ourselves to use these services, then we will not require the currency, we will not need notes, we will not need coins. Businesses will function automatically, resulting in a certain transparency. Under-hand dealings will stop; the influence of black money will be reduced. So I appeal to my countrymen, that we should at least make a beginning. Once we start, we will move ahead with great ease. Twenty years ago, who would have thought that so many mobiles would be in our hands! Slowly we cultivated a habit and now we can't do without it. Maybe this cashless society assumes a similar form. But the sooner this happens, the better it will be.

Cultivating the Spirit of Sportsmanship

My dear countrymen, whenever the Olympic Games come around, and when these begin, we sit, clutch our heads and sigh, "we were left so far behind in the tally of gold medals... did we get a silver or not... should we do with just a bronze or not..." This happens. It is true that in the field of sports we face a lot of challenges. But an atmosphere for sports should be created in the country.

To encourage the sportspersons who are leaving for the Rio Olympics, to boost their morale, everyone should try in their own way. Someone could write a song, someone could draw cartoons, someone could send messages with good wishes, somebody could cheer a particular sport, but on the whole a very positive environment should be created in the entire country for these sportspersons. Whatever may be the result, a game is a game, one can win or lose, medals are sometimes won and sometimes not; our spirits should always soar high. And as I speak, I would like to mention our Sports Minister, Shri Sarbanand Sonowal for a gesture that has touched my heart. Last week all of us were busy in the ups and downs of the Assam election results. Shri Sarbanandji himself was leading the campaign. He was the Chief Ministerial candidate—but he was also the Union Minister. And I was very happy when I came to know that one day before the Assam election results, he discreetly reached Patiala in Punjab. You must be aware of the Netaji Subhash National Institute of Sports—N.I.S.—where, the sportspersons going for the Olympics are trained. They all are there. He suddenly reached there, much to the surprise of the sportspersons. And it was a matter of surprise for the world of sports as well, that a minister personally cares for our sportspersons, inquiries about the arrangements for them. How is the food? Are they getting nutritious food according to their needs or not? Are the appropriate trainers for their fitness present there? Are all the training machines functioning properly? He surveyed everything in great detail. He personally inspected each and every sportsperson's room. He spoke to all the players in great detail. He had a word with the management and trainers; he himself ate with the sportspersons. With election results due, with the distinct possibility of a new responsibility as a Chief Minister, yet if one of my colleagues, in the capacity of a Sports Minister, displays such concern for his work, it gives me great joy. And I am confident that like this, we should all realise the importance of sports, we should encourage the people in the world of sports, encourage our sportspersons. This becomes a source of strength in itself, when sportspersons feel that 125 crore of their countrymen are with them, their his morale gets a great boost.

Last time I spoke to you about the FIFA Under-17 World Cup and recently I got to see the suggestions that have come pouring in. And these days I have noticed that a conducive atmosphere for Football can be seen in the whole country. Many people are taking an initiative to form their own teams. I have received thousands of suggestions on the Narendra Modi Mobile App in this regard. Maybe many people don't play the game themselves, but hundreds of thousands of young Indians have displayed such keen interest in the sport, that this by itself was a very delightful experience for me. We all know the bond that India has with Cricket, but I saw the same passion for Football as well, and this by itself heralds a very positive signal for the future. For all the selected candidates for the Rio Olympics, and for our favourite sportspersons, we should create a cheerful and positive atmosphere. We should not judge everything in terms of victory and defeat. India should be known in the world for its spirit of sportsmanship. I appeal to my countrymen to contribute their bit in creating an atmosphere that boosts the spirits and enthusiasm of our athletes.

Celebrate Your Success and Recognise Your Inner Strength

In the last week or so, results have been pouring in from all over the country and 'no', I am not talking about the election results. I am talking about those students who slogged for the entire year, those of classes Xth and XIIth. It is clear that our daughters are marching ahead triumphantly. It is a matter of joy. To those who have succeeded in these exams, I extend my congratulations and felicitations. And those who were unable to succeed, I would like to tell them once again that there is a lot to do in life. Life does not get stuck if we do not get results according to our expectations. We should live with hope, we should move ahead with confidence and a zeal to achieve something more.

But I have been confronted with a new type of question, to which, I had earlier never given a thought. I've received one email on MyGov.in, which drew my attention. One Mr Gaurav Patel of Madhya Pradesh writes that in the M.P. Board exam he has secured 89.33% marks. Reading this I felt elated. But as he continued, he told us his tale of woe. Gaurav Patel says that 'Sir, after securing 89.33% marks when I reached home, I was thinking that I would be congratulated by my family and friends, I would be applauded. But I was amazed when everybody in the house, friends and my teachers said the same thing, "Oh Dear, if your had secured just 4 more marks, you would have made it to 90%." So it seems that my family, my friends, my teachers, nobody was pleased with my 89.33% marks. Everyone was lamenting that I missed my 90% by four marks. Now I'm perplexed and don't know how to handle the situation. Is this all to life. Was what I did not good enough? Did I not prove myself? I don't know, but I feel a heavy burden weighing on my heart and mind.'

Gaurav, I have read your letter very carefully. And I feel that perhaps this pain is not just yours; like you there are lakhs and crores of other students who share the same pain. Because, nowadays there is a trend that instead of finding satisfaction in what we have achieved, we tend to express our dissatisfaction in not achieving unrealistic goals. This is another form of negativity. We can never guide society towards the path of satisfaction if we always find dissatisfaction in everything. It would have been better if your family members, your class mates and your friends had appreciated your 89.33%. Then you would have felt motivated enough to do a lot more. I would like to urge guardians, parents and people all around, to please accept, welcome and express your satisfaction over your children's results, and motivate them to surge ahead in life. Else, it might happen that a day will come when they bring 100% marks and you will still express shock and say, "you have got 100 percent! But still, had you done something more, it would have been better!" There is a limit to everything and that should be accepted.

Santosh Giri Goswami has written something similar to me from Jodhpur, almost along the same lines. He says that the people around him just don't accept the results. They say that you should have done something better. There was a poem I had read long ago. I don't remember the complete poem. The poet had written something like this:

> *I painted a picture of my anguish on the canvas of life. And when it was exhibited, almost all the visiting people commented that it needed some touching up. Someone said, 'yellow here would have been better in place of blue.' Someone said, 'This line would have been better situated there instead of here.' I wish some odd visitor had also shed a tear or two over the picture of my anguish.*

I don't remember if these were the exact words of the poem, as I read this poem way back in time. But nobody was able to grasp the pain depicted in that picture; everyone just spoke of touching it up.

Santosh Giriji, you have the same problem that Gaurav has. And there must be crores of students like you. You have the burden on yourself of fulfilling the expectations of millions of others. All that I would like to say to you is that in such a situation, don't lose your balance. Everyone expresses their expectations; just keep listening, but stick to your point and make an effort to do something even better. But if you are not satisfied with what you have got, you will never be able to create something new. The strong foundation of one success becomes the foundation for another greater success. The dissatisfaction arising out of success can never become a ladder to another success; it guarantees failure. And so, I would like to appeal, that you should sing in celebration of the success that you have achieved. Possibilities of newer successes will arise out of success achieved earlier. I would like to appeal to parents, friends and neighbours that please don't impose your expectations upon your children. And friends, does our life come to a standstill if we meet with failure sometimes. Sometimes one is not able to score good marks in exams, but he or she surges ahead in sports, or does well in music, or excels in the fine arts, or forges ahead in business. God has gifted each one of us with a unique talent. Please recognise your inner strength, build upon it and you will be able to march ahead. And this happens everywhere in life.

You must have heard of the musical instrument called Santoor. There was a time when the Santoor was associated with the folk music of the Kashmir valley. But it was Pandit Shiv Kumar (Sharma) whose magical touch transformed it into one of the prime musical instruments of the world. Shehnai once had a limited space in the world of music. It was mostly played at the threshold of the courts of emperors and kings. But Ustad Bismillah Khan's mastery over the Shehnai made it one of the finest musical instruments in the world; it has now carved an identity of its own. And so you should stop worrying about what you have and how that is. Just concentrate on what you have and devote your utmost strength on it; with that you are sure to reap handsome rewards.

Practicing Yoga to Lead a Balanced Life

My dear countrymen, sometimes I notice that the money that our poor families have to spend on their healthcare, throws their life off the track. It is true that while one has to spend little on preventing illness, the expenditure incurred on regaining health after you have fallen ill, is a lot more. Why can't we lead life in such a way that we don't ever fall sick and no financial burden falls upon the family? Cleanliness is one of the strongest protections from disease. The greatest service that can be rendered to the poor is by maintaining cleanliness. And the second thing that I constantly urge you to do is Yog. Some people also call it Yoga. 21st June is the International Day for Yog. People are not only attracted to Yog the world over, they have implicit faith in it and the whole world has embraced it. This is a priceless gift handed over to us by our ancestors, which we have given to the world. To the world which is filled with stress, Yog gives the power to lead a balanced life. Prevention is better than cure. A person practicing Yog, can easily have the achievements of staying healthy, maintaining balance, being richly endowed with a strong will power, nurturing supreme self-confidence and to have concentration in every task one does. 21st June, the International Yog Day is not just a mere event. It should spread wide; it should find a place in every person's life. Each person should take 20 to 30 minutes out from his daily routine and spend it on practicing Yog. And for this, the International Yog day on 21st

June gives us the inspiration. These collective occasions do become a reason for effecting positive change in an individual's life. I do hope that on 21st June, wherever you may be, please take the initiative; you have a month with you. If you visit the website of the Government of India, the syllabus for this year, the '*asanas*' you have to do, and how one has to do them, all that has been described in it. Have a look at it. Do get these followed in your village, in your *mohallas* [localities] in your city, in your school, in your [neighbourhood] institution, even in offices. Start it from now, one month in advance and you will be a participating partner on 21st June. I have read it several times that there are offices where on a regular basis, when they first meet in the morning, they begin with Yog and Pranayama and the efficiency of the entire office increases. The whole culture of the office gets transformed and the environment also undergoes a positive change. Can we make use of 21st June to bring Yog into our lives? Can we use it to bring Yog into our social life? Can we use it to bring Yog into our surroundings? I will be going to Chandigarh this time to participate in the programme on 21st June. I shall be doing Yog with the people of Chandigarh. You too must connect yourself with it when the whole world will be doing Yog on that day. I urge you all not to get left behind. Your staying healthy is very important to make India healthy.

My dear country men, through 'Mann Ki Baat', I connect with you regularly. I had given all of you a mobile number earlier, which you could use for listening to 'Mann Ki Baat' by giving a missed call on that number. But now we have made it a lot simpler. Now, to be able to listen to this programme, all you have to do is to dial just four digits and the four digit number is 1-9-2-2. I repeat—One-Nine-Two-Two. By giving a missed call on this number, you will be able to listen to

'Mann Ki Baat' at any time, wherever you are and in any language of your choice.

My dear countrymen, Namaskar to all of you once again! Please don't forget what I had said about water. You will remember it, won't you? Okay!

Thank You. Namaste!

For listening to the audio, please log on to http://www.narendramodi.in/mann-ki-baat or scan the given QR code.

CHAPTER 21: June 2016

My dear countrymen, my greetings (namaskar) to you all.

Last year, we had to endure so many trials – the scorching heat of the summer, scarcity of water, drought conditions and so on. However, the past two weeks have been the harbinger of the welcome news of rainfall from different places, bringing in its wake a feeling of freshness. You too must have felt it. Going by the predictions of the scientists, this time there should be good rainfall, far and wide and throughout the rainy season. This news in itself charges us with a lot of enthusiasm. I extend my greetings to all our farmer brethren hoping for a bountiful rainfall.

Nurturing Young Scientists

In our country, like the toiling farmers, our scientists are also achieving success on many fronts to take our country to new heights. I have believed it right from the beginning that the new generation should nurture the dream of becoming scientists, should have keen interest in science, and our youngsters should step forward with the zeal to do something for future generations. I also want to share another bright news with you. Yesterday I had gone to Pune, on the occasion of the anniversary of the Smart City Project. Over there I met those students of the Pune College of Engineering, who have on their own made a satellite, which was launched on 22nd June. I had called them to meet me, as I had a wish to see these young friends of mine, to interact with them and to experience first-hand the energy and enthusiasm in them. For the past many years, several students have made their contributions to this project. In a way, this academic satellite is a living example of the soaring flight of courage and ambition of young India. That has led these students to make this satellite. The dreams behind this small satellite are big and lofty; they soar high into the sky; the efforts put in by them are very intense. On similar lines as achieved by these Pune students, the students of Satyabhama University of Chennai in Tamil Nadu also created their satellite; and their SathyabamaSAT has also been launched. We have been hearing these things since childhood, and every child wishes deep inside his heart, to touch the sky and grab a few stars. Keeping this in mind, in my opinion, these two satellites made by students and launched by ISRO, are extremely important and most valuable. All these students deserve hearty congratulations. I also want to congratulate the people of the country that on 22nd June, our scientists at ISRO launched 20 satellites simultaneously into space, and in the process set a new record, breaking their own previous records. And this is also a matter of joy that of the twenty satellites which were launched in India, 17 satellites were from other countries. Along with America, the satellites of many other countries were launched on Indian soil by Indian scientists and along with these, those two satellites made by our students also reached outer space. And it is also noteworthy that owing to its guarantee of success with lesser cost, ISRO has carved its special place in the world. And for this very reason, many countries of the world are today looking towards India for the launching of their satellites.

My dear Countrymen, "Save the Girl Child, Educate the Girl Child" (*Beti Bachao, Beti Padhao*), has already become the 'Mann Ki Baat', the heartfelt wish of all the people of India. Still, some incidents infuse a new life into this slogan. This time in the results of 10th and 12th classes, our daughters have been doing wonderfully well, this is a matter of pride. And my dear countrymen, there is another significant event that all of us should take pride in. On 18th June, the Indian Air Force for the very first time inducted its first batch of women fighter pilots. You get goose pimples just at the mention of 'women fighter pilots'; we feel so proud that these three Flying Officer daughters of ours—Avni Chaturvedi, Bhawna Kanth and Mohana, have achieved this great feat. What these three daughters have accomplished is truly special. Flying Officer Avni is from Rewa in Madhya Pradesh, Flying Officer Bhawana is from Begusarai in Bihar and Flying Officer Mohana is from Vadodara in Gujarat. You must have noticed that all these three daughters do not hail from metro cities of India. They do not even come from the capital cities of their respective states. Despite hailing from small cities and towns, they nurtured dreams as high as the sky, and they have also made them come true. I extend my heartiest wishes to these three daughters Avni, Bhawana and Mohana as well as their parents.

Celebration of International Yoga Day

My dear Countrymen, a few days ago on 21st June, the whole world organised grand shows in observance of the anniversary of the International Day for Yoga. As an Indian, when we witness the entire world coming together through Yoga, we realize that the entire world is getting linked with our past, present and future. We are forging a unique bond with the rest of the world. In India too, the International Yoga Day was celebrated at over 1 lakh places, with a lot of fervour and enthusiasm in myriad forms and hues, and in an atmosphere of gaiety. I also got an opportunity to perform Yoga in Chandigarh amidst thousands of Yoga lovers. The zeal of the young and old alike was worth watching. You must have seen that last week the Indian government issued a postage stamp on 'Surya Namaskar' on the occasion of International Yoga Day. This time, people all over the world, on Yoga Day, were witness to two special events. One was at New York City where the United Nations Organisation Headquarters building is located. A special projection depicting different postures of the various yoga *asanas* on top of that building was organised. And passers-by kept taking pictures of these, and these pictures were soon being shared all over the world. Tell me, which Indian would not have felt proud at such happenings? One more interesting thing happened. Technology is at work. Social media has created an identity of its own. And this time Twitter carried out a light hearted pleasant experiment in Yoga with its 'Yoga imaging'. As soon as we typed 'hash tag yoga day', we would immediately get a picture of a yoga image on our mobile. And this image too went viral all over the world. Yoga by itself means adding–getting connected. Yoga has the power to connect the entire world. But for that to happen, first all of us need to get connected to Yoga.

Swati Srivastava from Satna in Madhya Pradesh called me up on telephone after the Yoga Day and left a message for all of you but it seems that it pertains more to me:

> *I wish that my entire country should be healthy and all the poor people also should remain free from diseases. For this I want that among the many ads that are played on Doordarshan, there should be one ad on Yoga, how it is to be done, and what are its benefits?*

Swati ji, your suggestion is very good, but if you observe carefully you will notice that not just on Doordarshan, but these days in India and outside India too, the Indian T.V. channels and channels of other countries are pitching in with their contribution to propagate Yoga. They all are shown at different times, and if you observe carefully, all these things are being done to disseminate information about Yoga. And I have seen that there are some countries in the world which have T.V. channels exclusively dedicated to Yoga 24 hours a day. And you probably know that, during the month of June, in view of the International Yoga Day, I used to share a video everyday of one particular asana of Yoga through Twitter and Face Book. If you go to the website of the Ministry of Ayush, you will find a very good video there a 40-45 minutes, of demonstrating one after another, different kinds of yoga *asanas* for different parts of the body that you can do, people of all ages can do. To you and through you to all the people interested in Yoga, I would like to exhort to get connected to it.

This time I have made an appeal. When we say that Yoga is a way to rid oneself of illnesses, then why don't we bring together all different schools of thought of Yoga, which have their own methods, their own priorities and their own experiences? But all of them share the same final goal. All the prevalent systems of Yoga, all the functioning Yoga institutions, all the different Yoga

Gurus, I have urged all of them to run a successful campaign this entire year on how to defeat Diabetes through Yoga. Can we control Diabetes through Yoga? Some people have been successful in that. Everyone has looked for a way in this regard. And we know that there is no definite cure for Diabetes. One has to manage it with medicines. Diabetes is the master switch that triggers all other illnesses. It becomes an entrance for many other diseases. And so everyone is wary of Diabetes. A lot of people have worked in this direction. Some diabetic patients have also been able to control it through their yogic practice. Why don't we share our experiences with other people to impart a momentum to this endeavour and create a kind of atmosphere for it for an entire year? I urge you to use–"Hashtag Yoga Fights Diabetes" I repeat—"Hashtag Yoga Fights Diabetes". Use this Twitter handle and share your experiences on social media. Or send them to me on NarendraModiApp. Let us see what the various experiences are. At least, give it a try. I invite you to share your experiences on "Hashtag Yoga Fights Diabetes".

Democratic Strength of Our Country

My dear countrymen, sometimes my 'Mann Ki Baat' is ridiculed a lot and is criticized much also. However, this can only happen because all of us are committed to democracy. But today, as I speak to you on 26th June, and I want to especially say this to the new generation that this democracy that we take pride in, this democracy that has granted great power to us, every citizen has been empowered… but 26th June 1975 was also a day… the night of 25th June and the next morning, was a dark hour for the democracy of India when Emergency was imposed in India. All the rights of the citizens were suspended. The country was turned into a prison. Lakhs of people along with *Jayaprakash Narayan*, thousands of leaders were put behind bars, many organisations were banned. Many books have been written about that dark period. Many discussions have been held on it. But today, as I talk to you all on 26th June, we should not forget that our strength lies in our democracy. Our strength lies in the people's power. Our strength lies in each and every citizen of our country. We have to carry forward this commitment and make it stronger. And it is this people's power which has sustained democracy as its living embodiment. There might have been locks on newspaper houses, radio might have been speaking just one kind of language, still on the other hand, given an opportune moment, the citizens gave an example of the power of democracy. A great example of the democratic strength of the common people was witnessed during Emergency. And we must keep reminding our country of its democratic strength from time to time. And our endeavour should be to make people aware of their power and to always have the tendency to further strengthen it by linking more and more people to it. I always stress that Democracy doesn't merely mean that people vote for you and give you the contract to run this country for five years. Certainly Not! Voting is certainly an important component but there are many other facets of democracy. And the biggest dimension is that of people's participation, their attitude, their thinking. And the more the governments get connected with the people, the stronger they become. The chasm between the governments and the people leads to ruin. My endeavour has always been to ensure that the nation moves forward on the strength of people's participation.

Recently, when my government completed two years, some young people with a modern outlook suggested, "When you talk such big things about democracy, then why don't you get your government rated by the people also." In a way it had a tone of challenge as well as advice. But that stirred my mind. I raised this topic with some of my senior colleagues. Their first reaction was, "Oh no! Sir! What are you thinking of doing? These days technology has changed so much that if people get together and form a group and if they decide to misuse technology, then who knows in which direction they might take this survey." They thus expressed their concern. But I felt that we should go ahead even if it is a risk. We should give it a try and see what happens. Now a lot of surveys are conducted after the elections, during the elections, at other times also over some issues, sometimes to gauge the popularity, but the sample size of these surveys is not very big. However, my dear countrymen, I am happy to state that when, through the medium of technology, using different languages, I appealed to the masses to rate my government, a lot of people amongst you have expressed your opinion on 'rate-my-government—MyGov. in.' Lakhs of you displayed your interest in this but 3 lakh people devoted their time and put in serious effort for answering each and every question. I am grateful to these 3 lakh people that they displayed a lot of self-initiative in rating the government. I won't discuss the results. Our media persons are sure to do that. But I can say for sure that it was a good experiment. And this was a matter of joy for me that people speaking all languages of India, residing in every corner of the country, hailing from all types of background, all of them participated in it. And the biggest thing was, and this, of course, came as a surprise to me..., that maximum number of people took part in this exercise through the portal of the website of the Rural Employment Scheme which is being run by the government. Thus, my primary impression is that there has been a large and active participation of people connected to rural India and poverty issues. This I liked the most. So you have seen that while on 26th June some years ago the voice of the people was stifled, now is the time, when the people make their decisions, they judge whether the government is doing the right thing or not, is performing well or poorly. This is the real power of democracy.

Disclose the Undisclosed Income

My dear countrymen, today I want to make a special appeal for one thing. There was a time when taxes were so pervasive, that it became a habit to avoid taxation. There was a time when there were many restrictions imposed on bringing foreign goods into the country which gave rise to a lot of smuggling. But gradually, times have changed. Now it is not very difficult for the taxpayer to get connected with the taxation system of the government. But even then, old habits die hard. One generation still feels that it is best to keep away from the government. Today I want to impress upon you that we end up losing our peace of mind by trying to escape from rules and regulations. As a result, anybody can trouble and harass us. Why should we let this happen? Why don't we, on our own, give the correct details of our income and property to the government, so that we can rid ourselves from the burden of hitherto undeclared assets? I appeal to my countrymen to do this. To the people who have undisclosed income, the Government of India has given a chance to declare such income. The government has presented before the country a special facility to disclose undisclosed income by the 30th of September.

We can be free ourselves of various burdens just by paying a fine. I have also promised that for those who voluntarily declare their assets and their undisclosed income to the government, there will be no enquiry conducted. Not once will it be asked as to from where all this wealth came and how it was acquired. And so, this is a good chance for you to become a part of a transparent system. At the same time, I want to tell people that please consider this plan, which is up to 30th September as your last chance. In between, I had even told the Members of the Parliament that after 30th September if any citizen is put through any difficulty, the ones who do not want to follow government rules, then it will not be possible to help them. I want to say this to the people, that we do not wish that after 30th September anything should happen that will cause difficulties for you. And so I say that please avail of this facility before this date and save yourselves from any possible trouble after the 30th of September.

My dear countrymen, I had to talk about this in 'Mann Ki Baat' today, because recently I held a two-day conclave with the Revenue Departments—all the officials of the Income Tax, Customs and Excise Departments. And I have told them in clear words that we should not perceive citizens as crooks. We should have trust and faith in the citizens. We should hold hands with them. If they want to follow rules, we should encourage them, and lovingly help them cross over. It is important to build an atmosphere of trust. We shall have to bring about a change through our conduct. We shall have to reassure the taxpayer. I stressed this upon them and I noticed that they too realized that today when the nation is surging ahead, all of us must contribute to it. And when I was taking inputs from them in this conclave, I gathered information which I want to share with you as well. None of you will believe that in a country of 125 crore people, one and a half, only one and a half lakh people exist, whose taxable income is more than 50 lakh rupees. Nobody will be able to swallow something like this. People having a taxable income of more than 50 lakh rupees can be seen in big cities in large numbers. Just looking at their bungalows worth 1 or 2 crores, one wonders how they can be in a tax bracket of less than 50 lakhs. This means that there is something wrong somewhere. We have to change this situation. And this has to change before 30th September. Before taking any extreme steps, the government must give a chance to people. And so my dear brothers and sisters, this is a golden chance for you to disclose your undisclosed income. And in another way, this is the way out to save yourself from any trouble that could arise after 30th September. I urge you to come forth in this task for the betterment of our country, for the upliftment of the poor. And I do not want that you should face any problems after 30th September.

Contribution in the Cleanliness Campaign

My dear countrymen, the common citizen of this country is always looking for a chance to do something for the country. When I asked the people to give up their cooking gas subsidy, more than 1 crore families of this country voluntarily gave up their subsidy. And now I want to cite an example especially for those people who have undisclosed income. Yesterday when I went to Pune for the Smart City programme, over there I got the chance to meet Shri Chandrakant Damodar Kulkarni and his family. I had called them especially to meet me. And what was the reason? Anyone who has ever evaded tax, my words may or may not inspire that person, but the example of Shri Chandrakant Kulkarni is sure to inspire him. Do you know what the reason is? Shri Chandrakant Kulkarni is an ordinary man who belongs to an average middle class family. He used to work for the government. Then he retired. He receives a pension of sixteen thousand rupees. And my dear countrymen, you will be surprised to hear, and those who are in the habit of evading tax will get a shock to know that Chandrakant Kulkarni ji, who gets a pension of only rupees sixteen thousand, some time back wrote a letter to me saying that out of his pension of 16,000, he voluntarily wants to donate Rupees 5000 per month for the Cleanliness Campaign. And not just this, he sent me 52 cheques, post-dated, which bear a date for each forthcoming month. We certainly do not have any right to evade tax in this country where there is one such government employee, who after retirement, out of a pension of mere sixteen thousand rupees, gives five thousand for the Cleanliness Campaign. No one can be a greater source of inspiration than Chandrakant Kulkarni. And for the people who are associated with the Cleanliness Campaign also, there could be no better and inspiring example than Chandrakant Kulkarni. I called Chandrakantji face to face. I met him and his life has touched my heart. I express my felicitations and admiration for the Kulkarni family, I congratulate them. And surely there must be countless people like them about whom I have no information. These are the very people and this is the power and strength of the masses. A man with a pension of sixteen thousand rupees sends me cheques worth two lakhs, sixty thousand in advance. Is this a small thing? Come, let us search deep down inside our hearts, and ponder over the fact that the government has given us an opportunity to disclose our incomes. While thinking of Chandrakant Kulkarni, let us also follow him.

My dear countrymen, Santosh Negi from Pauri Garhwal in Uttarakhand, has called up to narrate one of his experiences. He has given a message regarding water conservation. Friends, his experience can be of use to you as well:

> *Drawing inspiration from you, in our school, before the onset of monsoon we dug 250 small trenches which were 4 feet deep, along the side of the playground, so that rainwater could be collected in these. This way the playground remained unspoilt and there was no danger of children drowning in these... and we managed to save crores of litres of rainwater which fell on the playfield.*

Santoshji, I would like to thank you for sending me this message. Pauri Garhwal is a hilly area where you have done such splendid work. You deserve to be congratulated for that. The people of our country should certainly enjoy the rains but let us also be mindful that this is a holy gift from the Almighty. This is a limitless wealth. We should make every effort to conserve every single drop of water. How can we retain rainwater of the villages there itself and similarly preserve rainwater of cities. To recharge Mother Earth once again, how can we replenish water back to the earth? If there is water today, only then can there be a tomorrow. Water is the basis of all life. An atmosphere has certainly been created in the country. Lately, in all the states a lot of measures have been taken for water conservation. But now that we are going to have the bounty of rain water, we must see to it that it doesn't just flow away. We are so concerned about saving lives; we should be equally concerned about saving water.

My dear countrymen, you already know that number 1922, it must have become a part of your memory by now. 1-9-2-2. This 1922 is one such number that if you give a missed call to it, you can listen to 'Mann Ki Baat' in the language of your choice. By listening to 'Mann Ki

Baat', at the time of your convenience, in the language of your choice, you too can make up your mind and resolve to contribute to the journey of the nation's progress.

My Namaskar once again to all my countrymen, Thank You.

*For listening to the audio, please log on to **http://www.narendramodi.in/mann-ki-baat** or scan the given QR code.*

CHAPTER 22: July 2016

My dear countrymen, Namaskar!

Early this morning, I had an opportunity to spend some time with some young people from Delhi. And I believe, in the days to come, the spirit and fervour of sports will envelop every young person in the country. All of us know that in a few days' time, the world's largest sports event, the biggest sports carnival will take place. Rio is going to resound in our ears time and again. The entire world will be at play, every country in the world will keep a close watch on the performance of its sportspersons; you too will be doing the same. All of us harbour a lot of hopes and expectations, but keeping the morale of our sports contingent at Rio high is also the solemn duty of us 1.25 billion countrymen. In Delhi this morning, the Government of India had organised a very good event, 'Run for Rio' and 'Play and Live', 'Play and Blossom'. In the days to come, wherever we are, let us do our bit to encourage our sportspersons.

Sportspersons' *Tapasya*

A sportsperson, who makes it to this stage, does so after putting in a lot of hard work. It's a kind of severe and dedicated 'tapasya'. However much one cherishes all kinds of food, one has to sacrifice that. However much one would like to snuggle up in warmth during a harsh winter, one has to just get up and leave for the track and field. And this happens not just to the players. Even their parents leave no stone unturned for the sake of their children. Sportsperson are not made overnight; it takes a long and sustained perseverance to attain that stature. Victory and defeat are certainly important, but what is even more important is reaching this level in a game or sports discipline and, therefore, let all of us Indians join hands in wishing our Rio contingent the very best. I'm also ready to do this on your behalf; the Prime Minister of the country is ready to be a postman to convey your good wishes to these players. Do send your best wishes to our sportspersons in Rio on the 'NarendraModi App'. I'll convey these to our contingent. Just like 1.25 billion Indians, I too as a citizen would like to join you in encouraging them, cheering them up. Come, over the next few days, let us try to the fullest extent possible to make each one of our sportspersons feel proud, to reward them for their endeavours and exertions; and today, as I speak on the Rio Olympics, I would like to mention the name of a poetry lover, Suraj Prakash Upadhyay, a student of the Punjab Central University, who has sent me a poem. It's possible that many poets may have written poems, a few may be planning to write, some may even compose their verses into songs, in all languages. But here I would like to share with you the poem sent by Suraj ji.

The games bugle's been sounded
The festivities of competitions
In this mega sporting odyssey
Amidst the melodious chimes of Rio
May India commence on a grand note
May it rain gold, silver and bronze!
May India commence on a grand note

May it rain gold, silver and bronze!
May the turn be ours also this time
May we be amply prepared this time
Set your sight straight at the Gold
But let a loss not deject you
You are a hero to a billion hearts
You are the heartbeat of your sport
March ahead and set records
Let our tricolour flutter with pride in Rio
Let our tricolour flutter with pride in Rio.

Suraj ji, I dedicate your sentiments to all our sportspersons and extend to them the warmest and heartiest wishes from my side and on behalf of us 1.25 billion countrymen, so that our tricolour indeed flutters with joy and pride in the skies of Rio.

Tribute to Abdul Kalamji—Atal Innovation Mission

A young man, Mr Ankit, has reminded me of the death anniversary of President Abdul Kalamji, which was observed last week. The country, in fact the world, paid glowing tributes to him. The mere mention of Abdul Kalamji's name brings to mind vivid images of science, technology, missiles – in fact the entire spectrum of strengths and capabilities of India in the days to come. And that's why Ankit asks me—What is your government doing to ensure that Abdul Kalamji's dreams come true? You are right. The future is going to be technology driven. And technology is extremely dynamic. Day by day, technology keeps updating, changes form, transforms its impact. You cannot shackle technology. If you strive to hold it still, it would move beyond your grasp assuming new looks and forms. If we have to match its strides and move ahead, research and innovation are the keys, these are its lifelines and moving spirit. In the absence of research and innovation, technology will become a burden, just as still water stagnates and even stinks. And if we go on just using old technology without recourse to research and innovation, we will become outdated in this rapidly changing world and age. And that is why the government too has taken steps to attract the new generation toward science and research and innovation in the field of technology. And that is why I say 'let us aim to innovate'. And when I say 'let us aim to innovate' my AIM stands for 'Atal Innovation Mission'. This Mission is being promoted by the Niti Aayog. The purpose is to create an eco-system in the entire country through the Atal Innovation Mission, to forge a vibrant chain of innovation, experiment and entrepreneurship, which would also enhance the possibilities of new employment generation. If we have to develop the next generation innovators, we shall have to link our children with it. And that is why the Government of India has taken the initiative of 'Atal Tinkering Labs'. Wherever such Tinkering Labs are established in schools, these would be given 10 lakh rupees and a further sum of 10 lakh rupees will be provided for maintenance during a period of five years. Similarly, innovations are directly connected to Incubation Centres. If we have strong and well-equipped Incubation Centres, a system comes into place for innovations, for start-ups, for experimentation and to bring these efforts to a certain level. Creation of new Incubation Centres is essential just as it is necessary to strengthen the older Incubation Centres. And when I talk of Atal Incubation Centres, the government has considered allocating the huge sum of 10 crore rupees for this also. India is grappling with diverse challenges. We see problems in daily life. We shall now have to look for technological solutions for these. Through the 'Atal Grand Challenges' we have exhorted the younger generation of the country that if they see problems, they should search for solutions taking the path of technology, doing research, applying innovations and bring those on board. The Government of India wants to specially reward technology developed to find solutions to our problems. And I am happy that people have evinced interest in these things. When we spoke of Tinkering Labs, about 13,000 schools applied and when we talked of Incubation Centres, over four thousand academic and non-academic institutions came forward. I firmly believe that the real tribute to Abdul Kalamji will consist in harnessing research and innovation for developing technology to find solutions to problems we face in day-to-day life, ridding us of the difficulties we face to make things easier for all of us. The more the new generation devotes itself to this task, the greater will be their contribution with immense significance for the modern India of 21st century. That will be the real tribute to Abdul Kalamji.

My dear countrymen, while some time ago, we were concerned about a drought like situation, these days, on the one hand, we are enjoying the rains, but on the other, reports of floods are also coming in. Central government and state governments are working hand in hand with their utmost efforts to provide relief and assistance to the flood-affected areas. Despite causing some hardships, rains make every human heart rejoice, since rains and agriculture are the focal point of our entire sphere of economic activities.

Prevention of Dengue

There are times when one has to face an illness that leaves a scar for a lifetime. But if we are aware, alert and active, the prevention is also very easy. Take the case of Dengue. It is preventable. Pay attention to cleanliness, be alert, try and be safe and take special care of children. And the mindset that such diseases strike poor neighbourhoods only is not valid in the case of Dengue. Dengue first enters affluent localities and we should try and understand this. You must be watching advertisements on TV but there are times when we neglect taking proactive and informed action on it. The government, hospitals and doctors will of course do their job, but I urge that we should also be alert in ensuring that Dengue doesn't enter our homes, locality, family, for that matter, any illness connected with stagnant water.

Need for taking Proper Dose of Antibiotics

I would like to draw the attention of my dear countrymen to another menace. In today's fast paced, rat race of life, at times we don't have time to think about ourselves. When we fall sick, we want to get well as soon as possible and as a result pop in just any antibiotic that we can lay our hands on. It may give you instant relief, but my dear countrymen, this random pill-popping habit can land you in deep trouble. It may give you temporary succour, but we should completely stop taking antibiotics without the advice of a doctor. Avoid it till a doctor gives you a prescription. Do not use the shortcut method; it can lead to serious complications. Although random and rampant use of antibiotics gives immediate relief to the patient, but gradually the disease causing bacteria get accustomed to that drug. The drug then loses its efficacy and one has to fight the battle anew, develop new medicines, do new research; it takes years and till then these diseases create other complications. That's why we have to be very aware about that too. One more problem has presented itself. Suppose the doctor advises you take an antibiotic and he tells you to take 15 tablets of that over a period of five days, I urge you to complete the entire course of medication as prescribed by the doctor. Because if the treatment is abandoned halfway, it would benefit the bacteria. If the medicine is taken more than what is required, that too would be in the favour of the bacteria. And that is why, it is essential to take the entire course of antibiotic medicines in terms of number of tablets as well as days. If we leave the treatment halfway due to improvement in our condition, we are only helping that bacteria getting more sturdy and making it difficult to treat. Microbes spreading TB and malaria are bringing about rapid mutations in themselves, rendering medicines ineffective. In medical parlance it is called antibiotic resistance. Hence it is indeed necessary to follow rules in the administration of antibiotics. The government is committed to prevent antibiotic resistance. You must have seen, these days, on the antibiotic medicine strips there is a red line to make you aware. You must pay attention to that.

Prime Minister Safe Motherhood Campaign

While we are on the subject of health, I would like to talk about one more issue. I feel very concerned about the lives of pregnant women of our country. In our country, close to 3 crore women become pregnant every year but some of these mothers die during childbirth. Sometimes the mother loses her life, at times the infant does. There are times when both die. It is true that in the last decade there has been a decline in maternal mortality rates but even now, we are not able to save the lives of a large number of pregnant women. Anaemia during or after pregnancy, pregnancy related infections, high BP, any such complication can have devastating effect. Keeping in view these issues, in the last few months, the Government of India has launched a new campaign 'Prime Minister Safe Motherhood Campaign'. Under this, on the 9th of every month, all pregnant women will get a check-up at government health centres free of cost. I urge all poor families to ensure that all pregnant women avail of this benefit on the 9th of every month, so that if by the time they reach the 9th month any complication arises, it can be dealt with suitably on time and the lives of both mother and child can be saved. I have specially asked the gynaecologists whether they could offer their services for free on the 9th of every month, for the sake of under privileged mothers! Can't my doctor brothers and sisters spare just 12 days in a year for this service to the under privileged? Over the last few days, many have written to me. There are thousands of doctors who have implemented what I said. But India is such a vast country. We need lakhs of doctors to join this campaign. I do believe that you will indeed do so.

People's Movement for Planting Trees

My dear countrymen, today, the whole world is concerned deeply about climate change, global warming and the environment. These are discussed collectively in the country and across the world. In India, this has been accorded great importance for centuries. In the battlefield of Kurukshetra too, Bhagwan Shri Krishna talks of trees. Showing concern towards trees even in the midst of a battle, underlines the importance that was attached to trees. In the Gita, Bhagawan Shri Krishna says, '*ashvattha sarvavrikshanam*' which means amongst all trees, I am the Peepal Tree. It is proclaimed in Shukracharya Neeti that '*naastimulam anaushadham*' meaning that there is no plant that does not have medicinal values; the Anushasan Parva of Mahabharata elaborates this concept at greater length. It is stated in the Anushasan Parva that whosoever plants a tree begets an offspring in the form of that tree. There can be no doubt about this fact. He who donates a tree, that tree in return becomes a ladder to salvation just like children. Therefore, it is appropriate that parents desiring their well-being should plant trees and rear them like their own children.

Our scriptures like Gita, Shukracharya Neeti and Anushasan Parva of the Mahabharata contain such lofty ideals. However, there are certain individuals in the present generation also, who live up to these ideals. A few days ago, I came across a mention of Sonal, a young daughter from Pune. It touched my heart. It is mentioned in Anushasan Parva in Mahabharata that a tree is like an offspring and becomes means of salvation in after life, Sonal has not only taken it upon herself to fulfil her parents' wishes but society's expectations also. Shri Khandu Maruti Mhatre, a farmer of Narayanpur village of Junner Taluka of Pune got his granddaughter Sonal married in a very inspiring manner. What did Mhatre ji do in Sonal's marriage? He gifted all his relatives, guests and friends with a sapling of 'Kesar' variety of mango. I saw a picture of this marriage in social media. I was surprised to see that in the marriage festivities, instead of members of the wedding party, saplings were more visible! That picture really touches one's heart. I think that Sonal, who herself is an agriculture graduate, came upon this idea. And to present Mango saplings in the marriage, just think, reflects the love for nature in a brilliant manner. In a way, Sonal's marriage in an everlasting story of love for nature, I congratulate Sonal and Shriman Mhatre ji for this innovative effort. And such experiments are done by many people. I remember, when I was the Chief Minister of Gujarat – the temple of Ambaji there, is visited by lakhs of devotees travelling by foot in the month of Bhadrapad. A certain NGO decided to distribute saplings as 'Prasad' to the devotees, and the devotees were told that Mata Ambaji will keep on showering her grace, if they took care of the saplings, till the matured into trees in their homes and villages. And lakhs of such saplings were distributed to the devotees travelling on foot to the Ambaji temple that year. Other temples too can start the practice of distributing saplings instead of 'prasad' during this rainy season. It can easily grow into a people's movement for planting trees. I repeatedly tell my farmer brethren that instead of wasting our land in building fences around our fields, why don't we start planting timber trees there. Today, India has to spend billions and trillions of rupees to import timber wood from abroad for construction of houses and furniture. If we plant timber on the boundaries of our fields trees can be utilised for constructing houses and furnitures. They can also be cut and sold after 15 to 20 years with the permission of the government. This way, not only can these become a new source of your income, but can also save India from importing timber.

Green India Mission

Some days ago, a few states taking advantage of this weather have started a number of campaigns in this direction and the Government of India has also passed the CAMPA [Compensatory Afforestation Management and Planning Authority] law, under which about 40 thousand crores rupees will go to the states for planting trees. I have been told that the Maharashtra government planted about 2 crore saplings in the entire state on 1st July and next year they have taken a pledge to plant about 3 crore trees. The Maharashtra government has transformed this activity into a people's movement. Rajasthan, a desert region, has celebrated Van Mahotsav in a very big way and pledged to plant 25 lakhs trees. To plant 25 lakhs sapling in Rajasthan is not a small matter! Those who know the soil conditions of Rajasthan would know how mammoth this task is going to be. Andhra Pradesh, too has decided to increase its green cover by 50% by the year 2029. Under the Central Government's ongoing 'Green India Mission', Railways too have joined in this endeavour. Gujarat too has an illustrious tradition of observing Van Mahotsav. This year Gujarat has undertaken many projects like 'Aamra Van', 'Ekata Van' and 'Shaheed Van' as a part of Van Mahotsav and launched a campaign to plant crores of trees. I am not able to mention every state but all deserve to be appreciated.

Visit to South Africa

My dear countrymen, sometime back I had the opportunity to visit South Africa for the first time. During a foreign visit, diplomatic parleys are undertaken, there are trade deliberations and discussions about security and as is customary, many MoUs are concluded. But for me the visit to South Africa was more like a pilgrimage. When we think of South Africa, it is very natural to remember Mahatma Gandhi and Nelson Mandela. Whenever we hear the words – non-violence, love and forgiveness, the inspiring faces of Gandhi and Mandela appear before us. During my South Africa tour, I visited the Phoenix settlement where Mahatma Gandhi's home is known as 'Sarvodaya'. I also had the good fortune of travelling from Pietermaritzburg station in the same train in which Mahatma Gandhi had travelled, and which was the site of the incidence that sowed the seed of the transformation of Mohandas into Mahatma Gandhi. But what I want to tell you is that this time I had an opportunity to meet those great men who had devoted their young lives for society, fighting shoulder to shoulder with Nelson Mandela for the ideals of equality and equal opportunity; who had spent 20 to 22 years of their lives in prison with Nelson Mandela, effectively sacrificing the entire period of their youth for their society. I had the privilege of meeting these great personalities, these close associates of Nelson Mandela such as, Shriman Ahmed Kathrada, Shriman Laloo Chiba, Shriman George Bizos and Ronnie Kasrils. All were of Indian origin but had dedicated themselves to wherever they had settled and decided to offer their lives for those amidst whom they lived. They had so much strength! And the greatest thing was that while I was talking to them and listening about the experiences of their imprisonment, they had no bitterness or ill will for anyone. There was not a single trace of desire, to get something, to become somebody even after living such a great life of 'Tapasaya'. The essence of performing one's duty as explained in Gita was embodied in their persona. I will remember that meeting forever. Equality and equal opportunity are the two biggest 'mantras' for any society and government. Equality and equal opportunity, compassion and fraternity, these are the paths leading us to a bright future. We all want a good future for our children. Everybody has different needs and different priorities but there is one common path of development—equality, compassion and fraternity. Come, let us be proud about these Indians who have lived their lives in South Africa embodying our highest and fundamental ideals.

Beware of Digital Fraud

My dear countrymen, I have received a message from Shilpi Varma, to whom I am grateful. Her concern is very genuine. She has made me aware of an incident:

> *Pradhan Mantri ji, I am Shilpi Varma speaking from Bengaluru. Some days ago, I read in a news article that a lady became a victim of fraud and cheated on email, lost 11 lakh rupees and committed suicide. Being a woman, I feel an empathy with her family. What is your opinion about such cheat and fraud emails.*

She has pointed to a particular incident, and you must also be aware that we get messages on our mobile phones and emails, proclaiming attractive offers that you have won a jackpot of so many rupees; if you pay a certain amount then you become eligible for that greater amount. People get duped by this money trap. These are new ways of technology that are spreading in the entire world of cheating people. And just as technology plays an increasingly bigger role in our economic system, it also invites those who misuse it. A retired gentlemen, who not only had to get his daughter married but also to build his home, one day received an SMS, that there was a gift that had arrived from abroad and could be obtained if he deposited 2 lakh rupees as customs duty in a bank account and this gentlemen without giving any thought took out 2 lakh rupees from his hard earned life savings and sent it to some stranger. That too on the strength of just an SMS! And in a little while, he understood that he had been looted! You too must be getting similarly confused sometimes! These people write a letter in such style that it seems perfect. They use fake letter pads while sending these letters. They obtain your credit card number and debit card number and empty your bank account through technology. This new means of fraud is digital fraud. I believe that we must be aware against such lure, must remain cautious and if such false communications come to our notice, then we must share them with our friends and make them aware also. Shilpi Varma has brought this important thing to my notice, which although even you must have encountered, you may not have taken seriously. But I feel there is need to look at it seriously.

My dear countrymen, these days the Parliament Session is going on, and during the Parliament Session, I get to meet many people from across the country. Our MPs also bring people from their constituencies and introduce them to me; they tell me many things, their difficulties also. But recently I had a pleasant experience, a real pleasant experience! Student from Aligarh had come to meet me. You should have seen the enthusiasm of those boys and girls. They had brought a big photo album with them and their faces were lit with joy. They showed me the pictures of how they had beautified the Aligarh railway station! These were artistic paintings drawn on the station. What is more, they had looked for and collected plastic bottles and oil cans lying in the garbage in the villages and by filling those with soil and planting saplings, they have transformed those pots into a veritable garden. And by creating this garden on the site of railway station, they have given it a new look. If you go to Aligarh, do visit the railway station. I am receiving news from many railway stations in the country, where the local populace has through their arts taken to depicting their area's identity on the walls of the railway stations. They have brought about a refreshing feeling. This is a prime example of the great transformation, which can be brought about through people's participation. I felicitate all such citizens involved in these kinds of activities and especially congratulate friends from Aligarh.

Gifting *Pradhan Mantri Suraksha Bima Yojana* or *Jeevan Jyoti Bima Yojana*

My dear countrymen, with the onset of the rainy season, there is also an onset of festival season in our country. There will be fairs everywhere, festivities will be observed in temples and in places of worship. You too will become a participant at home and outside during the festive celebrations. The festival of Raksha Bandhan is a festival of special significance. Just like last year, can't you gift the *Pradhan Mantri Suraksha Bima Yojana* or *Jeevan Jyoti Bima Yojana* to mothers and sisters of our country on the occasion of Raksha Bandhan. Think about it, we should gift such a present to our sisters, which really provides her with security in the future. Not only that, we may have at home a lady preparing food for us or a lady who cleans our house, a daughter of an impoverished mother! To them also, you can gift *Pradhan Mantri Suraksha Bima Yojana* or *Jeevan Jyoti Bima Yojana* on this festival of Raksha Bandhan. And this is what social security in reality is all about; this is the true meaning of Raksha Bandhan.

My dear countrymen there are many among us who were born after independence. And I am the first Prime Minister of this nation who was born in free India. 'Quit India movement' started on 8th August, and this year would be the 75th year of 'Quit India—Quit Bharat' and on 15th August, it would be 70th year of our Independence. We are enjoying our independence and are proud to be free citizens, but this is an occasion to remember those who sacrificed their all for winning our Independence. The 75th year of Quit India and 70th year of Independence can be a source of new inspiration, a source of new enthusiasm and an occasion to take a pledge to do something for our nation. The whole nation should be imbued with the spirit of those great patriots and we should once again experience anew the fragrance of freedom. Let us all create such an atmosphere. Independence Day should not be a government event, it should be the celebration of the entire people. Just like Diwali, it should be our own festival. I hope that you too become inspired with the spirit of patriotism and do something good in that vein. Do send a picture of it on 'Narendra Modi App'. Let us create such an atmosphere in the nation.

Dear countrymen, I have the good fortune to talk to the nation from ramparts of the Red Fort on 15th August, it is a tradition. You too must be having certain thoughts that you wish were proclaimed from the Red Fort. I invite you to write to me about your thoughts which I, as your representative, as your Pradhan Sevak should talk about from the Red Fort. Send me suggestions, your advice and new thoughts, I will try to convey your thoughts to the rest of our countrymen. I do not wish that whatever I speak from the ramparts of the Red Fort should just be the opinion of the Prime Minister; it should be the collective voice of 125 crores of my countrymen. Do send me something, either on 'Narendra Modi App' or on MyGov.in. Today the platforms of technology are such that your message can reach me very easily. I invite you once again, come, let us remember and salute our great freedom fighters, who sacrificed their lives for India and let us move ahead with the pledge to do something for our nation. My best wishes to you all and many thanks.

*For listening to the audio, please log on to **http://www.narendramodi.in/mann-ki-baat** or scan the given QR code.*

CHAPTER 23: August 2016

My dear countrymen, Namaskar,

Tomorrow, 29th August, is the birth anniversary of hockey wizard Dhyan Chand. This occasion is celebrated as 'National Sports Day' throughout the country. I offer my tributes to Dhyan Chand ji and wish to remind you all about his invaluable contribution. He played a pivotal role in helping India win Hockey Gold Medals in Olympic Games of 1928, 1932 and 1936. All of us cricket lovers know Bradman's name very well. He had complimented Dhyan Chand ji by saying that 'he scores goals like runs'. Dhyan Chand ji was a living example of sportsman spirit and of nationalism. During a match in Kolkata, one player from the opposite team hit him on the head with the hockey stick. At that point, there were only 10 minutes left in the game, and Dhyan Chand ji scored three goals in just those ten minutes and said – 'I avenged the hit by scoring goals'.

India's Performance in Rio Olympics

Dear countrymen, as the time of Mann Ki Baat draws near, a very large number of suggestions are received on MyGov or on NarendraModiApp. These are on diverse topics. But, I saw that this time in most of these suggestions, people had asked me to say something about the Rio Olympics. I find it a very positive sign that our common people have such attachment and awareness about the Rio Olympics and they are insisting that the Prime Minister of the country says something on this matter. It shows that besides cricket, our people have so much involvement in and awareness and knowledge about other sports and games also. For me, even reading these messages proved to be a source of inspiration. One Shri Ajit Singh ji has written on NarendraModiApp – 'Please, this time in "Mann Ki Baat" do talk about the education of our daughters, our "Betis" and their participation in sports because they have brought laurels for the country by winning medals at the Rio Olympics'. One Shri Sachin has written urging that in 'Mann Ki Baat', this time, a mention may please be made about Sindhu, Saakshi and Deepa Karmakar. Whatever medals we have won have been earned by our daughters. These *Betis* have once again proved that they are second to none in any respect. One of these daughters is from North India while there is one who belongs to South India and then there is one from the Eastern part. All in all, they represent all corners of our country. It seems that our daughters in the whole of India have decided to take up the responsibility of bringing glory to the nation.

Shikhar Thakur has written on MyGov that we could have performed better at the Olympics. He has written – 'Respected Modi Sir, first of all, congratulations on our winning two medals at Rio. However, I want to draw your attention to the question – was our performance really good? And, the answer is 'No'. We have to go a long way in the field of sports. Our parents, even today, insist on focusing on studies and academics. Sports are considered a waste of time in our society. We need to change this mindset. Society needs motivation for this. And, no one can do this better than you'.

Similarly, one Shri Satya Prakash Mehra ji has written on NarendraModiApp – 'In Mann Ki Baat, there is a need to focus on extra-curricular activities, especially on encouraging children and youth to play'. Thousands of people have expressed similar sentiments. There is no denying the fact that we could not perform up to the expectations. During these Games, some of our players could not even repeat their own performance levels which they had achieved during domestic events in India. In the medals chart, our tally was only two medals. However, it is also a fact that if we look closely, we shall find that despite missing medals, Indian players gave a very good account of themselves for the first time in some of the events.

See, our Abhinav Bindra very narrowly missed the medal and got fourth place in Shooting. Dipa Karmakar produced a superb performance in gymnastics, although she remained at the fourth place and missed a Bronze by a very narrow margin. But, how can we forget that she is India's first daughter to qualify in gymnastics for the Olympics and also to reach the final round. The pair of Sania Mirza and Rohan Bopanna met almost a similar fate in tennis. Our athletes this time gave a creditable performance. After 32 years of PT Usha's feat, Lalita BaBar qualified for the finals in track and field. Our Women's Hockey Team qualified for the Olympic Games after a space of 36 long years. Men's Hockey Team reached the knockout stage after 36 years. Our team is quite strong. And the interesting part is that Gold Medalist Argentina lost just one match in the entire tournament and the team which defeated them was India. Thus, the future surely seems bright for us.

Vikas Krishna Yadav reached the quarter finals in boxing but could not win Bronze. Many players like Aditi Ashok, Dattu Bhokanal and Atanu Das performed very well. But my dear countrymen, we do have to go a long way. And if we stick to the same routine, we may perhaps keep facing the same disappointment. I have announced setting up of a committee. The Government of India will make an in depth in-house analysis and will study the practices being followed around the world. We shall prepare a roadmap on how we can do better. We have to prepare a far reaching plan keeping in view the Olympics in 2020, 2024 and 2028. I urge the State Governments also to set up similar committees to find out as to what we can do in sports. What can each state do? The states can take up one or two sports of their choice and display their strength.

I urge our sports associations also to do objective and impartial brainstorming on this. And, I also request all citizens of the country who have interest in this matter to mail their suggestions on NarendraModiApp. They may write to the government; associations may discuss these issues and submit their memoranda to the government. State governments too should deliberate on this matter and provide their suggestions. But, we must prepare ourselves fully and thoroughly. And, I am confident that we, the nation of 125 crore people comprising 65% youth population can reach an exalted status in the world of sports too. We have to move ahead with this resolve.

Invaluable Contribution of Teachers

My dear countrymen, 5th September is 'Teachers Day'. For many years, I have been spending a lot of time with students on Teachers Day and that too as a student myself. I used to learn quite a lot from those young children. For me, 5th September was Teachers Day as well as an Education Day. But, this time I have to leave for the G-20 Summit and so I felt that I should express my feelings in this regard in 'Mann Ki Baat' today.

In our life, a teacher holds the same place which a mother does. We have also seen such teachers who care more for their pupils than for themselves. They devote their lives for their disciples, their students. These days, after the Rio Olympics, Pulela Gopi Chand ji is being talked about everywhere. He is a player first but he has set up a glorious example of how a good coach, that is, a teacher should be. I see Gopi Chand ji today as an excellent teacher besides being a very accomplished player. And, on Teachers Day, I salute Pulela Gopi Chand ji for his hard work, his dedication towards sports and his manner of finding happiness in the success of his disciples. We always feel the contribution of our teachers in our lives. 5th September happens to be the birthday of India's former President Dr Sarvapalli Radhakrishnan ji and the country celebrates this as Teachers Day. Regardless of which post held in his life, he always tried to live like a teacher, an educator. Not only this, he always said that 'a good teacher can only be one who keeps the student within always alive'. Dr Radhakrishnan ji showed this by living as a teacher and by keeping alive the student within him despite holding the highest office of the President.

Some times when I think of it, I remember so many incidents related with my teachers because they were our heroes in our small village. However, I can happily say that even now I receive a hand written letter every month from one of my teachers, who has turned 90 now. In this letter, he mentions books read by him during that month along with quotations. He also gives his comments on what he deems correct or otherwise in whatever I have done during the month. It is as if he is, even now, teaching me in the class room. In a way, he is conducting a correspondence course for me even today. And, about his handwriting even at the age of 90, I marvel that he writes so beautifully whereas my own handwriting is very poor. That is why, whenever I look at somebody's good handwriting, I have a great respect for it. You may also have had a similar experience. If you tell the world about whatever good has happened in your life because of your teachers, people's attitude towards teachers would change. It will be a matter of pride and it is our duty to enhance the honour of our teachers in the society. If you have a photograph with your teacher or an incident connected with your teacher or an inspirational thing associated with your teacher, please do share the same on NarendraModiApp. Looking at the contribution of teachers in the country from the point of view of students is also immensely valuable in itself.

Ganesh Utsav—Festival of National Awakening and Social Refinement

My dear countrymen, Ganesh Utsav is drawing near. Ganeshji removes all obstacles and let us all wish that our country, our society, our families and each one of us may lead a life free of obstacles. But, when we mention Ganesh Utsav, it is natural to remember Lokmanya Tilak ji. The tradition of public celebration of Ganesh Utsav is Lokmanya Tilak's gift to us. By publicly celebrating Ganesh Utsav, he turned this religious occasion into a festival of national awakening and social refinement. These Ganesh festivities included the holding of wide-ranging discussions on issues that touched our lives and society, and comprised such programmes which provided a new vigour and vitality to our social fabric. Also, his mantra 'Swaraj, that is, freedom is my birthright' was the main focus thereby strengthening the freedom movement. Now, not in Maharashtra alone but in each corner of India, Ganesh Utsav is celebrated publicly. Young people make elaborate preparations, they are full of vigour. Some people even now try to follow the path shown by Lokmanya Tilak ji. They organise debates on topics of public interest, and hold essay competitions and rangoli competitions. Tableaus depict issues of social concern in a very artistic manner. In a way, a mass campaign of public education gets underway through these Ganesh festivities. Lokmanya Tilak ji gave us the inspirational mantra – 'Swaraj, that is, freedom is my birthright'. But now we live in independent India. So do we through these public Ganesh festivals, now move on to SURAAJ, that is, good governance by proclaiming 'SURAAJ is my birthright'. Good governance, SURAAJ, should be our priority; can we not recite this mantra and give a message for it in the public celebrations of Ganesh festival? Come on, I invite you all.

Environment Preservation While Celebrating Festivals

It is true that festivals express the vitality of a society. Festivals infuse new life into individuals as well as the society. Life seems to be impossible without festivals but these have to be moulded according to the needs of the changing times. I have seen that this time, many people have written to me mentioning Ganeshotsav and Durga Puja. They are worried about the environment. One Shri Shankar Narayan Prashant has strongly urged– 'Modi ji, kindly tell the people through your Mann Ki Baat that they should not use Ganesh idols made of Plaster of Paris. [POP] Why should we not use Ganeshji idols made of clay from the village pond. POP idols are not environment friendly'. He has expressed a great pain, as have others also. I request you all, why should we not use clay in making Ganesh and Durga idols and revert to our old tradition. This will help in environment preservation, prevent pollution of our rivers and ponds and also provide protection to small creatures living in water. This is also the service of God. Ganeshji removes obstacles. So, we should not make such Ganeshji idols, which create problems. I do not know how you will take my suggestions, but it is not just me but many other people saying the same thing. I have heard about many such people including the Pune based sculptor Shri Abhijit Dhondphale, Kolhapur institutions, Nisarg-Mitra and Vigyan Prabodhini, Nisarg Katta in Vidarbh, Gyan Prabodhini of Pune and Girgaoncha Raja of Mumbai. Many such institutions work hard to promote Ganesh idols made from clay and they also propagate it. Eco-friendly Ganeshotsav is also social service. There is still time left before the start of Durga Puja festivities. If we resolve now, our efforts will lead to employment generation for those families which traditionally made clay idols in the past. Also the clay will return and get dissolved in the pond or the river and will thus help in protecting the environment. I offer my best wishes to you all for Ganesh Chaturthi.

My dear countrymen, Bharat Ratna Mother Teresa will be canonised, that is, accorded sainthood on 4th September. Mother Teresa devoted her entire life to the service of the poor in India. Though she was born in Albania and her mother tongue was not English, yet she transformed her life and did everything to be able to serve the poor. When Mother Teresa, is accorded Sainthood, it is quite natural for us Indians to feel proud. Indian government will send an official delegation under the leadership of our External Affairs Minister Sushma Swaraj to represent 125 crore Indians at the canonisation ceremony to be held on 4th September. We keep learning something or the other from great men and women, saints, sages and holy people. We shall continue to receive something, learn something from them and keep on doing some good things.

Swachhata Abhiyan

My dear countrymen, when development becomes a mass movement, a big transformation takes place. Peoples' power is, in a way, considered to be a divine incarnation. Government of India has made a successful effort to clean Ganga and involve the people for this project with the cooperation of five State governments. Pradhans of villages situated on the banks of the river Ganga were invited to Allahabad on the 20th of this month. They included men as well as women. They came to Allahabad and took an oath before Mother Ganga that they will make all out efforts to immediately stop the practice of open defecation in their villages situated on the banks of Ganga, start a campaign of building toilets. They also pledged that these villages will make their full contribution in cleaning up Ganga and will ensure that Ganga is not polluted from now on. I congratulate all Pradhans who had assembled in Allahabad with this resolve from different States; they had come from *Uttarakhand*, from Uttar Pradesh, from Bihar, from Jharkhand and from West Bengal. I also congratulate all those Ministries of the Government of India and also those ministers who turned this vision into reality. I also want to thank the Chief Ministers of these five States for taking the vital step in the direction of making Ganga clean by involving people's power.

My dear countrymen, certain things touch me very deeply and my heart bows in respect to those who visualise such heart-warming initiatives. In Kabirdham district of Chhattisgarh, more than 1.25 lakh students from about 1700 schools collectively wrote letters to their parents. Some students wrote in English, some wrote in Hindi and some in Chhattisgarhi to their parents telling them that there should be toilets in their houses. They demanded that toilets be built. Some students even wrote that they would rather remain without celebrating their birthdays but that toilets must be constructed.

Students aged between seven to seventeen took up this task. And this had such an impact, such an emotional impact that while the students were going to school the next day, their parents handed over reply letters to them addressed to the teacher in which they promised to build toilets by a certain date positively. My compliments to those who visualised this idea, compliments to these students and special compliments to those parents who took their childrens' letters so seriously and also took a decision to construct a toilet. This is what inspires us.

In Koppal district of Karnataka, a 16-year-old girl, Mallamma started a Satyagraha against her own family. She launched the Satyagraha and stopped eating and she did that not to ask something for herself, not to demand good clothes or have sweets. This daughter Mallamma was adamant to have a toilet built in her house. But, the family was not in a good position economically. The daughter stuck to her demand and was not prepared to end her Satyagraha. The village Pradhan Mohammad Shafi came to know about this. He was told that Mallamma had protested to press for her demand for getting a toilet built in her house. Now, look at the gesture of village Pradhan Mohammad Shafi, he arranged 18,000 rupees and got a toilet built within a week. Just see the power and strength in Mallamma's protest, and also consider the grand gesture of a village Pradhan like Mohammad Shafi. Look how the solutions to problems are found, this is the power of the people.

My dear countrymen, Swachha Bharat has become the dream of each Indian. Some Indians have made it their resolve. Some Indians have made it their aim and purpose. But, each one is connected to it in one or the other way and everyone is making a contribution. Daily we hear about the various innovative efforts in this direction. Acting on one such idea, the Government of India has called upon the people to make short films of 2-to 3-minutes duration on Swachhta, that is, cleanliness and send these to the Government. You can find details of this plan on the website. A competition will be held and the winners will be awarded prizes on Gandhi Jayanti Day on 2nd October. I request TV channels also to invite such films and hold a competition. Creativity can give a new strength to Swachhata Abhiyan or the cleanliness campaign. New slogans will emerge, newer methods will come to knowledge, a new inspiration will be generated and all this will happen with the great support of the people. Lesser known artists could be taken and it is not necessary to have a big studio and a big camera. You can even shoot a film these days using your mobile phone camera. I call upon you all to come forward and participate.

Inauguration of Akashvani Maitree Channel

My dear countrymen, India has always tried its best to have close, cordial and vibrant relations with its neighbours. A very important event took place recently. The Honourable President of India, Shri Pranab Mukherjee, inaugurated a new radio channel named 'Akashvani Maitree Channel' at Kolkata.

Now, some people may wonder whether Honourable President should inaugurate a Radio Channel? But this is no ordinary Radio Channel, it is a very big and very important step. We have Bangladesh as our neighbour. We know that both Bangladesh and West Bengal continue to have a common cultural heritage. So, Akashvani Maitree on this side and Bangladesh Betaar on that side will mutually share the content and Bengali speaking people on both sides will enjoy the programmes of Akashvani, that is, All India Radio. This people to people contact is a big contribution of Akashvani. The President launched this radio channel. I extend my thanks to Bangladesh also for collaborating with us in this initiative. I congratulate friends at All India Radio too for making their contribution in our foreign policy also.

My dear countrymen, although you have entrusted me with the responsibilities of Prime Minister but I also am a human being just like you. At times, sensitive events touch me a little too deeply. Such sentimental incidents generate new energy, give new inspiration and this is what motivates us Indians to do some remarkable things. I received a letter recently which touched my heart. A motherly lady of about 84 years of age who is a retired teacher wrote to me. Had she not forbidden me from revealing her name, I wanted from the core of my heart to announce her name while talking to you. She wrote in her letter that after my appeal to the people to forego their cooking gas subsidy, she had given up her subsidy and then she even forgot about it. However, a few days ago a person on my behalf went to her and delivered a letter in which she was thanked for giving up the subsidy. And, she has said that a letter from the Prime Minister was no less than a Padma Shree honour for her.

Dear countrymen, you may know that I have tried to send a letter, to be delivered personally through my representatives, to all those who have surrendered their cooking gas subsidy on my appeal. My effort is to send letters to more than one crore people. Under this plan, my letter had reached this mother, who wrote back to me saying that I was doing good work under the campaign of providing relief to those poor ladies who are being freed from the smoke of a Chulha [Smoke oven]. I am a retired teacher and will cross the age of 90 within a few years and I am sending you a donation of 50,000 rupees which you can use in this mission of providing relief from Chulha smoke to poor women. You may well imagine the missionary spirit of this retired teacher living on pension and donating an amount of 50,000 rupees for the sake of providing gas connection to the poor mothers and sisters, in order to save them from the ill effects of Chulha smoke. It is not a question of 50,000 rupees but the basic issue is this old lady's empathy and it is the blessings of this lady and of crores of our other mothers and sisters which strengthens my confidence in the future of the country. And, she did not write to me this letter as a Prime Minister but she straightforwardly wrote – 'Modi Bhaiya!' I salute this wonderful mother and I also salute crores of similar mothers in India who keep doing something or the other all the time for the benefit of others despite facing many difficulties themselves.

My dear countrymen, we were struggling with drought-like conditions last year, but this August we have been facing the fury of floods all through. In some parts of the country, there have been repetitive floods. State governments, the Union government, local self-governing bodies, social organisations and the citizens did whatever could be done best. Yet, even amidst reports of these floods, some such events happened which should be remembered. Which show the power of unity, and how big results can be achieved by working together?

The month of August this year has become memorable. In August 2016, about 90 political parties in the country, many of these parties in the Parliament, which were staunch opponents of each other and which do not miss the slightest opportunity to go against each other, all these parties got united and passed the GST Act. The credit for this goes to all the parties. And, this is an example which shows that great tasks can be accomplished by working in unison to move ahead. Similarly, about the incidents that took place in Kashmir and all that happened in Kashmir, all political parties in the country collectively expressed their views in one voice. A message was sent to the whole world, a message also went to the separatist forces and our sympathy was also expressed towards the people of Kashmir. Any interaction that I had on Kashmir, with whoever resounded with these views quite prominently, and if I may try to summarise these views and comments, the gist and essence were unity and affection; these two were the fundamental points. And, we are all of the view, and this is the view of all 125 crore Indians, right from the village Pradhan to the Prime Minister that every loss of life in Kashmir – whether it is of a young man or of a security personnel – it is our own loss, a loss of our people, a loss for the nation! Those trying to disturb peace in Kashmir by pushing children to the front and hiding behind them will have to be answerable to these very innocent children some day.

My dear countrymen, ours is a vast nation, full of diversities. To keep this country of manifold diversities united, all of us as citizens, as a society and as the government, have a responsibility to encourage things which strengthen our national unity and highlight these with full vigour, only then can we make our country's future bright, and, of course, this will be achieved. I have full faith in the power of my 125 crore countrymen. That is all for today, many many thanks.

For listening to the audio, please log on to http://www.narendramodi.in/mann-ki-baat or scan the given QR code.

Conclusion

Two years and counting…an eventful journey

'Mann Ki Baat' completed 23 episodes (which means two full years) on Sunday 25th September 2016. On the same day the Prime Minister devoted a few minutes of the programme to speak about what 'Mann Ki Baat' means to him.

He said:

My dear countrymen, we started with 'Mann Ki Baat' on Vijayadashmi two years ago (in 2014).

It is my sincere effort that 'Mann Ki Baat' should not become a programme about praising and highlighting only the achievements of government; 'Mann Ki Baat' should not become a programme to demonstrate political one-upmanship, make allegations and counter allegations. Despite numerous pressures during these past two years–sometimes one may even be tempted due to the surrounding atmosphere, be provoked to say something–overcoming all such impulses over these two years with your blessings, 'Mann Ki Baat' has emerged as a means to connect with the common citizens.

On 8th November 2016, the Prime Minister addressed the nation during which he announced that the thousand and five hundred rupee notes would cease to be legal tender. Rules were put in place on withdrawals and transactions.

Naturally, this step by the Government led to intense discussion among the people. Here was a move that affected every Indian, be it in India or overseas.

It was thus not surprising that when the Prime Minister called for inputs for the November 2016 'Mann Ki Baat,' an overwhelming majority were on the Government's decision to demonetise the thousand and five hundred rupee notes.

The Prime Minister addressed the issue extensively and directly during the 'Mann Ki Baat' programme on 27th November 2016.

He gave glimpses of the three types of letters, mails, MyGov posts and Mobile App comments he received:

(1) Those who wanted to know more about the decision taken by the Government.
(2) Those who were sharing their own experiences, of how they bore temporary pains for long term gains.
(3) Those who said that the step taken by the Government on 8th November was great and that this should be complimented by even more anti-corruption measures.

Narendra Modi saluted the people of India for becoming active participants in the movement against corruption and black money. A strong case was presented on how these two evils have adversely affected and slowed down the growth of the nation.

The Prime Minister explained to the small traders and the daily wage earners how the decision taken by the Government presents unprecedented opportunities for them.

He urged small businesses to use demonetisation as an opportunity to scale up and expand their business using technology and cashless transactions. He added that corruption and black money have affected small businesses very negatively and that would not happen with the decision of the Government.

Narendra Modi addressed India's workforce and reminded them of the glaring anomalies that take place because of transactions involving cash. It often happens that a daily wage worker never receives the money he is supposed to–the money is shown as paid only on the records. In an era of increased cashless transactions, the exploitation of workers would reduce drastically. Every worker will get what he or she deserves and the scope for corruption or harassment by middlemen will be minimized.

In light of these advantages, the Prime Minister made a spirited appeal to the youth of the nation to help him increase cashless and digital transactions.

A substantial part of the episode on 25th December 2016 was also devoted to the demonetisation decision. The Prime Minister introduced the Lucky Grahak Yojana and the Digi Dhan Vayapar Yojana to the people. He expressed joy that awareness and support to the Government's efforts towards ending corruption and black money have increased.

Narendra Modi told the people of India that every single day, the suggestions of the people were considered very seriously, which is why rules were revised whenever required.

He thanked the people and the youth in particular for using their creativity to disprove every canard that was being spread on the demonetisation drive since 8th November.

The Prime Minister shared that a strict law on Benami Property was very much on the cards and that no one who is supporting or furthering corruption would be spared.

Those working with the Prime Minister narrated how he personally read a large number of letters and comments on his Mobile App on demonetisation. The public support, the ability to withstand pain for the larger good and the constructive feedback convinced him about the strength of 125 crore Indians and their support to the Government.

Every 'Mann Ki Baat' episode has been memorable, with each episode having a mix of something new and a continuation of themes like cleanliness.

The fact that this is a powerful platform with a pan-India reach was seen during many instances. It is through the radio that Narendra Modi has given a consistent clarion call for cleanliness. He used the radio to talk about farmer welfare, irrigation practices and water conservation. He used the radio to reach out to exam giving students. 'Mann Ki Baat' was used to talk about the Kashmir issue in August 2016. Carrying forward the 'Jamhuriyat, Insaniyat and Kashmiriyat' pitch made by Atal Bihari Vajpayee, Narendra Modi gave the twin principles of 'Ekta' (Unity) and 'Mamata' (Compassion) while talking about Kashmir. While talking about the dastardly Uri attack in September 2016, Narendra Modi made it clear that the safety and well-being of the people of Kashmir was of utmost importance.

'Mann Ki Baat' follows a very simple format. There is neither an anchor nor is the programme celebrity driven. What drives it is a citizen-centric approach, celebrating relatable human success stories and endeavors.

Similarly, the set-up of the room where 'Mann Ki Baat' is recorded is spartan to say the least. The number of people in the room when the Prime Minister is addressing the nation is limited, perhaps the bare minimum technical staff and an aide from the PMO. "Since it comes from the heart, the need for pomp and show is limited," remarked an aide who has been present for many episodes.

There were often times when the 'Mann Ki Baat' programme would be held on a particular Sunday at 11 A.M. and just after that, Narendra Modi would be addressing a political rally in some part of the nation. Both programmes, being held minutes after each other had nothing overlapping. There was a stark contrast in hearing the Prime Minister address his citizens through the radio and hearing Narendra Modi reaching out to voters at a rally. This is an ability very few leaders possess–to delineate the political with the non-political, to talk about governance and social issues and to reach out to citizens directly.

Narendra Modi's point of not using 'Mann Ki Baat' for politics is worth thinking about. Often, it is not surprising to find political opponents seeking answers through 'Mann Ki Baat' the morning it is to be held. However, come what may, Narendra Modi has, and most feel rightly, resisted such temptations. Naturally, those seeking a response from the Prime Minister are disappointed.

Those in the Prime Minister's team share that issues relatable to youngsters always receive a good response. The anecdotes on cleanliness are also well received, particularly in the area from where the anecdote comes. Both the episodes for exam-going students, particularly the one in 2016, were popular.

In an era where sensationalism occupies a prime space in setting discourse, where even a courageous act by the apolitical armed forces is seen with so much suspicion, 'Mann Ki Baat' stands apart as the golden exception. What does India's most powerful orator and Prime Minister in decades use the radio for? Not for sensationalism, which anybody could, tempted by the power of the medium. Instead, he uses it to highlight efforts that are contributing to national transformation.

The source of inspiration is the skills and strengths of the people of India.

It would be interesting to see the programmes in the months to come, but one thing is certain– as a communicator par excellence, who has always been above the curve when it comes to modern communication, Narendra Modi through 'Mann Ki Baat' has demonstrated how to connect with people across India, rising above politics and focusing on matters that inspire citizens and initiate a social revolution through the airwaves.

Narendra Modi said it very well when he said that his inspiration remained the common citizen of India, whose joys and sorrows he wanted to share.

> *The citizen of this country keeps inspiring me... For our countrymen, 'Mann Ki Baat' may (also) be a source of information. For me, 'Mann Ki Baat' has been the means to feel the strength of my 1.25 billion countrymen and women, to (celebrate) their great strengths...'Mann Ki Baat' has become a new opportunity of social transformation rather than just remaining a mere talk show of 15-20 minutes. What can be more satisfying than this for any one?*

Index